The Power of Sustainable Thinking

Dedicated to my nieces Becky and Laura and nephews Jeff and Brian, and to all of the children who follow them, who will be forced to deal with unprecedented change in their lives unless humanity quickly alters its thinking and behaviour and resolves global warming.

The Power of Sustainable Thinking
How to Create a Positive Future for the Climate, the Planet, Your Organization and Your Life

Bob Doppelt

publishing for a sustainable future
London • Sterling, VA

First published by Earthscan in the UK and USA in 2008
Reprinted in 2009

Copyright © Bob Doppelt, 2008

ISBN: 978-1-84407-595-9

Typeset by Domex e-Data Pvt. Ltd, India
Printed and bound in the UK by TJ International Ltd, Padstow, Cornwall
Cover design by Andrew Corbett

For a full list of publications please contact:

Earthscan
Dunstan House,
14A St Cross Street
London, EC1N 8XA, UK
Tel: +44 (0)20 7841 1930
Fax: +44 (0)20 7242 1472
Email: earthinfo@earthscan.co.uk
Web: **www.earthscan.co.uk**

22883 Quicksilver Drive, Sterling, VA 20166-2012, USA

Earthscan publishes in association with the International Institute
for Environment and Development

A catalogue record for this book is available from the British Library

Library of Congress Cataloging-in-Publication Data

Doppelt, Bob.
    The power of sustainable thinking / Bob Doppelt.
        p.   cm.
    Includes bibliographical references and index.
    ISBN: 978-1-84407-595-9 (hardback : alk. paper)
  1.   Sustainable living. 2.   Human ecology–Psychological aspects.
  3.   Conservation of natural resources. 4.   Self-reliant living.
  5.   Energy conservation. 6.   Appropriate technology. I. Title.
    GF78.D66 2008
    333.72–dc22

                                                    2008015714

The paper used for this book is FSC-certified. FSC (the Forest Stewardship Council) is an international network to promote responsible management of the world's forests.

Mixed Sources
Product group from well-managed forests and other controlled sources
www.fsc.org Cert no. SGS-COC-2482
© 1996 Forest Stewardship Council

Contents

Part I   The Imperatives of Change

Part II   The Path Forward

List of Figures, Tables and Boxes

FIGURES

TABLES

BOXES

Acknowledgements

The past always influences the present, and, although the words on these pages were written by my hands, the substance is the result of the work of many people with whom I've had the opportunity to study or learned from over the years. First and foremost, I want to thank the systems dynamics, change management and global warming specialists who have taught me so much. The late Jerry Kransky, Ray Lowe, Donella Meadows and Will Schutz, along with Russell Ackoff, Daniel Kim, Bryan Smith and others fall into the first group. Intergovernmental Panel on Climate Change (IPCC) members Phil Mote, Stephen Schneider and other climate scientists, and aquatic ecologists James Karr, Gordy Reeves and Jim Sedell are included in the latter group.

I give enduring thanks to Wayne Velicer, James Prochaska, Colleen Redding and Lynn Stein from the University of Rhode Island Cancer Prevention Research Center, and Janice Prochaska of Pro-Change Behaviour Systems for educating me about the 'ins and outs' of the trans-theoretical model of change and for assisting with my research. Thanks also go to Rushworth Kidder from the Institute for Global Ethics for allowing me to modify his approach for the resolution of global warming-related ethical dilemmas.

A very special thank you goes to Ray Anderson, Larry Chalfan, Reverend Richard Cizik, Sue Klobertanz and Rusty Rexius for taking the time to talk with me and sending emails describing their climate and sustainability change initiatives. Many of these people provided valuable editorial feedback as well.

I want to thank Mayor Kitty Piercy of Eugene, Oregon, for her willingness to risk valuable political capital to engage her community in these issues. The world needs more elected officials like her.

Mike and Carleen McCornack, Dick Lamster and Maeve Sowles, and some of our other friends provided valuable editorial feedback. Judy and Paul Harte of Harte Media provided valuable editorial assistance with the book.

A financial contribution from Jon and Vivian Lovelace made writing this book possible. It would not have happened without their support.

Jon and Vivian, along with Jim and Jane Ratzlaff, the Carolyn Foundation, and other donors and foundations helped to launch the Climate Leadership Initiative at the University of Oregon, which generated much of the material in this book.

I want to also thank the board of the University of Oregon (UO) Climate Leadership Initiative. Each board member makes a substantial contribution in their own right to climate protection and sustainability. Over the years they have taken time out of their busy lives to support and provide direction to the Climate Leadership Initiative (CLI).

Kathy Lynn, CLI associate director, and all of the other CLI staff have my deepest respect and thanks for their ongoing commitment, savvy and outstanding work in advancing climate protection and sustainability. I also want to thank Robert Ribe, Director of the Institute for a Sustainable Environment at the University of Oregon, and Dorothy Bollman, ISE administrator, for their never-ending support, guidance and assistance.

When I write, I often find myself exploring deep and sometimes painful truths about myself. I also become intensely focused and preoccupied. My wife and life partner Peg not only put up with these ruminations, she also provided honest editorial advice and constant encouragement throughout the process. This book would be just a concept were it not for her.

DISCLAIMER

Although statements by numerous people are used throughout this book, the content and views expressed here are solely my own. I did my best to double-check all facts and figures. I apologize in advance for any errors or misrepresentations I may have made.

Foreword

Bob Doppelt gave the world the first truly effective book on how to implement sustainable ways to run a company, operate a government or conduct any organization more sustainably. His landmark book, *Leading Change Toward Sustainability*, is a text in several of my classes at Presidio School of Management; no doubt Bob uses it in his classes at Bainbridge Graduate Institute, the two business schools in which sustainability is woven throughout the entire curricula.

I recommend Bob's new book, *The Power of Sustainable Thinking: How To Create A Positive Future For The Climate, The Planet, Your Organization and Your Life* to anyone trying to implement change in helping a corporation, a community or a country capture the opportunities that behaving more responsibly confers. As Bob points out, many books now exist to tell change agents what to do; his first book is a brilliant manual of how to do it. This book focuses on the far more important 'why' to change, and how to sort through competing priorities, and on how to change ourselves before we seek to change others or our organizations. He tackles the difficult psychological issues behind our daily choices to change (which the challenges facing our world demand of us) or to bury our heads and change the channel. He addresses how each of us can tackle our internal contradictions and motivations, and find the will to change.

Margaret Mead once said that the only person who likes change is a wet baby. And I'd add that even a baby squalls throughout the process, only quieting down when it's all over.

But change we must. Bob rightly focuses on the climate crisis as the most urgent driver of change. But of course there are others. When Royal Dutch Shell undertakes what it calls scenario planning, in attempting to understand what the future might hold for its business it looks for what are called 'drivers of change'. These are forces that will determine that business as usual cannot endure, and a sign to a smart manager to seek 'no regrets' strategies: ways of ordering a company's affairs that will be robust regardless of how the future plays out.

Our world faces some pretty formidable drivers of change. We are losing every major ecosystem on earth, energy prices are soaring perhaps because the world has reached peak oil production, food is scarce and costly, population continues to rise, water shortages may prove even harder to solve than energy, and China, with India right behind, has entered the world market for essentially everything. At the same time, companies, communities and countries are facing the 'sustainability imperative'.

In April 2005, the United Nations released the Millennium Ecological Assessment. The work of 1360 experts in 95 nations from 22 national science academies, the study reported that over the past 50 years a rising human population has polluted or over-exploited two-thirds of the ecological systems on which life depends.

At the heart of this assessment is a stark warning: 'Human activity is putting such strain on the natural functions of earth that the ability of the planet's ecosystems to sustain future generations can no longer be taken for granted.' UN Secretary-General Kofi Annan added, '. . . the very basis for life on earth is declining at an alarming rate.'

The business leader Ray Anderson, rightly asks, 'What is the business case for ending life on earth?' And Bill Becker, who is running the Presidential Climate Action Project observes, 'If we're going to ruin the planet, we've got to stop claiming we're a superior species.'

The only interesting question is how hard we're going to make the change on ourselves. In *The Power of Sustainable Thinking*, Bob comes to grips with just that question. He reminds us that it isn't a question of technology; it's about us. He's right. We have all the technologies we need to implement ways of living that can manifest a vision all living things can share.

It's not about economics, either. At least six recent studies have shown that the companies who are leaders in environmental, social and good governance policies are outperforming their less sustainable competitors. The first such study by Goldman Sachs showed that the sustainability leaders outperformed the Morgan Stanley Capital International's world index of stocks by 25 per cent since 2005. Seventy-two per cent of the more sustainable companies outperformed industry peers.

Similar studies from such diverse sources as the Economist Intelligence Unit, IBM, Xerox and Sustainable Asset Management all show that companies which use resources more efficiently, that redesign how they make products using such approaches as biomimicry and Cradle-to-Cradle, and who manage their operations to enhance people and intact ecosystems are prospering beyond their slower competitors.

Communities, companies and countries that implement sustainability are gaining commanding competitive advantage. Interestingly, the companies that are the economic laggards turn out to be the most likely to have no one in charge of sustainability. Making the changes we need to make can drive a stronger economy, and more profitable companies. They are demonstrating the practicality of a transition to a sustainable economy.

But enhanced profitability will only drive the transition so far. Dr Bernard Amadei, the saintly founder of Engineers Without Borders – US, who was recently recognized for his years of work by the Heinz Award, reflected, as we discussed how to transform development policy in places like Afghanistan, that the spread of poverty about the globe reflects an inner poverty, and that we cannot address the one without coming to grips with the other. Dana Meadows, author of the now prescient *Limits to Growth*, and *Beyond the Limits*, observed that much of our materialistic, consumer-mad society is derived from seeking to meet non-material needs with material things. It'll never work, but we may destroy life as we know it trying.

Bob offers an alternative: a way to reach inside ourselves to find the capacity to change, and courage to implement it.

It's easy to say that what I do makes no difference. But that's wrong. For starters, the only person we can truly change is our self. More importantly, the rest of the world is watching the west. If we continue to live unsustainable lives, so will they. The Chinese and Indians, for example, have made clear that if we feel it necessary to burn coal for electricity, own several cars per person and consume as much as we can, they demand the right to do just the same thing. Lester Brown points out that if the Chinese continue to grow their economy at the rate that it is currently growing, they will, by 2030, want more oil than the world now lifts, or can ever lift. And more coal, and cars and concrete and. . . At that rate, the future's not possible – unless each one of us shows that there is a better way to live, and unleashes the human capacity to be very fast followers. As Bob points out in this book, it matters what each one of us does.

We also need a new form of leadership. I rather like the line from Lord of the Rings, when Gandalf said:

> *The rule of no realm is mine. But all worthy things that are in peril as the world now stands, those are my care. And for my part I shall not wholly fail if anything passes through this night that can still grow fair, and flower and bear fruit in the days to come. For I too am a steward, did you not know?*

Not a bad maxim. But remember in the end, it was the fun-loving, unassuming little hobbits, who took on their shoulders the awesome task. They were scared, and they didn't know which way to go. But in the end, all the kings and warriors and wizards could only stand by as the little people saved the world.

I think real leadership is extraordinary courage from ordinary people.

The Power of Sustainable Thinking will give you the insights, tools and encouragement to become extraordinary leaders for change.

The fate of the world depends on it.

L. Hunter Lovins
Natural Capitalism Solutions
Eldorado Springs, Colorado
May 2008

Introduction

'Is that it?' I asked my wife. 'Are we finally finished remodelling the house?' Much to my displeasure, Peg replied: 'Not quite.'

After three years of exhausting work that seemed to consume every weekend and many evenings, we were making the final touches to the dilapidated house we had purchased on 24 beautiful acres. The poor condition of the dwelling had reduced the price and made the purchase possible. Unfortunately, our infatuation with the land had led to a grave misjudgement about the house. It was in much worse shape than we had thought.

Exterior walls had dry rot. Windows leaked and provided almost no protection from cold or heat. Almost every exterior door was rotten. Paint was peeling and where it did stick, it looked like it had been applied before World War I. Carpets reeked of cat urine. Electrical plugs and wires hung from the walls. The kitchen and bathrooms were filled with fake plastic butcher-block counter tops and other accessories that must have been all the rage in the 1960s. And that was just the initial list.

My wife and I wanted to fix up the house using the most environmentally and socially positive practices and materials we could find. After all, my field is climate change and sustainability and I know that global warming is the formative issue of our time. I wanted to walk the talk and practise what I preach. My wife felt the same way. She works with small animals. Our house is always filled with cats and dogs and we wanted a safe, non-toxic environment for them.

We also wanted to learn. What was involved with designing a truly climate-positive sustainable household? What did it take to think through the issues and make decisions that were environmentally sound and socially and economically beneficial? Could the work be done without massive consumption of raw materials or producing huge amounts of greenhouse gas emissions and waste? If we found that thinking and acting sustainably were relatively straightforward, we felt confident that anyone could do it.

We had basic construction skills (mostly in demolition), so to reduce costs my wife and I did as much of the work as we could on our own. It was arduous. Unfortunately, it wasn't just the physical aspects of rebuilding the house that were difficult. Keeping our vision of a climate-positive sustainable home from being lost in the minutia of constant problem-solving proved to be even more challenging. A few decisions were easy to make because they involved choices between clear right and wrong options. For example, we met and exceeded all building codes and energy efficiency standards. Most decisions, however, were much more difficult because they required thinking through complex issues and making choices between options that all seemed to have good qualities. We wondered whether it was better for the climate and natural environment to install super-efficient windows and in other ways increase the building's energy efficiency or to invest in technologies such as solar energy panels. We pondered the effects on communities both here and abroad if we purchased products made of natural materials made in a foreign country as opposed to synthetic ones made locally.

Motivating the contractors we hired to help us rebuild the house to use climate-positive sustainable practices and products was also challenging. As a rule, they had very little knowledge about, or interest in, sustainable design and construction. Instead, their thinking was oriented towards keeping their costs as low as possible by using the cheapest, easiest to obtain materials, many of which were made with toxic substances, doing just enough to meet local building codes, and then quickly moving on to their next job while leaving behind large amounts of waste. Doing the minimum was better for them, but would increase our operating costs and produce more environmental and social impacts over the long run. Their mind frame was myopic, meaning they focused only on their immediate needs and could not see how their activities affected the ecological and human systems of which they were part. Ongoing diagnosis and intervention were required to move the contractors from a state of non-awareness and resistance to understanding and action.

Most taxing of all, however, was the constant need to examine our own thinking and behaviours. Due to the relentless stream of obstacles we faced, my wife and I both had to work hard to remain open to new options and continually consider the effects of our activities on the climate, natural environment and people today and tomorrow. Luckily, my wife had the good sense to say 'stay the course' and suggest a glass of wine (organic, of course) at the end of the many days when our heads throbbed from the stress.

Our school-of-hard-knocks education shed some light on why the road to climate protection and sustainability has been so problematic. A good deal of information is available on the web and in books describing *what* people should do to reduce greenhouse gas emissions and behave sustainably. Books describe '50 things you can do to save the Earth', for example, and no less than 39 sets of sustainability principles have been established (Edwards, 2005).

Although they offer helpful tips, reality often quickly overwhelms standards and lists with complexity, making these tools of limited use. Few resources are available to help people think through and decide *why* and *how* to make climate-positive sustainable decisions given the complicated nature of the issues. These questions are much more important than catalogues of actions that individuals can take. People need reasons, not directives, to guide their thinking and behaviour when fundamental change is required.

Most people also don't know how to adjust their habitual thinking or behavioural patterns to incorporate climate-positive approaches, especially if, like the contractors, their mind frame is oriented to the myopic take–make–waste model. In addition, most individuals are unaware of how to motivate other people or the groups and organizations they associate with to implement climate-positive sustainable solutions. As a result, confusion, fear and discouragement seem endemic today, leading to precious little meaningful action to resolve global warming, protect the natural environment or improve social equity.

This is disturbing to me because the fields of psychology as well as organizational change have long known that people, teams and organizations evolve through a series of fairly predictable stages whenever they undergo any significant transformation in their thinking and behaviour. Very different types of change mechanisms are necessary for people who are not yet interested in new approaches than for people who are considering a change, planning or actively engaged in new behaviours.

Research also shows that a systematic relationship exists between the weight people give to the costs and benefits of a change and their readiness to make a shift. The more the downsides of new thinking and behaviour dominate, the more people resist new approaches, and the more the upsides rule, the greater the likelihood that change will occur. The different interventions used to help people progress from the initial stage of not being ready to consider new thinking and behaviour to the later stage of change where new patterns are firmly embedded must increase their perception of the benefits and decrease their concerns about the downsides of change. Change interventions must also increase the confidence people have in their ability to make a shift. In some cases, this may involve skill building and other times may require addressing countervailing cultural and social norms or other perceived or real obstacles.

Information about the process of change does not seem to have made its way to those promoting climate protection and sustainability. Often, no systematic change strategy exists at all, or if one does exist it is based on a one-size-fits-all approach that reaches only a small number of people.

Generally, 80 per cent or more of any group of people are not prepared to quickly alter their thinking and behaviour on an issue. This is especially true when the changes involve deeply held beliefs and assumptions about other people or the natural environment. It should therefore be no surprise that many climate protection and sustainability initiatives struggle. Most tend to emphasize either generic information campaigns or, conversely, action-oriented policy initiatives. The implicit assumption seems to be that people are either totally unaware of the issues or, on the other hand, are ready to act. The vast majority of people and organizations, however, usually lie somewhere between those two poles. People whom climate and sustainability-change initiatives fail to address naturally ignore or resist the need for new thinking and behaviours.

Said differently, change experts have long known that information alone is not sufficient to foster fundamental change. Action without some degree of increased awareness, however, also usually fails. Communications embedded in strategically targeted cognitive, experiential and behavioural change interventions are necessary to address the needs of people no matter what their stage of change may be.

One very successful model that meets these needs is what I call the 5-D 'staged-based' approach to change. The 5-D staged approach applies to individuals, teams and organizations, and, I believe, to society as a whole. It employs a suite of specifically tailored change interventions to help people move from their current stage of change, no matter what it may be, to the next, all the way to action.

My concern over the scarcity of resources available to help individuals and groups institute effective global warming and sustainability communications, behavioural change and policy initiatives led to this book. It is not filled with lists of things you can do to reduce greenhouse gas emissions and become more sustainable. This book is about the process of new thinking and change, not the outcome.

In one sense, this volume is a follow-up to my previous book, *Leading Change Toward Sustainability: A Change Management Guide for Business, Government and Civil Society* (Doppelt, 2003), which describes how organizations can alter their systems of governance, culture and leadership to embrace sustainability. People I spoke with during my research for *Leading Change* often told me they wanted to learn how to shift their personal thinking and behaviours from unsustainable to sustainable, and help people whom they know and work with do the same. This book is my attempt to honour those requests.

In another sense, this book is an altogether new venture. Through my work directing the Climate Leadership Initiative at the University of Oregon, it has become abundantly clear to me that we will not protect the climate or adopt a path towards sustainability unless a vast number of people reorient their thinking and behaviours.

For instance, many people – in particular, environmentalists – hold the perception that climate protection and sustainability are about the natural environment. This is wrong. Sustainability is about *us*. It's about altering the way in which we humans imagine, design, build and operate our economic and social systems. The climate and natural environment are just some of the many beneficiaries of more mindful and effective human behaviours.

Despite the fears of many in the business community, climate protection and sustainability are also not about constraining the economy. To the contrary, only by increasing prosperity, well-being and security around the globe will we protect the climate and achieve sustainability.

Although many politicians would have you believe that new technologies and policies lie at the heart of climate protection and sustainability, this is also erroneous. New ways of providing goods and services and the policies needed to foster them are merely the outcome of something much more fundamental, which is a deep-seated change in how we perceive and respond to the world around us. At their core, climate protection and sustainability are about *new ways of thinking and behaving*. Until this is understood by a majority of the population, little progress will be made.

The struggle to resolve global warming and today's other pressing environmental and social challenges thus reflects, more than anything, a crisis of thought. In fact, I believe that climate change represents the greatest failure of thought in human history. The most urgent need is for all of us to look inside and decide if our core beliefs and perceptions, and the behaviours that they spawn, match the nature of today's reality and if we are living up to our most deeply felt values and aspirations. If people and organizations can become motivated to engage in this type of deep-rooted appraisal and then be helped to progress through the normal stages of change all the way to action, solutions that increase economic prosperity and social well-being and that protect the environment will inevitably follow. It is my hope that this book will, in some small way, contribute to this goal.

REFERENCES

Doppelt, B. (2003) *Leading Change Toward Sustainability: A Change Management Guide for Business, Government and Civil Society*, Greenleaf Publishing, UK

Edwards, A. (2005) *The Sustainability Revolution*, New Society Publishing, Gabriola Island, BC

List of Acronyms and Abbreviations

°C	degrees Celsius
CEO	chief executive officer
CFC	chlorofluorocarbon
CLI	Climate Leadership Initiative
CO_2	carbon dioxide
CRT	cathode ray tube
DDT	dichlorodiphenyltrichloroethane
DNA	deoxyribonucleic acid
EPA	US Environmental Protection Agency
°F	degrees Fahrenheit
GDP	gross domestic product
GHG	greenhouse gas
HDPE	high-density polyethylene
HFC	hydro-chlorofluorocarbon
IPCC	Intergovernmental Panel on Climate Change
kg	kilogram
km	kilometre
kWh	kilowatt hours
lb	pound
LED	light-emitting diode
NAE	National Association of Evangelicals
NASA	US National Aeronautics and Space Administration
ppm	parts per million
PSA	public service announcement
PVC	polyvinylchloride
SBI	Sustainable Business Initiative
STB	sustainability thinking blunder
SUV	sports utility vehicle
TTM	trans-theoretical model of change
UK	United Kingdom
UO	University of Oregon
URI	University of Rhode Island
US	United States
VOC	volatile organic compound
WHO	World Health Organization

Part I The Imperatives of Change

1
The Gift

To most of the world, especially those of us living in the West, this seems like a particularly troubled time. From global warming to terrorism, growing poverty, war in the Middle East and uncertainties over the supply and affordability of oil, it sometimes feels as though the wheels of our civilization are all coming off at once.

At some point, every society finds itself confronted by forces that the reigning worldview cannot successfully address. Some forces arise from uncontrollable natural events. After Hurricane Katrina devastated the US Gulf Coast in 2005, many people were forced to re-examine their perspectives about the role of government in overseeing construction, land use and emergency management systems. Others are self-inflicted, such as when a nation overextends itself in war and, as a result, must alter its entire foreign policy. Still other forces result from purposeful acts of enquiry that lead to entirely new understandings. The discovery of coal-driven steam power that triggered the Industrial Revolution comes to mind.

No matter what the cause, when societies come face to face with these core inflection points, the successful practices of the past quickly become failures because ideas and solutions that seemed pertinent under previous circumstances lead to disaster under new conditions.

It is at this point that societies rise or fall. Human history is filled with defining moments when, faced with new conditions that only altered perspectives could surmount, people were forced to make fundamental choices that determined their fate. Grasping the significance of such moments and making the deep shifts in thinking, perception and behaviour required in order to succeed in the new reality is what historian Thomas Berry (1999) calls *The Great Work* of a people.

Seen from this perspective, human history is the story of how societies responded to their defining moments. Occasionally in the past, tragedy resulted when a society failed to rise to the challenge. Archaeologists believe the Mayan culture in Mesoamerica collapsed, in large part, because they failed to heed the warning of depleted soils, silted lakes and declining water supply in dry years. Geographer Jarred Diamond (2005, p248) suggests that the Norse culture in Greenland collapsed predominantly because they did not adapt their thinking and perspectives to cooler weather conditions.

Yet, at other times, when societies altered their core beliefs and thought processes, greatness resulted. New perspectives opened the floodgates of inspiration, creativity and possibility. The Renaissance, which followed the Middle Ages, a time described as a period of darkness and ignorance, unleashed a flourishing of European artistic and scientific achievement, starting in Italy during the mid 1300s. Many historians today view the roots of the Renaissance as an intellectual and ideological change, rather than a substantive one.

One of the most important solutions to global warming is a deep-seated shift in the type and way in which energy is used. Transformations in the energy regimes that power societies have long been at the heart of many of history's defining moments. Every major economic revolution throughout time, for example, has been driven by a fundamental shift in energy regimes because energy powers every aspect of human activity. The transition to new forms of energy inevitably alters a society's beliefs and thought patterns in a fundamental way. With new thinking comes a shake-up of the prevailing economic, social and political power structure. The upheaval and stress that accompany these transformations typically marshal in legions of doomsayers and end-of-times religious revivals. Yet, looking back, one can see that each major energy transition offered the gifts of increased prosperity and well-being.

The first major energy shift came about 230,000 years ago when humans discovered how to control fire. The ability to kill germs by cooking food and to provide warmth in cold and damp weather dramatically reduced illness and death. The change from wood and organic material – for most of human history the dominant source of energy – to coal over 200 years ago launched the Industrial Revolution. In the first four decades of the 20th century, the transition from coal to oil, and then from the direct to the indirect use of fuel through electricity for commercial and residential uses, and from horses and coal-fired trains to electricity and oil-fuelled cars and tractors in the transportation sector, triggered wealth creation in the West on a scale never before seen in human history.

Despite the turmoil and difficulty involved in each of these transitions, changing conditions provided an offering that, with a suitable response, not only avoided the social calamity predicted by the pessimists, but dramatically improved human well-being.

Today, through circumstances only partly our doing, it is our turn. We have been offered a gift. We must decide if we will accept it. The offering has come about due to the profound risks posed to us and future generations by global climate change and many other interlinked environmental and social problems. These perils are the result of humankind's failure to align our thinking and behaviours with the fundamental laws of ecological and human systems.

Human-induced global warming is perhaps the most serious threat that the whole of humanity has ever faced. It is the result of the most profound failure of perception and reason in the history of humanity. Climate change is not really new. Since time began, living beings have had to adapt to changing climatic conditions. However, most of the adjustments humans have made in the past were in response to short-term regionalized climate variations caused by natural events, such as volcanic eruptions and fluctuations in solar radiation. Today, for the first time in history, climate change threatens the entire world and humans are the dominant cause.

Global warming is the ultimate issue of sustainability. Although few people, as of yet, seem to grasp this, it will be the defining issue for all of humanity for decades to come.

In their *Climate Change 2007: Synthesis Report* (IPCC, 2007) the United Nations-sponsored Intergovernmental Panel on Climate Change said that it is unequivocal that global warming is happening now and that the consequences will be serious even if worldwide greenhouse gas emissions can be immediately reduced. For example, a global mean warming of 2° Celsius (3.6° Fahrenheit) is almost unavoidable due to the greenhouse gases already emitted into the atmosphere. Sea-level rise of up to 1.4m (4.6 feet) may now be inevitable. If global temperatures rise high enough to cause a partial deglaciation of the polar ice sheets, over a time frame of centuries or less sea levels may rise an additional 3.7m to 6m (12 to 20 feet).

Even a little less than a 2°C (3.6°F) warming would put millions of human beings at risk from coastal flooding, drought-induced famine and other effects. Up to 30 per cent of species on the planet could be pushed to the brink of extinction (IPCC, 2007). Temperature increases much above 2°C (3.6°F) compared to pre-industrial levels are very likely to force the climate beyond a point where dangerous risk to human societies and ecosystems rises substantially. Limiting warming to 2°C (3.6°F) must therefore be the goal for mankind.

James Hansen, head of the US National Aeronautics and Space Administration's (NASA's) Goddard Institute for Space Studies and one of the first imminent scientists to warn the public about global warming, suggested in March 2008 that to limit temperature increases to 2°C, atmospheric concentrations of greenhouse gases must be stabilized at no more than 350 parts per million (ppm). Climate models had previously suggested that keeping emission levels to between 450ppm and 550ppm would be sufficient, and the European Union and many of the big environmental groups had advocated for the lower end of this target. The concentration of greenhouse gases in the atmosphere has already reached 385ppm, which means that if Hansen is correct, emission levels may already be above the range that could trigger dangerous climate change.[1] This may explain why Arctic ice sheets are melting faster than climate models first predicted.

Time is therefore of the essence. To keep warming below 2°C, the Intergovernmental Panel on Climate Change's (IPCC's) chairman, Rachandra Pachuari, said in 2007 that changes instituted in the *next two to three years* must halt global emission increases in less than ten years (*by 2015* was the date given) in order to avoid tragedies of an almost unimaginable scale. This must be followed by an unbending effort to reduce emissions by 50 to 80 per cent or more by mid century or earlier.

The need for dramatic emission reductions means we now live in a carbon-constrained world. For the next 100 years, and more likely for centuries, humanity will be forced to meet its needs while generating significantly less – and some would say almost zero – greenhouse gas emissions. The Kyoto Accord, the world's first international treaty aimed at controlling global warming, requires industrial nations to reduce their greenhouse gases by 5 to 8 per cent compared to 1990 levels by 2008 to 2012 (targets and due dates are nation specific). Most of the nations that signed the accord are struggling to meet even these modest targets. A 50 to 80 per cent or more reduction seems especially daunting.

The ecological impacts of uncontrolled climate change, such as increased droughts, floods, wildfires, heat waves, disease, storm intensity and sea-level rise, will cause damage to the global economy on the scale of the great depression of the 1920s and 1930s or either World War. This was the conclusion of a major study released in 2006 by Nicholas Stern, head of the UK's Government Economic Service and former chief economist for the World Bank. The report found that the economic impacts are likely to be between 5 and 20 per cent of the world's gross domestic product (Stern, 2006).

The main culprit is our use of fossil fuels. However, deforestation and land-use changes also contribute to the problem. Since the early 1800s, fossil fuels have powered the growth of Western industrial economies. More recently, coal and other fossil fuels have also powered the expansion of economies in nations such as China and India, processes that have elevated millions of people out of poverty. Whether burned in industrial or developing nations, however, fossil fuels produce carbon dioxide (CO_2) that accumulates in the atmosphere. Too much CO_2 heats up the Earth and unbalances the global climate. The climate crisis resulted from economic development that drives energy production and use in industrialized economies; but some developing nations, such as China and India, have now become major contributors as well.

So far, much of the attention on reducing greenhouse gas emissions has focused on power plants and large manufacturing facilities. Big energy producers and industrial plants, however, are not the sole problems. They generate energy and manufacture products for consumers. This means the problem is all of us. Ordinary people like you and me are the ultimate drivers of global warming through the greenhouse gases that we directly generate through our transportation choices, the way in which we power and manage our buildings and homes, and the waste that we generate. Consumers are also responsible for emissions that we indirectly influence through the type and amount of goods and services we purchase and use. One study found that consumers in the UK are directly or indirectly responsible for 60 per cent of that nation's greenhouse gases (CBI, 2007). Another study in the UK found that at least a third of the carbon savings achievable from households result from behavioural changes as opposed to new technologies (Boardman, 2007). Almost two-thirds of the energy used in the US today comes from consumer-driven industries, including residential energy use and vehicle transportation (McKinsey and Company, 2008).

Solving global warming will therefore involve much more than modest efficiency improvements or cap-and-trade policies. Although they are absolutely essential, new legislation and market-based tools represent just a few of the tools needed to fight the climate crisis. Successful solutions will require altogether new perspectives and ways of thinking that produce behavioural changes, as well as technological and policy changes at every level of society: individual, household, organizational, community, state, national and international.

Climate change may be humanity's most pressing environmental problem today, but it is far from the only challenge. The *Millennium Ecosystem Assessment*, a four-year international study of the status of the world's environment, found in 2005 that two-thirds of the globe's ecological services, such as the clean air and water provided by nature, are degraded or are used unsustainably (United Nations Environment Program, www.millenniumassessment.org/en/About.aspx). A separate study by a dozen academic institutions in five countries predicted that due to over-fishing, pollution and other environmental factors, all of the world's fishing stocks will likely collapse by mid century unless major changes are made (Worm et al, 2006, 2007). Given the unanticipated emergence of many recent environmental concerns, we should also expect new and, as yet, unforeseen risks to suddenly appear.

These issues influence the global climate, and the way in which global warming unfolds will exacerbate existing environmental problems. Environmental degradation also aggravates and, in turn, is aggravated by poverty and other forms of social distress. Poverty has many faces. It is hunger. It is lack of adequate shelter. It is being sick and not having access to healthcare. Poverty is the death of a child due to illness caused by polluted air or water. The World Bank estimates that in 2001, 1.1 billion people had consumption levels below US$1 a day – one fifth of the world's population – and 2.7 billion lived on less than US$2 a day (Chen and Ravallion, 2004). A 2007 study by the World Health Organization (WHO) found that approximately 40 per cent of deaths worldwide today are caused by water, air and soil pollution. Furthermore, of the world population of about 6.5 billion, 57 per cent are malnourished, compared with 20 per cent of a world population of 2.5 billion in 1950, with most of the increase concentrated in non-industrialized nations.[2]

In addition to the human suffering that these figures represent, the interplay between environmental degradation, poverty and disease increases social and ethnic tensions and produces political instability, which reinforces the cycle. The severe drought caused by a shifting climate, coupled with unsound environmental practices, led to social chaos and violence in Sudan, Somalia, Ethiopia and across the Sahel in sub-Saharan Africa, forcing millions of subsistence farmers and herders to become refugees. A similar explanation has been given for the guerrilla war in Mexico's Chiapas Province, where more than half the farmers cultivate steep hillsides. Seventy per cent of Mexico's agricultural land is affected by erosion, which could be one of the reasons for the steady migration northward into the US.

Ironically, just as concern grows over the environmental impacts of fossil fuels, the supply and price of oil seems to be rapidly changing. A number of oil experts believe that the global supply of oil may already have peaked or will soon do so. The major concern about peak oil is not so much that supplies will run out; in theory, half the supply is still available. Fossil fuels are also fungible, meaning that oil can be made from shale, coal and other resources. The problem is that supplies will now be on a downward slide even as demand continues to rise, which means prices will continue to rise. And making oil from shale, as is now being done in Canada, or from other fossil fuels is extremely costly and produces even greater environmental impacts than the direct use of oil. When it occurs, peak oil therefore promises major economic, social and environmental disruptions.

If global warming, ecological degradation and peak oil cause economic opportunities to decline, many experts fear that instability will grow around the world. Forced migration of refugees, civil unrest, expanding regional and global conflict, and the collapse of governments and expansion of authoritarian practice will likely result.[3]

In short, the Earth's natural capital – ecological wealth not created by, but essential for, human survival – as well as social and economic well-being are at grave risk. The way in which society responds to these challenges will define the winners and losers of the future.

A four-part response that I call 'RPEG' is needed to resolve global warming and today's other pressing challenges. We must quickly and simultaneously: Reduce greenhouse gas emissions by 80 per cent or more below 1990 levels; Prepare our natural (e.g. ecosystems and biodiversity), built (e.g. water, transport infrastructure), human (e.g. health care, emergency response) and economic (e.g. industry, agriculture) systems to withstand and adapt to the now unpreventable impacts of a warming planet; Educate everyone around the globe about how to live in a much warmer carbon-constrained world; and Grow prosperity and security through low and non-carbon industries and jobs.

This means that no silver bullet can solve our challenges. They are interlinked and must be tackled together. Economic development must be decoupled from the environmental and social impacts that it now generates, allowing prosperity and security for people across the globe to increase while greenhouse gas emissions and environmental degradation decrease. As the signers of the Kyoto Accord have found, achieving an 80 per cent reduction in global warming emissions while expanding economic and social well-being cannot be accomplished simply through modest energy efficiency improvements and other slight adjustments. Nothing less than a fundamental redesign of our economic development paradigm and the social systems that support it will accomplish this type of absolute decoupling.

Because fossil fuels are central to most economies, deep-seated changes in the type of energy and the way in which it is used offer a way to start the emission reduction component of the REPG processs. Indeed, increased energy efficiency and a shift to clean energy are the focus of most current climate protection efforts.

Changes in energy regimes, however, are just one piece of the solution. Almost every consumer product today seems to be constructed in whole, or in part, with fossil fuels, from the plastics in computers and most household goods to the natural gas in industrial fertilizers and the plastic bags that litter the landscape. Whole new ways of designing goods and services, new sources of renewable material feedstocks, and new ways of using and disposing of end-of-life materials will, consequently, be needed.

Because the Earth's ecological systems are in such peril, fundamental shifts to sustainable mining, agriculture, forestry and land use must also be integral elements of any solution.

Although rapidly reducing emissions is vital, it is just as important now for people across the world to assess the vulnerabilities and increase the resilience of their natural, built, human and economic systems to withstand and adapt to the impacts of climate change. Extensive education and training will be necessary to help people understand the risks, reduce emissions and prepare for climate change. And, of course, none of this will occur unless people feel secure, which will require extensive efforts to increase prosperity through the expansion of sustainable industries and jobs.

Some type of human behaviour is involved with designing, constructing, using, managing and disposing of every gizmo, plan and educational curriculum we develop. Significant changes in behaviour will therefore be a core element of any successful effort to protect the climate and adopt a path towards sustainability. And each of these transformations must increase economic prosperity and personal security in industrial and developing nations alike if they are to have any chance of long-term success.

New solutions always start with fresh perspectives. Whole new visions and forms of reasoning must drive the transition. New thinking begins with an accurate understanding of our current challenges and the beliefs, assumptions and values that produced the problems in the first place. It also requires rethinking what we stand for, how we want to live and what we want to achieve in the future.

Global climate change and today's other environmental and social challenges may produce bumps and bruises for a while; but, paradoxically, they may also be the shock that humanity needs to sweep away tired old ideas and allow new ones to flourish. Many people seem aimless today, with little sense of purpose. Lacking any other source of meaning, rampant consumerism and other personally and socially destructive behaviours have come to dominate. If we get our heads screwed on correctly, however, today's challenges could be just the ticket needed to focus individuals, organizations and society at large on achieving a higher purpose that ushers in a whole new era of prosperity and security, while resolving our environmental challenges.

New thinking among early adopters offers a glimpse of the possibilities to come. Industries producing low-carbon goods and services are rapidly growing, for example, and the global market for these technologies alone is projected to exceed US$500 billion and could exceed US$2 trillion per year by 2050 (Stern, 2006). The market for renewable energy technology is expected to grow from just less than US$60 billion in 2006 to almost US$240 billion by 2016 (Clean Edge Inc, 2006). Worldwide investment in clean energy could be as much as US$100 billion by 2009. More than 2 million people are already employed in the renewable energy field globally, and more than 170,000 jobs were created just in 2006. Investments in renewable power reached US$71 billion in 2006, almost 50 per cent more than in 2005. And the market capitalization rate of the 85 largest renewable energy companies reached US$50 billion in 2005, double that of 2004 (The Climate Group, 2007).

Renewable energy, such as solar, biomass and wind, holds special promise in developing countries because of the potential for small distributed systems that avoid the need for huge centralized infrastructure and for its job creation potential. The most important need is financing. International carbon trading is seen as one of the most economically efficient means of financing renewables in developing nations. Other ideas are also being explored.

The market for bio-based products is also rapidly growing. Bio-based products include commercial and specialty chemicals, fuels, and materials produced from the direct or indirect physical or chemical processing of biomass, such as cellulose, starch, oils, protein, lignin and terpenes.

Big corporations are getting into the act. In 2007 alone, for example, Dell Inc, the computer maker, pledged to become the greenest technology company in the world and become 'carbon neutral'. FPL Group, a Florida-based utility, announced plans to invest US$2.4 billion in a clean energy programme. In Texas, regulators approved a US$45 billion buyout of utility TXU Corp, but only after its new owners, investment firms Kohlberg Kravis Roberts & Co and TPG, agreed to cancel 8 of 11 coal-burning power plants that it had planned, increase investments in renewable fuels, reduce its carbon emissions, and take other steps to address global warming. Google Inc launched one of the biggest solar power arrays in the world at its headquarters and pledged to become 'carbon neutral'. Google also launched a programme to reduce energy consumption in its huge data centres and said it was investing hundreds of millions of dollars to figure out how to make renewable fuels as cheap as environmentally unfriendly coal (The Climate Group, 2007). Although some of this is likely to turn out to be greenwash, these activities represent growing awareness of the need for innovation and change.

Early adopters in the public sector have also begun to engage in climate protection. At the national level, Germany, for example, has already reduced emissions by 19 per cent below 1990 levels and expects to reduce them by 21 per cent by 2010 and by 40 per cent by 2020. Germany is aggressively pursing renewable energy and now has more wind power capacity than the US. Through a combination of a carbon trading scheme and corporate reductions involving 44 industrial sectors and 6000 companies, efforts to reduce greenhouse gas emission in the UK have exceeded expectations and been accomplished more cheaply than anticipated as well.

Some municipal governments have engaged in far-thinking innovation. For example, since 2006, Barcelona – Spain's second largest city – has required all new and renovated buildings to install solar panels to supply at least 60 per cent of the energy needed to heat water. Vaxjo, a town of 78,000 on the shores of Lake Helga in Sweden, has cut greenhouse gas emissions by 30 per cent since 1993 through a combination of replacing oil with wood chips from local sawmills at its heating and power plant. Ashes from the furnace are returned to the forest as nutrients in a truly closed-loop system. Toronto, Canada, has saved Cdn$23 million since 1993 from energy efficiency improvements. The city also receives Cdn$1.5 million in revenue annually from the sale of electricity generated from methane gas that is captured at three of its landfills (The Climate Group, 2007).

Innovative ways of improving the environment, while creating jobs for low-skilled individuals, are also sprouting. Richmond, California, for example, is spending US$1 million annually to train low-income residents in solar installation as a way of preparing them for jobs in the solar industry. During 2007, Oakland, California, designated US$250,000 for a Green Collar Jobs Program that will train unemployed people in solar and green roof installation, green building and home weatherization. Since 1994, the City of Chicago has spent US$2 million on a programme that trained 265 participants in landscaping and tree pruning, and since 2005 in computer recycling and disposal of household chemicals, such as motor oils and paints. Sixty per cent of the people found jobs in government, the private sector or non-profits (*U.S.A. Today*, 2007).

The Climate Masters Program developed by my programme at the University of Oregon, which as helped private citizens reduce their greenhouse gas emissions by an average of 2 tons per person, and other community-based programmes are helping households and individuals in the US reduce emissions while also saving money, and improving personal health and quality of life.[4]

Similar efforts are emerging in developing nations. Cleaner, more efficient wood fuel cooking stoves, for example, are being distributed in southern developing nations. Traditional cooking stoves are inefficient, generate large amounts of greenhouse gas emissions and are linked to 1.6 million deaths per year from indoor air pollution.

These and many other examples signify the exciting possibilities that new thinking offers for increasing prosperity and security while resolving global warming and other environmental challenges. They represent just the tip of the iceberg, however, of the new perspectives and economic opportunities that will be needed and can emerge in the future if we reorient our thinking and behaviours around the mission of stabilizing the climate in a way that increases global prosperity and security.

And so, in these early years of the 21st century, through circumstances created by previous generations and amplified by our own behaviour, we have been chosen for the great work of fundamentally reframing the thinking and behaviours that created and buttressed our economic and social systems around the higher purpose of protecting the climate and adopting a path towards sustainability. We did not set out to create this moment. Ironically, the unbridled success of our industrial economy and related social systems brought it upon us.

As in previous times, we have the ability to choose our own destiny. Defining moments like this do not come along all that often. They also do not endure. The window of opportunity slams shut if left open too long. Failure to act will just as surely determine our future, as will active engagement. The choice is ours to make.

The journey that lies ahead is certain to be fraught with hazards. No matter how fast or effectively we act, humanity must learn to live with some global warming and climate change. Some regions of the world and certain people will be particularly hard hit. Doomsayers will undoubtedly fan the flames of fear and despair. The transition will not be painless. Yet, if we follow the path of previous societies who rose to the challenge of their defining moment and made fundamental adjustments in their sense of purpose and way of thinking, we can make the transition to a climate-positive sustainable future and end up better off.

Seen from this perspective, we have been offered the opportunity to write the first act of a whole new script about how humanity meets its economic, social and environmental needs. This is, indeed, a gift – and a great responsibility.

NOTES

1 Tim Flannery interview on 'Landline', Australian Broadcasting Corporation, 9 October 2007.
2 Online edition of the journal *Human Ecology*, www.ingentaconnect.com/content/klu/huec, June 2007.
3 For more on this topic, see the report by 11 US admirals and generals produced in April 2007 by the CNA Corporation, an Alexandria Virginia national security think tank, entitled *National Security and the Threat of Climate Change*.
4 For more information, see http://climlead.uoregon.edu.

REFERENCES

Berry, T. (1999) *The Great Work: A Way into the Future*, Bell Tower, New York
Boardman, B. (2007) *Home Truths: A Low-carbon Strategy to Reduce UK Housing Emissions by 80% by 2050*, Environmental Change Institute, University of Oxford, Oxford, UK

CBI Climate Change Task Force (2007) *Climate Change: Everyone's Business*, CBI, London, www.avtclient.co.uk/climatereport/docs/climatereport2007summary.pdf

Chen, S. and Ravallion, M. (2004) 'How have the world's poor fared since the early 1980s?' World Bank, www.wds.worldbank.org/external/default/main?PagePK=64193027&piPK=64187937&theSitePK=523679&menuPK=64187510&searchMenuPK=64187282&theSitePK=523679&entityID=000112742–20040722172047&searchMenuPK=64187282&theSitePK=523679

Clean Edge Inc (2006) *Clean-Energy Trends 2006*, www.cleanedge.com/reports-trends2006.php

CNA Corporation (2007) *National Security and the Threat of Climate Change*, CNA Corporation, Alexandria, VA, http://securityandclimate.cna.org/report/National%20Security%20and%20the%20Threat%20of%20Climate%20Change.pdf

Diamond, J. (2005) *Collapse: How Societies Choose to Fail or Succeed*, Viking Books, New York

IPCC (Intergovernmental Panel on Climate Change) (2007) *Climate Change 2007: Synthesis Report*, Fourth Assessment Report, United Nations Environment Programme, www.ipcc.ch/pdf/assessment-report/ar4/syr/ar4_syr_spm.pdf

McKinsey and Company (2008) 'The case for investing in energy productivity', www.mckinsey.com/mgi/reports/pdfs/Investing_Energy_Productivity/Investing_Energy_Productivity.pdf

Stern, N. (2006) *The Stern Review of the Economics of Climate Change*, 30 October, London, www.sternreview.org.uk

The Climate Group (2007) *In the Black: The Growth of the Low Carbon Economy*, May, http://theclimategroup.org/index.php/news_and_events/news_and_comment/low_carbon_products_and_services_bring_high_levels_of_jobs_and_revenues/

U.S.A. Today (2007) 'Cities cultivate 2 types of green', *U.S.A. Today*, 13 December, p3A

Worm, B. et al (2006) 'Impacts of biodiversity loss on ocean ecosystem services', *Science*, vol 314, no 5800, November, pp787–790

Worm, B. (2007) 'Response to comments on "Impacts of biodiversity loss on ocean ecosystem services"', *Science*, vol 316, no 5829, June, pp1285

2

Making Our Fate

It is the coward and the fool who says this is fate. But it is the strong man who stands up and says: 'I will make my fate.' (Sanskrit proverb)

The gods did not decree global warming or any other troubling outcome of our unsustainable economic system. Nor did the gods create the incredible advances in science, economics and governance that the world has seen over the aeons. Human behaviours produced them. Human activities result from choices they make about what is really important. Our beliefs and assumptions, and the thought patterns they engender, lead us to make certain decisions. A change in thinking results in different judgements and behaviours. Some great unknown force will not determine our destiny. The way in which we think will make our fate.

One of the reasons people fail to achieve new goals is that they try to change their behaviour without first altering their thinking. This always fails. Success of any new venture depends entirely upon how you think beforehand.

Even the most progressive among us can fail to adopt a climate-positive sustainable path when their thinking is flawed. The US organic food industry has long thought of itself as the vanguard of the sustainability movement. The first organic farmers were personally committed to caring for the land and providing healthy, nutritious food. Today, the organic food trade is outpacing conventional agriculture by leaps and bounds.

Although organic products are sustainable, through the work my staff and I have done over the years with the industry, I know that the business model used by the majority of organic food companies is not. Raw organic materials are imported, usually by air, to North American and European markets from far-off places such as South America, Africa and Australia. They are then transported yet again, usually by polluting diesel-powered trucks, to retail outlets across each country. All along the way, fresh organic food is refrigerated. Many organic products are vastly over packaged, often in non-recyclable plastic containers made from fossil fuels that end up in landfills or incinerators. The emission of greenhouse gases and other toxic substances produced by the constant cooling, long-distance travel, packaging and waste is immense. Produce in the US travels, on average, 2100km to 3200km (1300 to 2000 miles) from farm to consumer. At least 17 per cent of all greenhouse gas emissions in the US today are produced by the food production and distribution system (Pimentel, 1996). Similar patterns are true in Europe.

Climate-positive sustainable operations are the goal of many in the organic food trade, but few have made the fundamental changes in thinking required to achieve it.

Whether the challenge is at the family, organizational or societal level, overcoming a culture's prevailing worldview is never easy. Every culture has a shared way of comprehending the world. This mental frame helps people to make sense of events, decide right from wrong, and shape the way in which they think about family, work, other people and the natural environment. The mental frames held by a society are the glue that binds its culture together.

Since the dawn of the industrial revolution, Western societies have taught people to think of the economy as a 'machine' that operates in an automatic fashion following unalterable and amoral 'laws'. Although the machine provides goods and services for humans, it is itself soulless and inhuman (Nelson, 2006). People, we are not so implicitly told, are but cogs in the wheels of commerce, to be utilized as the economic machine deems necessary. The natural environment is nothing more than an endless source of resources for human use and a free receptacle for our waste.

Ethical and moral questions related to how the economy should be directed to serve human needs and respect the natural environment upon which we all depend are seen as irrelevant to the economic machine. Instead, the relentless pursuit of individual self-interest is viewed as a virtue and a fundamental right. Almost any behaviour not declared by law to be illegal is acceptable.

Industrial society's mental frame of the 'economy as an amoral machine' is actually quite new by historical standards. For most of human history, economics involved self-provisioning – a job shaped by longstanding cultural and religious traditions. The Industrial Revolution, which began in England during the late 18th and 19th centuries, altered things. The shift from slow-moving subsistence agricultural economies to fast-moving mechanized production profoundly changed the way in which people perceived the world. This shift in worldviews gave birth to today's economy-as-machine mental framework. Classical economics emerged from this change as well.

Up through the 17th century, most people saw their relationship with nature in largely religious terms. Because survival was a direct outcome of the food and provisions provided by the land, most people thought of themselves as part of a living sacred universe.

The underpinnings of this ancient worldview began to erode when scientific advancements, first by Galileo and René Descartes and later by Isaac Newton, began to form a new sense of the world as a giant clockwork mechanism. Nature was seen to be reducible to components controlled by laws and mathematics. This new mental frame shattered the old belief system and gave rise to technological innovations that spawned the Industrial Revolution.

Adam Smith was among the first to describe the economy using a machine metaphor. This is not surprising. Smith's thinking was a natural outgrowth of the prevailing worldview of his time. Smith argued that individuals' rational pursuit of their own self-interest would automatically be transformed by the 'invisible hand' of self-regulating market mechanisms into what is good for society as a whole. Self-interest to Smith was the 'energy source' driving the 'gears' of the economic machine.

Subsequent economists and scientists began to observe that the clockwork-like economic machine progressed on its own quite nicely with little concern for purpose, impacts or ethics. After all, machines have no minds or values. Economists increasingly saw their role to be the objective study of the 'drives' and 'mechanisms' that power the economic machine. Over time, as this shift unfolded, moral and ethical questions about the workings of the economy were increasingly dismissed as 'uneconomic' and shuttled off to the soft-hearted realms of philosophy and religion.

Industrial societies have embraced the economy-as-amoral-machine mental frame since at least the mid 1800s. This way of thinking is drummed into us from early childhood onward. If you question whether our society actually embraces the economy-as-amoral-machine worldview, ask yourself if your employer would replace you with a machine if it were possible. If the answer is yes, you are seen simply as a resource to be deployed, much like a computer or a drill punch, to keep the economic machine rolling along.

Critics of the machine worldview are usually dismissed by proponents as naive idealists who don't grasp the tough world of economics, as obstructionists (or Luddites) who want society to revert to the caveman era, or as lazy people not willing to invest the time or energy needed to succeed. With such powerful forces shaping our minds, it's no surprise that few of us dare to challenge the economy-as-machine mental frame.

THE TAKE–MAKE–WASTE ECONOMIC SYSTEM

The worldview of the economy as a machine unprejudiced by ethical questions led logically to the belief that nature exists for the unbridled use of humans. From this way of thinking emerged what is often called the '*take–make–waste*' economic system that today dominates industrial societies and is spreading to emerging economies such as India and China. Humans take resources such as minerals, metals, fish, wood, coal and other fossil fuels from the Earth's surface. We use these raw materials to power our economy and convert them to goods and services for human use. The massive amounts of often highly toxic by-products produced by the system are then dumped back into the very same resource base that we rely on for our raw materials as carbon dioxide and other greenhouse gases, air, soil and water pollution, as well as solid and hazardous waste.

Each step in the take–make–waste system is pursued as quickly and efficiently as possible. Ever-increasing labour productivity is seen as the way of increasing

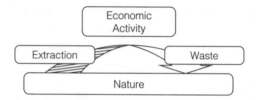

Figure 2.1 *The take–make–waste economic system*

Source: adapted from Doppelt (2003).

abundance. Little concern is given to how the take–make–waste system affects the climate, physical environment and people today or in the future: it is blind to its effects on the systems upon which it depends (see Figure 2.1).

Capitalism is not the only economic system to employ the take–make–waste approach. Communism, socialism and almost every other form of economic organization employed over the past 200 years have adopted this approach, meaning that this mental frame is not associated with any particular political ideology. It results from humanity's fundamental way of looking at the world. The human race has perfected the machine-like 'take it, make it, waste it' approach.

THE LINEAR TAKE–MAKE–WASTE SYSTEM

My wife and I like to think we are not accomplices in the take–make–waste system. We try to buy only what we need (a point of some debate in our household), don't purchase heavily packaged goods, and recycle everything we can. Yet, we throw a small amount of waste (heavily laden with cat litter) into a receptacle that our refuse company hauls away each Tuesday to the local landfill. As much as we want to deny it, we are part of the 'take–make–waste' system. It is very difficult to be good in an inherently harmful system.

I want to make a distinction here between the issues of competition and markets and the take–make–waste economic model. Competition is natural in both ecological and human systems. Similarly, since the dawn of time, humans have traded amongst each other. Thus, competition and markets are not in themselves intrinsically harmful. It is only when these processes fail to take into account the core ecological and human systems that all competitors rely on for life that they become destructive.

The straight-line 'take it–make it–waste it' approach has created tremendous material wealth over the past 200 years. However, because it has failed to account for the systems within which it is embedded, it has also produced serious unintended negative side affects that are now becoming apparent, such as global warming, rampant environment degradation and growing social inequity. If we are to protect the climate and adopt a sustainable path, we must alter the beliefs, assumptions and thinking that perpetuate this approach.

Conditions have changed but our mental frames have not

The take–make–waste economic model and the economy-as-an-amoral-machine mental frame that supports it are vestiges of a bygone era. When the Industrial Revolution began, resources were plenty, the human population was small, capital was in short supply, technological capacity was modest and the Earth had unlimited capacity to absorb human pollution and waste (Meadows et al, 1992). Under these conditions, it was logical for the take–make–waste economic system to take hold. In a world shaped by a mechanical worldview of nature and the economy, and unconstrained by resource limits, myopic thinking was the norm because there was little need to consider how anyone's actions could significantly affect ecological and human systems then or in the future.

The Industrial Revolution, however, dramatically increased the amount of capital available for economic growth and spurred radical technological transformations that significantly expanded the food supply and improved public health. Because populations of any organism normally expand to the limits of their food and energy supply, the human population grew exponentially, along with its capacity to consume resources and generate pollution and waste.

The escalation of humanity's impacts upon the biosphere fundamentally altered the factual basis upon which previous myopic thinking was based. Today, natural capital is scarce and it is people who are abundant: we are awash in capital, and have reached the limits of the Earth's physical capacity to provide more resources and absorb additional pollution and waste. More population growth, consumption, pollution and waste threaten a catastrophic breakdown of life supporting climatic and ecological systems. Economic and social upheaval will surely follow. Our worldview and the myopic thinking and behaviours it spawns, however, have not adapted to this new reality.

Advances in science since the time of Galileo, Descartes and Newton have also refuted the belief that nature and the economy operate through predictable laws that can be measured mathematically. It turns out that order and chaos exist as partners in both ecological and human systems, making them inherently unpredictable and unstable. Melting snow and ice in the Antarctic due to global warming, for example, create a vicious feedback cycle that previously seemed impossible. Less snow and ice exposes more land and water to solar radiation, which absorbs more heat from the sun rather than reflecting it back into space, which amplifies the melting of snow and ice.

Human systems also unexpectedly change on a dime. Think of the unexpected fall of the Berlin Wall and the rapid collapse of the Soviet Union. Numerous other examples of unknown and unpredictable feedbacks exist in ecological and human systems. Our mental image of ecological and social systems, however, still clings to the mechanical model and has failed to incorporate this new information.

The new science challenges the basic premises of modern economics. The so-called 'welfare theory' of contemporary economics says that perfectly functioning free markets will produce efficiency. Waste minimization is seen as a natural outcome of the pursuit of self-interest and profit. However, our economic system generates huge amounts of waste: wasted time, wasted motion, wasted energy and massive amounts of toxic molecular, gaseous, solid and liquid waste. Perfectly functioning efficiency-seeking free markets obviously do not exist. In the real world, the economy is complex, messy and distorted by people and institutions that hoard information, control vast amounts of resources, inundate people with subliminal marketing messages and in other ways force their will on others. It is also at the whim of surprise events. Most people today fail to comprehend this, leaving industrial societies controlled by the science and economics of an age long since passed.

Today's situation reminds me of the age-old story of people in a rowboat. They row and row, but never get anywhere because they forgot to untie the boat from the dock. Despite the many efforts to protect the climate and adopt a path towards sustainability occurring around the globe, little progress seems visible because we remain tied to the dock of the old myopic unsustainable take–make–waste mental frame.

BECOMING A SUSTAINABLE THINKER

Just as previous thinking was based on the conditions of the times, it is imperative that we rapidly formulate a new mental frame based on today's realities. All thinking today must be grounded, first and foremost, in the truth that protecting and restoring the Earth's climate and ecological systems is humanity's most pressing need. This is not something we should do after we deal with economic issues. The issues are one and the same. Stabilizing and restoring the climate and physical environment is a biological, economic and social necessary – a requirement for the survival of humanity.

All thinking today must also be based on the understanding that to protect the climate and natural environment, the most extreme forms of poverty, as well as social justice and global insecurity, must be resolved. Ironically, the limits imposed by the Earth's ability to provide more natural resources and absorb more greenhouse gases and waste can only be addressed by *increasing*, not decreasing, global economic prosperity and social justice. China, for example, will not reduce its greenhouse gas emissions if it means abandoning efforts to raise millions of its people out of poverty. Expanded food, shelter, healthcare, education and environmentally sound job opportunities are thus imperatives if we hope to resolve global warming and today's other challenges. The urgency of these needs can provide humanity, as a whole, and industrial nations, in particular, with the clear mission and higher purpose that seems to have been absent since the great depression and World War II.

This means that all economics today involve moral questions. In the past, people saw their resource use and waste generation as morally desirable in order to lift humanity out of subsistence conditions and poverty. The size of the capital base, the number of people alive and the degraded condition of the climate and physical environment today, however, means that a continuation of similar thinking and behaviour will negatively affect people or ecological processes somewhere, somehow, now or in the future. These are morals issues. Continued unconstrained freedom to generate greenhouse gas pollutants, degrade the environment, and harm individuals and communities in whatever way one wants may have made sense in a previous age; but today it brings humanity closer to the precipice of disaster.

On a now overtaxed finite planet, we are all in it together. Living together requires that humanity think and act in ways that acknowledge, protect and restore the ecological and social systems of which we are all part. Any form of thinking and behaviour that violates these precepts is simply self-destructive and unsustainable. What I call 'sustainable thinking', on the other hand, accounts for and enhances the systems we all depend upon for our survival. Sustainable thinking is the next logical step in the evolution of human thinking and behaviour.

Altering society's long standing perspectives from the myopic to a sustainable mind frame will not be easy; but it can be done. After all, worldviews are simply images people hold in their minds. By honestly examining and challenging the beliefs and assumptions that control our minds, we can see the perspectives that produce today's ecological and social crisis. New beliefs and assumptions make possible new thinking and behaviours. This means that anyone can become a sustainable thinker. Once you make a commitment to this higher purpose, you are in control of your fate. Once you are in control of your own fate, you can help to decide the fate of the world as well.

REFERENCES

Doppelt, B. (2003) *Leading Change Toward Sustainability: A Change Management Guide for Business, Government and Civil Society*, Greenleaf Publishing, UK

Meadows, D., Meadows, D. and Randers, J. (1992) *Beyond the Limits: Confronting Global Collapse, Envisioning a Sustainable Future*, Chelsea Green Publishing, Post Hills, Vermont

Nelson, J. (2006) *Economics for Humans*, University of Chicago Press, Chicago

Pimentel, D. (1996) *Food Energy and Society*, University of Colorado Press, Boulder, CO

3
Climate and Sustainability Basics

Sustain – to cause to continue (as in existence or a certain state, or in force or intensity); to keep up, especially without interruption, diminution, flagging, etc.; to prolong. (Webster's New International Dictionary)

Before you decide to become a sustainable thinker, you will undoubtedly want to know what you are getting yourself into. The term 'sustainable' seems to be applied to just about everything today. I recently had to laugh out loud when I was at a restaurant that listed 'sustainable chicken' on the menu. Seems to me, a sustainable chicken would live to a ripe old age. Maybe it would even be your pet chicken. How can a dead chicken you are about to eat be called 'sustainable'? What does sustainable thinking actually involve?

In principle, sustainability is a straightforward notion. *Webster's Dictionary* describes it as the ability to continue something without interruption for a long time. But if we focus on the climate, the natural environment or social well-being, what factors should be maintained over the long haul and how do we ensure that those features endure? A basic understanding of systems is essential to answer these questions.

FUNDAMENTALS OF SYSTEMS

A system is a set of interconnected parts that make up a whole. A car engine is a mechanical system composed of a battery, pistons, sparkplugs and other components that work together to move a vehicle. Ecological systems such as a pond or forest are composed of numerous living and non-living elements that continually interact to comprise a whole. Human systems, which I will often call social systems, function in similar ways. Two or more people interacting together to achieve a purpose, whether it is manufacturing a product, running an organization or planning a Saturday night out, comprise a social system.

It should not be a surprise that non-human and human systems function in much the same way. Although humans are more powerful and can do things that no other living organism on Earth can do, it is primarily the size and magnitude of our power, as well as our capacity for self-awareness and free will, that differ from other organisms. Humans are bound by the same fundamental laws of nature that apply to all other life on Earth. Systems have a number of distinct characteristics.

WHOLENESS AND INTERCONNECTEDNESS

Two fundamental attributes of systems are wholeness and interconnectedness. An ecological system is composed of an endless series of circular exchanges of energy and information between living things, such as plants and animals, and their physical surroundings, such as soils, water, sunlight and heat. Social systems are similarly composed of continuous interactions between people and their environments. None of the parts of either type of system on their own can accomplish as much as they do by interacting with the other parts. Soil without water will not support plants. A business without customers will not produce a profit. The constant exchange of information and energy between components makes a collection of individual parts into a system.

STRUCTURE DRIVES PERFORMANCE

Another unique distinguishing characteristic of systems is that the way in which they are structured determines how they perform. The term structure depicts the way in which the components of a system are organized and linked together. The arrangement determines how energy and information flow through the system and therefore how the system behaves.

Each organism in an ecological system performs a 'job'. In ecology, this is called a niche. Different organisms occupy different niches. There are food producers, for example, which are generally green plants whose niche (job) is to produce the nourishment upon which other organisms depend for sustenance. Food consumers, which include all animals and some parasitic plants, eat the material created by food producers. Another important niche in the food chain is filled by decomposers, which are mostly micro-organisms such as bacteria, yeast, moulds and other fungi. Their job is to break down the dead carcasses and excretion of organisms into simpler substances, which are then converted into nitrogen compounds that help green plants (food producers) grow. With few exceptions, ecological systems are thus structured so that one organism's waste becomes food for another in a continuous circular process. Each organism must fill its niche – that is, perform its job – at the right time and in the right way for the system to function effectively.

Social systems function in much the same way. Whether it is a village, organization or household, the way in which a social system is structured determines how it performs. In any community, we recognize certain standard niches or jobs. They may include the doctor, farmer, police officer, banker, teacher and so on. In a business, the jobs may include chief executive, bookkeeper, salespersons and machine operator. Each of these jobs plays a role and has more or less predictable behaviour. We usually know, for example, what a banker or salesman does in a different community or even in another nation, for that matter.

The way in which those roles are organized determines how the community functions. The justice system in most communities is composed of police officers who enforce laws, lawyers who defend people, prosecutors who act for the government (public) and judges who oversee the process. If the police communicate mostly with the doctor or teacher, rather than the prosecutor and judge, the justice system would function very differently, or not at all.

DISTURBANCES DRIVE CHANGE AND GROWTH

Due to positive feedback, both ecological and human systems exhibit the same pattern of slowly moving toward greater complexity and interdependency. In natural systems, this is called ecological succession. Over time, ecosystems evolve from simpler to more complex levels until a 'climax' stage is reached where the system achieves relative stability. Human systems evolve in much the same way. Human history, starting with the early hunters and gatherers, to the first farmers, to today's increasingly urbanized world, can be viewed as the story of increasing complexity and interdependency.

Such progression, however, is not guaranteed. Although it is not possible to know when they will occur, all systems are susceptible to disturbances, which can be considered negative feedback, and disturbances in both ecological and human systems have always changed the course of history.

Natural disturbances such as earthquakes, fires, floods, droughts and volcanic eruptions affect all living organisms in the area. Large forest fires, for instance, often destroy vegetation and eliminate the dominant organisms in the ecosystems that require large amounts of energy inputs. Similarly, human-caused disruptions such as wars affect natural systems by destroying biodiversity, as well as human systems, by altering the economic and social conditions of both the winners and losers.

However unpleasant they may appear at the time, ecological disturbances are both natural and essential for new growth. Unless they are severely depleted, the process of ecological succession begins again soon after a disturbance and produces ever-increasing productivity and diversity among species until a new disturbance occurs, and the system is reset once again. Each successional stage introduces to the system new larger and dominant organisms with greater power.

Disturbances in human systems also serve as catalysts for change. Families came to see me when I worked as a counsellor because they were in distress, not because everything was hunky dory. Their pain served as a much-needed stimulus to improve family relations. In capitalistic economies, the term 'creative destruction' is often used to describe disruptions that unleash tremendous productivity and enthrone new dominants. In rapid order, for example, the introduction of digital equipment and software essentially eradicated the typewriter and other simpler forms of communication, and made Microsoft and other high-tech companies economic dominants. I believe that, left unchecked, global warming will prove to be the greatest disturbance to human economic and social systems since the massive destruction produced by World War II.

RESILIENCY FOSTERS ENDURANCE

The structure of a system determines its resiliency. A system is said to be resilient if it has the capacity to defend against, adapt to and repair itself after disturbances. Ecological and social systems have self-maintenance and repair mechanisms embedded within their structures. As long as those processes remain robust, systems maintain their resiliency despite constant change in their environment – that is, they can be sustainable. Logging a few trees may reduce forest structure and basic functions for a short time period. However, ecological succession will begin anew as long as the forest's primary production mechanisms, including the soil structure, nutrient cycling and other core functions, remain whole.

An economy can recover after a recession as long as the fundamental elements of its primary production mechanisms remain robust, such as its capital base, communication and transportation infrastructure and an educated, skilled workforce.

In sum, systems will remain resilient, and will adapt and prosper after disturbances as long as their self-maintenance and repair mechanisms remain robust.

FEEDBACK IS VITAL FOR RESILIENCY

The consequences of a disturbance are heavily influenced by the patterns of interaction and feedbacks among the entities involved with the system. Endurance – the ability to sustain – depends upon the capacity to sense, prepare for and adapt to changing conditions over time. Feedback allows ecological systems to adapt to change. The pine trees on our property sense the threat and defend themselves against invading insects by emitting sap that traps bugs that try to burrow into them. Many organisms shut down in response to excessive heat in order to minimize energy consumption.

Social systems likewise depend upon feedback. A business can overcome lost market share as long as it gets timely feedback on the need to adjust its products or prices. Children learn what is acceptable through feedback from their parents. Feedback is integral to learning and the accumulation of knowledge.

Credible and timely feedback is vital for a system to successfully adapt to disturbances. Warm-bodied animals, for example, seek to maintain a certain internal body temperature. When I play basketball my heart works hard (even though, in my mid 50s, I don't move very fast), which raises my body temperature. When this occurs, my body's feedback mechanisms trigger perspiration – one of nature's self-maintenance and repair mechanisms – to cool my system back down to 37°C (98.6°F).

Social systems work in similar ways. A recession may push the US stock market downward. Financial signals of a slowing economy are feedback that the Federal Reserve may use to decide to reduce interest rates. Cheaper money, in turn, may boost investments and reinvigorate the market. When a system's feedback mechanisms function effectively, its adaptation and self-repair apparatus can defend itself from attack, repair afterwards and stimulate new growth.

Distorted or delayed feedback, on the other hand, can be deadly. Imagine how dangerous it would be if my body's feedback systems fail to trigger perspiration when I play basketball and my internal temperature rose to 40°C (104°F) or beyond. I might become seriously ill or die. If a delay is too long, the opportunity for a system's natural self-maintenance and repair mechanisms to correct a problem is significantly diminished. Despite the warnings about rising temperatures by scientists that started decades ago, most people in the US ignored the feedback. Atmospheric carbon dioxide levels have consequently continued to rise, making it more difficult to solve the problem.

Feedback is often non-linear

Feedback often does not occur as a simple one-to-one cause-and-effect relationship. Non-linear effects often lead to unexpected outcomes that overwhelm the self-maintenance and repair mechanisms of systems. If you eat one Big Mac a day, for instance, you may gain 1lb of weight. If you eat two Big Macs, you may gain 2lbs. So far, the relationship between Big Macs and pounds gained is linear and your body may be able to adjust to the added weight. However, if you eat ten Big Macs, it is not likely you would gain just 10lbs. This type of change is likely to overwhelm your body's self-maintenance and repair mechanisms. The result may be that you gain 30lbs or more, or even have a heart attack and keel over! With that many Big Macs, the relationship between Big Macs and weight gain is non-linear.

Scientists are very concerned that global warming and other forms of ecological degradation will accelerate due to non-linear feedbacks. Increased temperature is melting snow and ice in Greenland and west Antarctica, but not in a linear fashion. Snow and ice reflect sunlight. The more barren ground and ocean that are exposed as a result of melting snow and ice, the less sunlight that will reflect back to space. The more solar radiation that is absorbed, the warmer it will get, which will further hasten ice and snow melt. Thus, non-linear feedback produces surprises.

HUMAN AND NON-HUMAN SYSTEMS ARE INEXTRICABLY LINKED

Step back from this book for a moment and take a deep breath. Now, think about what just happened. The oxygen you inhaled was produced by phytoplankton, which is a one-cell plant that lives at the ocean's surface, and by trees, shrubs, grass and other land plants through the process known as photosynthesis. You would not be alive today if it was not for the complex interactions occurring in marine and terrestrial (land) ecosystems that produce the oxygen you breathe. Humans are but one organism in nature and are completely dependent upon the web of interactions that comprise it.

This underscores that human systems, such as economies, are merely subsets of, and exist within, the bounds of the Earth's climatic and ecological systems. All economic activities rely on the raw materials and energy created by nature. In fact, humans never really create anything. Only nature *creates*. Ecological processes create all the fibre, fish, water, minerals, metals and energy used by our economy. Humans only *convert* these substances into goods and services for human use. Even the synthetic materials so popular today are derived from natural substances and rely on wild seed stock for replenishment (Meadows et al, 1992).

This is a very important point. Through the process of obtaining food and shelter and excreting waste, all organisms modify the environment in which they live. When those changes become too great, organisms eliminate the conditions necessary for their own survival, which allows new organisms to move in and dominate the system. If the methods that humans employ to convert nature's raw materials into energy, goods and services severely degrade the climatic or ecological processes that created them in the first place, they will alter the conditions that allow humans to survive and prosper. This is what is occurring today and it is obviously self-defeating and certainly not sustainable.

EARTH'S COMPLEX SYSTEMS OF SOURCES AND SINKS

Now that you have a basic understanding of systems, let's apply it to the climatic, physical and social environment to see what sustainability entails. Figure 3.1 shows very clearly that the Earth is a finite system. No trade routes connect the Earth to other planets where we can obtain additional resources or dispose of our pollution and waste. Except for incoming sunlight (solar radiation) and an occasional meteorite, the resources we have now are all that we will ever have here on Earth. The pollution and waste we generate will always be with us in some form somewhere.

The finite nature of the Earth means that humanity must learn to live within the limits of the systems of which we are part. The limits are established by what are called sources and sinks. Sources and sinks make up the dynamic, complex and interdependent system that we call Earth.

Figure 3.1 *The Earth*

Source: NASA, Eugene Cernan, Ronald Evans and Jack Schmitt.

Sources provide material and energy resources for living organisms, including humans. Forests are sources of nutrients for plants, animals and people. Forests are also sources of fibre and energy for human habitation. The Earth's crust is the source of minerals, metals and fossil fuels for human systems. Streams and oceans are sources of food for humans and thousands of other organisms.

Sinks are the ultimate destination of material and energy flows used by a system. They absorb, break down and reintegrate pollution and waste back into the environment for future uses, or sequester them to prevent harm to other organisms or systems. The atmosphere, oceans and forests are natural sinks that sop up carbon dioxide and other greenhouse gases. Landfills are human-made sinks for the solid and hazardous waste we produce.

Some sources also serve as sinks. The ocean, for example, is a source of fish for human nourishment and a sink for human-produced carbon dioxide. Forests provide fibre for human use and also absorb carbon dioxide. Other sources function independently from sinks. Figure 3.2 describes the continual exchange of gases between the sources of carbon and their sinks.

ECOLOGICAL LIMITS AND OVERSHOOT ON A FINITE PLANET

In a sustainable system, the Earth's sources and sinks are always in a dynamic balance. Resources and energy are used at a pace that allows them to be naturally regenerated. Waste, including greenhouse gases, is generated no faster than nature's sinks can assimilate and break it down. The sources never get fully depleted and the sinks are never completely overwhelmed by waste.

An ecological limit is reached when the source of energy or raw materials is exhausted. When the food supply in a forest is depleted due to a drought or fire, a limit has been reached. Organisms that depend upon the food must either move to a different location or see their population reduced. When the water in a river

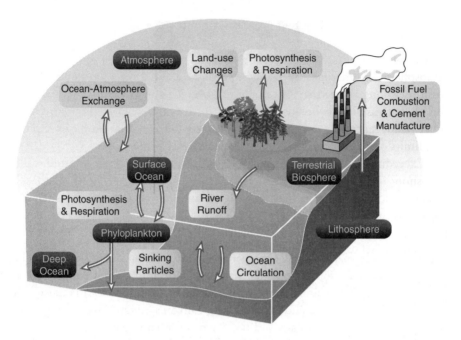

Figure 3.2 *CO₂ sources and sinks: The global carbon cycle*

Source: Sanders, 2005.

Note: The land and oceans can absorb some of the increased carbon from fossil fuel emissions; but as the emission rate increases, these sinks saturate and become less effective at removing carbon from the atmosphere.

dries up due to excessive irrigation or drought, a limit has been reached. Farmers must either find other sources of water or survive without.

Similarly, a limit has been reached when too much waste overwhelms a sink so that it cannot break down the substances fast enough to keep up with the incoming amount. Pollutants such as human-generated greenhouse gases, dioxin, industrial solvents, organophosphates, pesticides, petrochemical fertilizers, radioactive waste, fossil fuel-derived plastics, formaldehyde and many other toxic synthetic substances cannot be easily broken down by the Earth's sinks, causing them to accumulate in the climate and natural environment and to damage many organisms and even the sinks themselves. Landfills close when the available space has been filled.

Some limits are temporary. The well at our house almost goes dry each summer because the lack of summer rain draws down the water table. When the rain returns in the fall, the water table rises and the well once again has plenty of water. Other limits are permanent. Because it takes thousands of years to create petroleum, when humans consume all of the world's oil, it will be permanently gone.

Sometimes non-renewable materials are limited by their sources and sinks. Fossil fuels, for example, are a finite resource that will eventually run out. It is likely, however, that rising carbon dioxide emissions will overwhelm the atmospheric and marine sinks of these substances and force a limit on the use of fossil fuels long before they physically run out. This means that the use of fossil fuels is not sustainable because both their sources and sinks are limited. On the other hand, renewable energy sources such as wind and solar power have few, if any, limits on their sources or sinks. They are sustainable.

Exceeding the limit of an ecological source or sink is often called 'overshoot'. This condition is not always fatal. As long as accurate feedback is received and responded to in a timely way, and as long as a system's self-repair apparatus remains in good condition, it can regenerate after an overshoot. The forests of the Pacific Northwest began to recover from excessive logging once the spotted owl was protected under the Endangered Species Act and President Clinton gave the forests time to recover by reducing timber harvest levels. If we rapidly heed the feedback indicating overshoot provided by actual measurements, observation and scientific models, humanity can avert the worst of global warming.

However, when society fails to gather or respond quickly to feedback signalling overshoot by reducing the consumption of a key source or the amount of pollution and waste foisted on a sink, ecological systems will degrade. Ecological harm can be magnified when nature's sources and sinks themselves become damaged. This is evident, for example, when pesticides dumped into streams kill the aquatic organisms that naturally break down organic waste.

HUMANITY HAS REACHED THE EARTH'S LIMITS

Human-produced greenhouse gases are accumulating at unprecedented levels in the atmosphere. One of the Earth's most important sinks is overstressed. Fifteen out of 24 of the global ecosystem services examined by the Millennium Ecosystem Assessment are being degraded or used unsustainably. Key ecological services such as wild foods, genetic resources and freshwater are degraded or in decline. Essential regulating services provided by nature, such as air purification, erosion control, water purification, pest control, plant pollination and natural hazard management, are seriously impaired or in decline. In short, many of the Earth's sources and sinks are endangered.

These conditions indicate that humanity has reached the Earth's physical limits. We must acknowledge this fact and adjust our thinking and behaviour to this reality. Failure to respond to this feedback is already causing harm and, in the not too distant future, will lead to widespread calamity.

FUNDAMENTALS OF CLIMATE PROTECTION AND SUSTAINABILITY

From this discussion some fundamentals of climate protection and sustainability become clear. *First, ecological and social systems are sustainable only when they can successfully adapt to, and repair after, disturbances.* Sustainability does not mean an unchangeable state. Due to the natural happenstance of disturbance, it is the exception, not the rule, for any system, ecological or human, to remain the same for very long. A sustainable system has the resiliency to adapt to new circumstance, recover from disturbance and renew its march towards greater complexity and interdependency. As a practical matter, the basis of sustainability is the ability to adapt to change.

Second, robust feedback, self-maintenance and repair mechanisms are essential for successful preparation for, and adaptation to, change. As long as a system retains its capacity to obtain information about changes in its environment, and to defend and repair itself after disturbance, it can endure and prosper over time. When a system's feedback, self-maintenance and repair mechanisms are depleted or destroyed, disturbances of many types will cause it to degrade or collapse.

Third, humanity must preserve the self-maintenance and repair capacities of ecological and social systems in order to live prosperously and securely. Ample measurement and observational data indicates that many of the Earth's key sources of materials and energy are seriously depleted, and that critical climatic and ecological sinks are overburdened and in disrepair. So, too, are many social and economic systems. The most important task facing humanity today is to adjust our thinking to these realities. All future economic prosperity, social well-being and security depend upon humanity's ability to find ways of living within the limits of the systems of which we are part.

THE IMPERATIVE OF ENHANCED ECONOMIC PROSPERITY

Living within the limits imposed by the Earth's systems does not mean the end of economic prosperity. To the contrary, given the millions of people living in poverty today around the world who demand and deserve better nutrition, healthcare and economic opportunities, only by increasing prosperity can the fundamentals of climate protection and sustainability be maintained and restored. However, in order to protect the Earth's sources and sinks and to put humanity on a path towards sustainability, future economic paradigms must be of a very different type than the world has seen over the past 200 years.

It often takes hundreds or thousands of years for ecological systems to achieve a 'climax' stage of succession where plants and animals are able to propagate themselves indefinitely because they are in relative dynamic equilibrium with their physical environment and climate. All movement prior to the climax stage points in that direction through increased complexity and interdependency.

Human systems such as economies evolve much like ecological systems. I see little evidence, however, that the economies of industrialized nations are anywhere close to a climax stage. The up-and-down, boom-and-bust cycles that the economies of Western nations have experienced for the past century and a half appear more like the middle seral stage of succession where, through their own behaviours, the dominant organisms transform the conditions that allowed them to thrive to the extent that they can no longer survive, which allows new organisms to invade and repeat the same pattern.

If my perspective is correct, the world's economy still has ample room to evolve towards a climax, or sustainable, stage. This would not be a 'steady' state as we typically think about stability. Disturbances would continue to rock the system, forcing adaptation and adjustments. It does mean, however, that people who currently live in poverty can have higher standards of living. Wealthy industrialized nations can maintain high standards. A sustainable world would not be mundane, stagnant or poor. It would be filled with excitement, innovation and well-being.

These conditions will be possible, however, only if we avoid the fear and panic that the opposite of enhanced prosperity, which is contraction, will unquestionably trigger. Flexibility, free thinking, innovation and self-governing units that enable actors to respond quickly to changing circumstances are qualities that must be nurtured if we are to adapt to and resolve global warming and today's other challenges. Just as ecosystems suffer when a single organism exerts control over all of the nutrients, authoritarian political, military or religious despots who tend to seize power in periods of great anxiety will squelch these traits. Expanding prosperity will be vital if we are to prevent the consolidation of physical and psychological control that a prolonged economic contraction would bring.

CIRCULAR BORROW–USE–RETURN SYSTEMS

Since economic growth always depends upon the availability of abundant, reliable sources of energy and because today's fossil fuel-based energy regime depletes the Earth's sources and sinks, future economic prosperity must, of necessity, be powered by clean renewable sources of energy. Enhanced feedback and communication mechanisms, as well as technologies designed to operate within the context of closed-loop systems, will also be needed. In circular, or what I call 'borrow–use–return', systems, raw materials are extracted from the environment, materials and energy are then temporarily converted into goods and services, and the by-products of the system are then returned to the economy for future human uses or back to nature as nutrients for future growth without

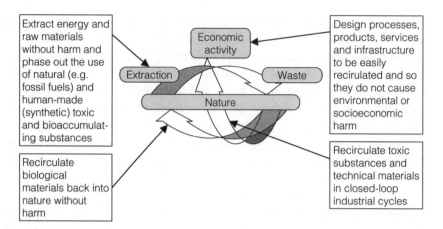

Figure 3.3 *The sustainable circular borrow–use–return economic model*

Source: adapted from Doppelt (2003).

degrading nature's self-maintenance and repair mechanisms or harming people (see Figure 3.3).

Circular borrow–use–return systems are not a major departure from the current economic model. To the contrary, they are the next logical step in human thinking about the economy, environment and social well-being. Rather than taking a myopic view that ignores the ecological and social systems in which humans are embedded, circular systems take a sustainable perspective that acknowledges those systems and links the two disconnected ends of the linear system. Closed-loop systems would not be possible without the accumulated knowledge and technological advances of the past.

CONDITIONS OF SUSTAINABLE THINKING

The need to increase prosperity and security while living within the limits of the Earth's systems requires whole new ways of thinking. Sustainable thinking must therefore meet three overall conditions:

1   *Endurance.* Sustainable thinking must lead to production and consumption systems that ensure that the Earth's critical sources of energy and materials persist into perpetuity. Thinking that leads to the per capita use of the Earth's renewable resources, such as forests, fisheries and water, at higher rates than can be naturally regenerated cannot be sustainable. Thinking that leads to the per capita use of the Earth's non-renewable resources, such as fossil fuels, minerals or non-rechargeable groundwater, at faster rates than a renewable alternative can be found cannot be sustainable (Daly, 1991).

2   *Cleanliness.* Sustainable thinking must lead to the production and use of clean sources of energy, raw materials and other substances that protect and regenerate the Earth's ecological sinks. Thinking that leads to actions that degrade these sinks through the continued release of greenhouse gases and other natural or synthetic toxic substances faster than the Earth's sinks can break down and reabsorb them without harm is not sustainable. Thinking that leads to the degradation or destruction of the sinks themselves – nature's own pollution abatement mechanisms – cannot be sustainable.

3   *Community.* Sustainable thinking must foster a basic sense of connection to, and mutual responsibility for, others, future generations and ourselves. This sense of solidarity and community, built on the awareness that all of humankind now shares a common fate, must lead to the formation of social capacity, governance mechanisms and leadership that enhances global prosperity and security while protecting the Earth's sources and sinks. Thinking that leads to a continued increase in human populations is not sustainable. Thinking that fosters the consolidation of social or political control, squelches free thinking and innovation, or leads to social inequity is not sustainable. Thinking that undercuts laws which regulate selfish and destructive behaviours by individuals, corporations or governments, undermines ethical codes of conduct, or in other ways weaken social capacity to enhance human welfare while protecting the Earth's sources and sinks cannot be sustainable.

In sum, sustainable thinking ensures that vital sources of materials and resources endure over long time periods, that they are clean, and that the way in which we organize and govern our economic and social systems supports theses processes and enhances all of humanity, not just a select few.

In the next chapter we will explore some of the ways in which today's dominant myopic ways of thinking and behaving undermine these conditions.

REFERENCES

Daly, H. (1991) *Steady State Economics*, Island Press, Washington, DC

Doppelt, B. (2003) *Leading Change Toward Sustainability: A Change Management Guide for Business, Government and Civil Society*, Greenleaf Publishing, UK

Meadows, D., Meadows, D. and Randers, J. (1992) *Beyond the Limits: Confronting Global Collapse and Envisioning a Sustainable Future*, Chelsea Green Publishing, Post Hills, Vermont

Sanders, R. (2005) In 'Faster carbon dioxide emissions will overwhelm capacity of land and ocean to absorb carbon', UC Berkeley News, graphic by Inez Fung, University of California, Berkeley, CA

4

Sustainability Thinking Blunders

For every complex problem there is an easy answer, and it is wrong.
(H. L. Mencken, from Teachout, 2003)

One of the first things my wife and I wanted to do after we purchased our new house was to replace the leaky old single-pane windows with super-efficient, triple-pane windows. We hired a contractor who had worked for us before because this seemed easier than obtaining bids from others. Unfortunately – or, perhaps, fortunately – we found out at the last moment that the contractor planned to purchase cheap vinyl windows at a discount window factory. Had these windows been installed, our energy bills and associated greenhouse gas emissions would have been permanently higher and the vinyl would have off-gassed toxins into our home forever. Our desire to take the easy route moved us precariously close to undermining both our environmental and personal financial goals.

This story underscores how easy it is for our thinking and behaviour to run counter to the climate and sustainability fundamentals of endurance, cleanliness and community. Despite the downsides, many of us are controlled by the myopic take–make–waste mind frame and continually engage in climate-damaging unsustainable thought and behavioural patterns. Much like addicts, we seem compelled to repeat the very things that cause us to suffer.

As with any addiction, admitting we have a problem is the first step towards recovery. This chapter discusses ten pervasive thinking and behavioural patterns that do harm to the climate and sustainability fundamentals of endurance, cleanliness and community. I call them sustainability thinking blunders (STBs). As you read the pages that follow, I'm sure numerous variations of the STBs will become evident and new ones may pop into your mind. My research and experience, however, suggest that people living in industrial societies tend to be most addicted to those described here. You can decide which, if any, you and the teams and institutions with whom you associate may be addicted to. You can use the chart provided (Table 4.1) to evaluate the extent of your STBs.

The overarching cause of the STBs is what I call systems blindness, which is discussed at the close of the chapter.

STRAIGHT-LINE THINKING

Our propensity for straight-line thinking is the most common STB and the foundation of many of the others. Mirroring the image of a machine that moves product from point A to point B in step-wise fashion, most people growing up in industrial societies have been taught to think in straight-line patterns. We see the world as a series of linear cause-and-effect relationships: 'A leads to B'; 'B causes C'; 'C brings about D'. We think, for example, that 'more recycling is good for the environment'. Everything around us is seen as resulting from simple cause-and-effect relationships.

Straight-line thinking implicitly assumes that circumstances are predictable and can be controlled. This may be an accurate assumption when only a few factors influence the outcome of a situation. When recycling allows a material to be reused for the same or a higher purpose, it is not unreasonable to think that it is good for the economy and environment.

If, however, there are numerous factors that could interact in unknown ways to influence an outcome, straight-line thinking becomes much less appropriate. If recycling allows toxic substances designed for one purpose to be used inappropriately for another, for instance, or leads people to believe that they can keep consuming ever-increasing amounts of resources as long as they recycle, recycling is not good for the environment.

The take–make–waste economic system is a linear model and straight-line thinking provides its intellectual foundation. Ray Anderson is the founder and chairman of Interface, a global manufacturer of modular soft-surfaced floor coverings, commercial panel and upholstery fabrics, and a pioneer in the sustainable manufacturing movement. He readily admits that he was addicted to straight-line thinking until he became aware of how harmful it was. 'We took natural resources, made carpet and other products from them, then threw the waste in a landfill without ever considering potential feedbacks. It was the system I grew up in. I took it for granted that everything worked this way.'[1]

One of the downsides of straight-line thinking is that we fail to see the big picture or long-term consequences. A 'single-use' mentality that depletes the Earth's sources and sinks is one example of the many negative outcomes produced by this thought process. Thousands of products are now designed for single uses, from cameras to packaging to medical supplies. Most single-use products require massive amounts of raw materials and waste to make, generate huge quantities of greenhouse gases throughout their life cycle, and then promptly lose all value when discarded as waste.

But it's not just single-use products that are harmful. Much of society is designed around this straight-line model. Manufacturing plants, for example, often generate waste heat from one process that is immediately vented into the environment, even though it could be used for other purposes, such as to heat buildings or hot water. Thousands of other examples exist of myopic single-use linear thinking.

Complex situations produce counterintuitive outcomes. They are understandable only in the most general way and cannot be easily controlled. For this reason, systems-based (not straight-line) thinking is required to protect the climate and adopt a path towards sustainability. When we think in systems, we take into account multiple factors that are likely to interact in unexpected ways. It involves looking at the big picture first and then seeing how the individual parts fit together and produce outcomes. Thinking systemically focuses on the root causes of dilemmas, not just their symptoms, and on seeing how our beliefs and thought processes, or that of the teams and organizations with whom we are associated, produce or exacerbate those problems. When we use straight-line thinking instead of a systems approach, we undermine the climate and sustainability fundamentals of endurance, cleanliness and community.

QUICK-FIX THINKING

The use of straight-line thinking often leads to a second STB: quick-fix thinking and its kissing cousin: short-term thinking.[2] These are reactive forms of cognition. They focus on the present and are oblivious to the future. We automatically respond to events by swiftly trying to solve the immediate problem and have no flexibility in how we respond. Quick-fix, short-term thinking is psychologically and emotionally easy because we avoid having to consider the unintended and long-term consequences of our decisions.

The origin of quick-fix, short-term thinking is our basic human instinct for survival. Every animal must be acutely aware of its external environment or risk being harmed by a predator. Due to our early days as hunters and gatherers, humans are no different. Quick-fix, short-term thinking is built into our DNA as a remnant of our evolution.

Few people living in industrial societies today, however, face immediate threats of being harmed by an animal. Nevertheless, we continue to think and behave as if we do. Because we have failed to adjust our thinking, we have transformed a formerly beneficial attribute from the past into a harmful psychological and social addiction.

Sometimes, quick-fix, short-term thinking is appropriate. When a chemical spill occurs, the best response is to stop the leak as rapidly as possible. However, when we rid ourselves of what we don't want, we do not necessarily get what we do want. Often we get less of what we want, or something as bad as or even worse than we had in the first place. Thus, although short-term quick fixes sometimes provide a foundation for longer-term solutions, more often than not the opposite occurs. We find ourselves unable to adjust and change.

This is because most often quick-fix, short-term thinking responds to *symptoms*, not the root causes of problems. Our 'solution' therefore fails to resolve the underlying cause of a dilemma. Although the issue may appear to be solved, eventually the same problem reappears, often in slightly different form. Even worse, quick-fix, short-term thinking frequently leads to surprises and unintended consequences.

My wife and I wanted to complete most of the remodelling on our newly purchased rundown house before we moved in. We had just a few weeks to finish the work because we had sold our previous home and the new owners wanted to move in right away.

We served as our own general contractor. It was our job to get everything ready before the workers we hired came to do their jobs. These circumstances made us feel as though we were in a race, trying to stay one step ahead of the contractors. This self-imposed pressure caused us to make some quick reactive decisions, each of which turned out badly.

After we pulled out the old carpet, for example, we found that cat urine had penetrated the floorboards below. We knew the odour needed to be removed or our cats would add their marks in the same location. New carpet was going to be installed the next day. To quickly solve the problem, we purchased a paint advertised as great for sealing in odour.

Our quick-fix, reactive thinking appeared to solve the immediate problem – we eliminated the smell of cat urine – at least in the short run. However, six months later we discovered that our cats were marking the spot with their urine and we had to tear up the floorboards anyway. Our reactive response also produced two other problems. The paint turned out to be highly toxic and I got a splitting headache immediately after applying it. Although the headache was my burden to bear, by using the paint we also released toxins into the atmosphere and burdened other people. We learned once again that quick-fix solutions usually fail and often create unintended side effects.

One of the reasons Rusty Rexius, co-president of Rexius Company, a 250-employee processor of wood and organics for the landscape, construction, irrigation and maintenance industries in Eugene, Oregon, began to consider engaging in sustainability was because he came to the realization that short-term thinking could destroy his company. 'I asked if our current business model would allow us to hand over a thriving business to the next generation of family members, and the answer was a resounding no. I had to think about the next generation, not just the immediate future, if we were going to survive'.[3] You'll learn later in the book how Rusty changed his thinking and behaviour and helped his company to become a sustainability leader in his community.

Often, the unintended effects of quick-fix thinking make it more difficult to resolve the root causes of a problem. In 1989, more than two dozen countries signed the Montreal Protocol intended to mitigate the degradation to the Earth's ozone layer by banning the use of chlorofluorocarbons (CFCs) in refrigerators, air conditioners and hair spray. Unfortunately, the people designing the protocol failed to realize that companies using CFCs would quickly turn to the cheapest alternative, which was hydro-chlorofluorocarbons (HFCs). HFCs are better for the ozone layer, but contribute to global warming. Scientists have found that the volume of greenhouse gases created as a result of the Montreal Protocol's phase-out of CFCs is two to three times the amount of carbon dioxide that the Kyoto climate change agreement is supposed to eliminate. The quick fix for the CFC problem made it much more difficult to solve global warming.

This example demonstrates that climate change and scores of today's other pressing challenges are in many ways the result of yesterday's quick-fix, short-term 'solutions'. A big picture perspective that prevents short-term actions from undermining long-term viability is needed if we are to increase prosperity and security while protecting the climate and natural environment.

TECHNOLOGY CAN SAVE US

A logical and yet subtle extension of both straight-line and quick-fix thinking is the view that technology can save us from the dilemmas we have created. This is a form of wishful thinking. It is based on the hope that some new invention will resolve our problems and relieve us of the need to alter our thinking or behaviour.

Technology has done marvellous things for humanity, including raising living standards and improving human health in much of the world. The reality, however, is that rather than lightening our burden, most of today's new technologies require more of everything – more resource extraction, more raw materials, more processing, more transportation, more energy, more complex organizations and more sophistication by the end-users. Given current designs, most new technologies generate huge amounts of greenhouse gases and often toxic waste. The more intricate a technology, the greater is its requirements.

According to a United Nations University study, manufacturing one desktop computer and 17 inch cathode ray tube (CRT) monitor uses at least 240kg (530lbs) of fossil fuels, 22kg (50lbs) of chemicals and 1500kg (3330lbs) of water – a total of 1.8 tonnes of materials – roughly the weight of a sports utility vehicle. A typical 60lb computer includes 13.8lbs of synthetic plastics, only 20 per cent of which can be recycled. Huge quantities of energy are required and massive amounts of hazardous emissions and waste are generated in making computers. They also include toxic substances such as lead, cadmium, polyvinyl chloride and other nasty substances that mostly cannot be recycled or reused. This means that they accumulate somewhere in the environment, including in human tissue (Kuehr and Williams, 2004).

In 2006, over 164 million computers existed in the US, Japan had 49 million, Germany 30 million, and the UK had about 26 million. And this does not even include printers, memory sticks and flash drives, connection cords, backup power sources and other peripherals associated with computers, nor does it include cell phones, iPods, CDs, DVDs and other electronic gadgetry flooding the market today. The scale of the impact upon the Earth's sources, sinks and communities that these gizmos produce is immense.

Although computers were supposed to create the 'paperless office', we use twice as much paper today as we did two decades ago, placing increased pressure on the world's forests.

Sophisticated technology is also mostly unavailable to the poor, who don't have the money to buy it, and is beyond the reach of those without the skills to use it. This allows the rich and powerful to remain top dog, undermining equity and community well-being.

Industry today produces thousands of synthetic substances, which are compounds that are made artificially through chemical reactions. Because they have only existed for a short time period, the Earth's sinks have not developed the capacity to break down these substances, so most accumulate somewhere in nature and often degrade the sinks themselves. The human immune system also has not developed effective defence mechanisms against synthetic substances and, as a result, many metabolic diseases such as cancer have been linked to these materials.

In short, our industrial society has become increasingly more sophisticated in the technologies and substances we produce, but not wiser about if, why or how to employ them.

At this point you may be panicked because if technology cannot resolve our problems, what options do we have? Relax. All economic progress is driven by new technologies, and new devices will, of course, be essential to protect the climate and resolve many of today's other pressing challenges. But we often forget that technologies reflect the goals, beliefs and thought patterns of the people who design them. And the way in which people use technologies determines their effect.

Technology itself, therefore, cannot save us. Only new purposes, thinking and behaviours can resolve our dilemmas. New technologies will be a positive force in resolving today's challenges only if people break free from the myopic take–make–waste mind frame and adopt thinking that leads to the design and production of non-toxic goods and services that function within circular borrow–use–return systems and are powered by clean energy.

More is better

Closely related to the previous STB is our tendency to think that if a little bit is good, more must be better. This STB comes in many flavours: more efficiency is better, bigger machines are better, larger organizations are better, and so on. At the root of this thinking is the core belief that all things in life must be maximized.

Unfortunately, more may not be better when global warming and today's other pressing challenges are taken into account. It often makes conditions worse.

The belief in increasing efficiency is a case in point. People often confuse short-term performance with long-term success. While both can be important, they are not the same. Many high-performing products or practices appear to perform well in the short run, but wane in the long run. In contrast, a number of approaches may be less productive in the short run but endure over very long time frames. In this sense, the lower-performing methods are much more successful – read sustainable – than the high-performing entities.

The differences between organic and industrial agriculture highlights this distinction. Conventional industrial agriculture today, with its dependence upon large inputs of pesticides and petrochemical fertilizers, increases yield in the short run but reduces soil productivity in the long run. Organic agriculture, on the other hand, may not achieve the same high yield levels as industrial methods in the short run (although new studies dispute this), but can sustain the soil and farm yields into perpetuity.

The relentless drive for increased efficiency also leads to counterintuitive outcomes. The mass production of the small US$2500 Tata car in India, for example, will provide much needed mobility to thousands of people. However, more cars will further clog already crowded roads and lead to increased fuel use, pollution and greenhouse gases. Increased efficiency will make things worse.

Thus, although resources that are in short supply must always be used as effectively as possible, the continual pursuit of more efficiency, as seems to be a compulsion in industrial nations, is often misplaced. Increased efficiency leads people to think that they can use more and do more and, consequently, often leads to greater consumption, whereas long-term success and sustainability are often derived from less efficiency.

The obsession with size offers another interesting dilemma. In both ecological and human systems, size does matter, but only up to a point. Larger organisms tend to be less vulnerable to harm by predators than smaller ones. Large businesses have a number of competitive advantages over small ones.

However, in nature, when a disturbance reduces energy supplies in any particular region over a long time period, it is the larger organisms that require great inputs of energy that disappear first. Smaller organisms adapt faster than larger ones. Macro-organisms such as insects and other bugs, for example, can adapt to changes more easily than can larger mega-fauna, which are animals that weigh over 100lbs, or trees.

Similarly, societies that depend upon huge amounts of energy are most at risk during prolonged economic downturns caused by energy constraints. Smaller societies that require fewer energy inputs are much more capable of eking along. Restrictions on fossil fuel use due to global warming and peak oil are likely to produce these very conditions if we fail to quickly develop clean energy sources. Larger is not better from this perspective.

If we are to resolve climate change and today's other pressing challenges, we must avoid the tendency to think that maximizing efficiency and size is always better. Instead, the emphasis should be on small self-governing units, flexibility, free thinking and long-term effectiveness. These are the qualities that will be vital to increase prosperity and security while resolving global warming and our other challenges.

LESS BAD IS GOOD ENOUGH

An insidious STB is thinking that climate change and other environmental problems can be resolved merely by 'minimizing' our impact upon the climate, natural environment and communities. Households religiously recycle their newspapers, glass and cans. Businesses install pollution-control equipment to comply with environmental laws. Although well intentioned, in today's world of burgeoning population and degraded ecological sources and sinks, reducing our impacts a little bit is just not going to cut it.

World population has ballooned to 6 billion today and is expected to continue to grow in the future, albeit at a slower rate. Six billion plus people behaving a little 'less badly', to paraphrase noted architect Bill McDonough, still produce a massive negative impact upon the Earth's climate, physical environment and communities (McDonough and Braungart, 2002). Reducing global greenhouse gas emissions by 10 per cent, for example, or even by 20 or 30 per cent will do little to prevent the most dangerous forms of climate change. Emissions must be reduced by at least 80 per cent by mid century, and possibly to a net of zero in the US, which requires going well beyond being a 'little less bad'.

Government regulations attempt to 'minimize' harm by setting minimum standards. However, regulations almost never ban harmful greenhouse gases, toxic chemicals, pollution or waste. To the contrary, as Bill McDonough said, most regulations are actually licences to pollute. Through the political process of compromise, they set 'acceptable' levels of emissions that may reduce local impacts, but when aggregated among emitters across a region or the globe never fully protect the Earth's sources or sinks. Meeting today's minimum legal requirements, while important, therefore cannot protect the climate or restore the Earth's ecological systems.

In addition, because the production and use of so few toxic synthetic substances are even regulated, simply meeting minimum legal standards will do little to protect the health and well-being of people from this dangerous stuff.

The contractor we first hired to install our new windows had a 'less bad is good enough' mind frame. When I asked him why he had not purchased the super energy star windows we had asked for, his response was: 'Well, the windows I purchased for you are better than those you have now.' He did not understand that having a little less impact is not the same thing as being climate positive.

It seems logical to believe that minimizing environmental and social impacts is a good thing. However, making conditions 'less bad' will not resolve global warming, nor will it set us on a path towards sustainability. Indeed, in many cases, minimization is a form of denial of the true nature of the climatic, ecological and social crises that we now face.

Although its usually necessary to begin with small steps and build step by step towards the ultimate goal, only by aiming for being 'totally good', meaning emissions free and fully sustainable, can we resolve global warming and adopt a path towards sustainability. Making this shift requires new forms of thinking.

CHEAPER IS CHEAPER

A frequent STB is our propensity to think that cheaper goods and services are actually less expensive than higher-cost sustainably produced items Yes, you read that correctly. In reality, the costs of 'cheaper' goods are often similar to, or greater than, more expensive climate-positive sustainably produced products; but the true costs have just been hidden from us or shifted elsewhere. This is a case of unknowingly getting more than you pay for.

Whether it is industry, government or individuals, people often shift their costs elsewhere in an attempt to reduce their own financial outlays. Economists call this process 'externalizing'. We externalize our costs when we fail to pay for depleting the Earth's sources and sinks or harming others, and instead force other people or future generations to bear the expense. Global warming is the ultimate case of externalization. The benefits from climate-damaging activities, such as burning fossil fuels when we drive a vehicle, accrue to those who engage in them today. The true costs of those activities, however, including the costs of the damage caused by sea level rise, intense storms, heat waves and drought, as well as the costs of rebuilding and recovery after damage, are shifted to individuals all around the world and to our children and grandchildren. The true costs of burning fossil fuels are thus much higher than you pay at the gas pump.

Corporations today scour the globe in search of the cheapest places to produce their goods. The least expensive locations usually pay minuscule wages and have few labour or environmental safety laws. As a result, goods made in developing nations have cheaper sales prices in Western markets than those made locally where higher standards exist, but only because they have been produced without safeguards. Workers, communities and the environment in the foreign locations where the products were manufactured have been forced to bear the unpaid costs.

Paying less today will make the future costs of climate change exorbitant. The UK Stern Report on the *Economics of Climate Change* found that future losses due to global warming would be between 5 and 20 per cent of global gross domestic product (GDP) by 2050, while the costs of solving the problem now would only be 1 per cent of global GDP (Stern, 2006). Any rational person would conclude that it makes sense to pay more today to avoid excessive (and possibly irreversible) costs in the not too distant future.

Looking back at the years before he became aware of the need to pursue a path towards sustainability, Interface's Ray Anderson realizes that he and his company ignored externalities: 'We never thought about the costs we were imposing on others due to the smoke coming out of our factory smokestacks. I now realize our production costs were intellectually dishonest'.[4]

Buying goods and services that are cheaper only because the costs have been externalized to other places or future generations actually costs much more since it undermines the fundamentals of endurance, cleanliness and community. Only when we pay the true costs of our actions now, rather than making others pay for them later, will we resolve the issue of global warming and adopt a path towards sustainability.

AWAY MEANS GONE

A natural outcome of the take–make–waste paradigm is thinking that once pollution and waste are out of sight, they are gone. This STB is based on a flawed understanding of how nature works.

One of the fundamental laws of nature is that everything eventually breaks down and disintegrates. Metals rust, wood rots and all living organisms, including humans, eventually die. This is called the first law of thermodynamics (the dilapidated house that my wife and I purchased demonstrated this law – everything was broken down!). There is no escaping this law. Everything that nature creates and humans produce eventually disintegrates (except for nuclear waste and some other synthetic toxins that may last thousands of years because nature has no mechanisms to break them down).

Another fundamental law of nature is that the resources we consume and the pollution and waste we produce never really disappear. When solid, liquid or gaseous substances break down, they either become nutrients that are recycled by nature for other uses, or they become pollution and waste that accumulate somewhere in the environment. Although your gas tank may be empty after driving your car, the liquid did not actually disappear. It has simply been transformed into a gaseous substance called carbon dioxide that accumulates in the atmosphere. The waste we send to the landfill does not go away. It just sits hidden underground, often for hundreds of years. This is called the second law of thermodynamics. (The junk my wife and I had to remove from the property we purchased brought this law to life. When something broke, the people who lived there before us apparently thought they could make it disappear by simply throwing it outside!)

These two laws of nature mean that in today's take–make–waste economic model the more physical stuff we produce, the more waste we generate. By thinking that 'away means gone', however, we assume that more products and substances can be produced forever without generating more harmful impacts. Unless that stuff can be continually recirculated in clean energy-powered closed-loop systems, the Earth's sinks eventually become saturated, degrade and collapse.

Larry Chalfan, who grew up in a former small rural timber town and went on to be chief executive officer (CEO) of Oki Semiconductor Manufacturing, gave little thought to the environment in his early years. As CEO of Oki, he 'Did not think much about what it meant to send our waste to the landfill.'[5] As will be discussed later in the book, Chalfan changed his thinking and went on to make Oki an environmental leader by realizing that he needed to cut its waste because 'away did not mean gone'. He also transformed his personal thinking to such an extent that he eventually became a leader in the zero waste movement.

There are real limits to the amount of pollution and waste that nature's sinks can absorb on a finite planet such as Earth. As Bill McDonough has so poignantly said: 'There is no away' (McDonough and Braungart, 2002). Only when we redesign our production and consumption systems along the lines of a renewable energy-driven circular borrow–use–return model will we begin to create opportunity and prosperity for humanity while restoring the Earth's sources and sinks.

ALL FOR ONE AND NONE FOR ALL

An almost universal STB is our propensity to love to death the things we value the most. This is the infamous story of the 'tragedy of the commons' (Hardin, 1968). Each of us tends to pursue the things we desire. We want inexpensive food. We want to move about as quickly and cheaply as possible. We want the latest electronic equipment in our home. If the source of the raw materials needed for these products is large enough and the pool of people pursuing the same resource is small, everyone can get what they want without trouble. If, however, the demand gets too great for the source to support or the waste becomes too large for the sinks to absorb, the source and sinks begin to degrade, leaving less for everyone.

Examples of this thinking blunder litter the landscape. We eat so much of our favourite fish that it is fished to extinction, depriving everyone of the joy of eating it. We build larger and larger houses requiring more and more wood and in doing so deplete the Earth's forests upon which everyone depends. We drive bigger vehicles longer distances and emit more carbon dioxide into already saturated atmospheric sinks, potentially restricting everyone's ability to drive in the future due to climate change.

For about six months my wife and I filled our vehicles with corn-based ethanol because we thought it would reduce our greenhouse gas emissions. Later we found out that our desire to reduce our own emissions with this form of ethanol (other types exist) was harming other people by contributing to higher food prices and depleting water supplies around the world. After we realized we were behaving selfishly, we stopped buying the product.

Harm to the Earth's sources, sinks and people are predictable when we place our own individual needs ahead of the broader community. We lose our perspective and become ethnocentric. The result is the Three Musketeers mantra in reverse: 'All for one and none for all.' Avoiding this deadly pattern requires that we prioritize the community as a whole, rather than just ourselves. In doing so, ultimately we all end up better off.

MY ACTIONS DON'T MATTER

Our propensity to think that our small everyday actions don't have an impact upon the climate, the natural environment or other people is another common STB because it allows us to justify business as usual and avoid responsibility for our behaviour.

As previously discussed, through the process of obtaining shelter, securing food and excreting waste, every organism modifies its environment. This is true for small organisms such as insects and for larger ones such as human beings. The deer that migrate through our land dig up the grass and chomp down leaves, bark, herbs – and my wife's newly planted flowers and shrubs! Similarly, we modified the land we bought by putting up a fence to keep our cats from roaming (and to hopefully prevent coyotes from eating them).

This means that every human activity, both positive and negative, has an effect. When few humans existed on Earth, resources were plentiful and modest amounts of waste were generated, each human's impacts made little difference in the aggregate. Today, however, each time we modify the environment we add more pressure on an already overstressed world.

Although per capita greenhouse gas emissions vary depending upon a person's location, habits and personal choices, for instance, the US Environmental Protection Agency (EPA) estimates that the average American emits 33lbs of carbon dioxide per day. Canada averages 18lbs, Sweden 11lbs and the UK 16lbs of carbon dioxide per day. The average worldwide is 7lbs of carbon dioxide a day (US EPA, 2006).

The average US household uses about 10,800 kilowatt hours (kWh) of electricity and 1070 gallons of gasoline each year. It takes the equivalent of almost 34,000kWh of energy, or more than 930 gallons of gasoline, to grow, process and deliver the food consumed by a family of four in the US each year. The average passenger car emits 2.39 tonnes of carbon dioxide each year. Even lawn and garden equipment emits an average of 0.03 tonnes of carbon dioxide annually.

All of this means that the simple acts of operating your homes, driving your vehicles, cutting your lawn or ploughing your garden have an impact.

Your purchasing decisions also have an impact. Every time you buy a product made of non-recyclable materials, or fail to fully re-circulate used materials items back into the economy or back to nature for further use, you reduce pressure on industry to develop closed-loop 'borrow-use-return' economic models and reinforce the unsustainable take–make–waste system. Every time you use toxic lawn, garden or household chemicals, you add toxicity to an already over-toxic environment.

I could go on about the many ways in which our daily mundane activities produce ecological and social impacts. My point is that there is no single source of harm to the climate, natural environment or communities. They are affected by a 'death of 1000 cuts'. Each of our small actions adds up and has an impact.

Unless we fundamentally alter our thinking and behaviours so they become neutral or restorative, each of us will continue to add to the causes of global warming, ecological degradation and social distress. To think sustainably is to acknowledge that everything is linked and every move we make has a consequence. When we fail to abide by these laws, we undermine the climate and the sustainability fundamentals of endurance, cleanliness and community.

IRON-CAGE THINKING

Each of the STBs described above are in some way linked to industrial society's mental frame of the economy as an out-of-control amoral machine driven by the media of self-interest, profit and power. In the early part of the 20th century, eminent sociologist Max Weber used the metaphor of the 'iron cage' to describe this thinking. Today, many people still think of the economy as an iron cage that controls their behaviour.

Iron-cage thinking lies at the heart of global warming and most of today's other pressing challenges because it breeds hopelessness. People believe they can do nothing to prevent conditions from growing worse. The iron cage, however, is not real. It is just a myth in our heads, promulgated mostly by those who get the most benefit from the existing system. The economy is not an amoral machine that humans cannot control. Self-interest, profit and power are not the only drivers of human behaviour, nor are worsening climatic, ecological or social conditions inevitable. A quick look around shows these views to be plainly false.

A wide variety of motives drive people's behaviour. Some do seek wealth and power. Others, however, are willing to live in near poverty conditions in order to pursue their creative and artistic drives. Many people are willing to accept less pay than they could get elsewhere because they want to be part of an organization committed to a higher social purpose. Still others desire to make just enough to care for their families and devote the rest of their energies to civic or spiritual endeavours.

Businesses also operate in different ways. Some are interested in continual growth. Others seem to be run for the personal enrichment of senior executives. Still others, however, prioritize the well-being of employees above all else. Some businesses are committed to public service, others to providing jobs for family members and others to offering quality service to customers even at the risk of reducing profits. Researchers Jim Collins and Jerry Porras point out in their book *Built to Last* that in the most successful corporations, profits are seen only as a measure of success and are not the primary goal.[6]

In addition, corporations are not required by law to 'maximize profit' above all else to benefit shareholders. Researchers that have examined US federal and state corporate legal codes have, at best, found vague language on this topic. In Delaware's corporate code, for example, a state where many US corporations choose to incorporate, the words 'profit' and 'return' never even appear. The articles of incorporation simply state that a corporation is required to engage in lawful activity permissible under state law (Nelson, 2006).

The principle that corporate directors and managers have a 'fiduciary duty' to the corporation has been established by case law. This phrase is often interpreted by corporate executives to mean that they are required to maximize profits above all else. However, language describing the duties of corporate directors simply states that they must 'act in a manner ... reasonably believed to be in the best interests of the corporation', which says nothing about profit maximization (Nelson, 2006).

Another rationalization given for the belief that corporations must always maximize profits is the fear of being sued due to precedents set by court decisions, such as the *Dodge versus Ford* court case of 1919, where a judge ruled that corporate directors do not have a right to reduce the profits of the organization. Few lawsuits against corporate directors, however, have ever resulted from this case. One reason is that legal scholars have countered the *Dodge versus Ford* decision by noting that 'no state corporation code in existence specifies that the directors of a corporation owe fiduciary responsibility solely to the shareholders'. Thus, shareholders face a steep uphill battle when they try to sue directors for breach of duty for not maximizing profits (Nelson, 2006).

The variety of motivations that people have for their behaviour and the flimsy legal underpinning of the profit maximization mandate means that the belief that greed, profit and power are the primary drivers of the economy is a mirage. The economy is not a machine over which humans have no control. These are false images that have taken on a life of their own over time because few people question them. On any given day, everywhere you look, you will see people making the choice to give of themselves, help others and promote the common good. It's not that individualism is wrong and should be rejected. Instead, it should be understood that it is just one part of human nature. At any moment people can make the decision to transform their individual drives into a force that promotes the higher purpose of resolving climate change and launching humanity on a path towards sustainability.

Here is just one example of what can happen if we channel individual self-interest into a force aimed at improving the common good. Despite the millions of people who live in poverty today across the globe, extreme poverty incidence actually *decreased* from 29 per cent in 1990 to 18 per cent in 2004. If current trends continue, the United Nations Millennium Development Goal of reducing extreme poverty by 50 per cent from its 1990 level by 2015 will be achieved (UN, 2006). Not only will this relieve untold human suffering, it will also reduce the social distress that is easily channelled into terrorism and other forms of extremism.

If extreme poverty can be cut in half in less than ten years, we can also resolve global warming and many of the world's other pressing challenges.

By failing to challenge the claim that only power, profit and greed matter and that there is little that humans can do to control their future, a self-fulfilling prophecy is created whereby those qualities become dominant. Breaking the myth of the iron cage, on the other hand, will help people see that we are in control of our fate.

EXAMINE YOUR THINKING

Take a moment to honestly examine your thinking and behaviour. Use the rating scale provided in Table 4.1 to evaluate the degree to which you employ the thinking patterns (don't feel bad: due to our training and indoctrination, most of us fall prey to them). Record your scores in the scorecard and add up the total. The higher the score, the more likely it is that your thinking and behaviour produce significant ecological or social impacts. We will use the scorecard again in Chapter 8.

To clarify the differences between the myopic take–make–waste mind frame and sustainable thinking, Table 4.2 presents ten core tenets of a sustainable perspective.

SYSTEMS BLINDNESS: THE ULTIMATE DRIVER OF UNSUSTAINABLE THINKING AND BEHAVIOUR

The most fundamental cause of STBs is 'systems blindness'.[7] By this I mean humans have difficulty overcoming two deep-seated limitations in our make-up: we find it difficult to see the effects of our actions on people or places outside of our immediate vicinity, and we struggle to realize that delays may cause the effects of our actions to appear in the future, not right away.

If people, plants or animals close to us do not appear to be affected by our actions, we assume that everything is fine. It rarely dawns on us that behaviour such as using high volatile organic compound (VOC) paint or driving vehicles

Table 4.1 *Sustainability thinking blunder scorecard*

On a scale of 1 to 5, with 1 being never and 5 being always, how often do you find yourself using the following sustainability thinking blunders?

Straight-line thinking	1	2	3	4	5
Quick-fix thinking	1	2	3	4	5
Technology can save us	1	2	3	4	5
More is better	1	2	3	4	5
Cheaper is cheaper	1	2	3	4	5
Less bad is good enough	1	2	3	4	5
Away means gone	1	2	3	4	5
My actions don't matter	1	2	3	4	5
All for one and none for all	1	2	3	4	5
Iron-cage thinking	1	2	3	4	5
Totals	—	—	—	—	—
					= Total score

Scoring

Total score of 10 = low effects

Total score of 11 to 20 = moderate effects

Total score of 21 to 30 = medium effects

Total score of 31 to 40 = high effects

Total score of 41 to 50 = extreme effects

Note: Even if your overall score is low, any question answered with a 4 or 5 suggests a potentially major effect on the climate, natural environment and social well-being.

that emit carbon dioxide may affect atmospheric conditions or people in other parts of our community – or in Bangladesh, for that matter. Humans have limited sight horizons. People see the parts but not the whole: out of sight, out of mind. This is *spatial* systems blindness (Oshry, 1996).

Delays cause the effects of our action to show up in the future, not immediately. Because they cannot be seen today, we don't consider the possibility that effects may arise down the road. The impacts of the slow build-up of human-produced greenhouse gases, for example, are only now becoming apparent despite the fact that industrial society began generating them over 150 years ago. People see the present without seeing the past or future. Humans have limited time horizons: if not now, then never mind. This is *temporal* systems blindness (Oshry, 1996).

Table 4.2 *Ten tenets of sustainable thinking and behaviour*

Sustainability thinking blunders (STBs)	Sustainable thinking tenets
Straight-line thinking	Systems-based thinking
Short-term, quick-fix thinking	Long-term thinking focused on fundamental solutions
Technology can save us	Borrow–use–return systems can save us
More is better	Small, flexible, self-governing units are better
Cheaper is cheaper	Pay full costs now
Less bad is good enough	Totally sustainable is good
Away means gone	There is no away
My actions don't matter	Every action matters
All for one, none for all	All for all, and all for one
Iron-cage thinking	Thinking can be changed at any time

Both types of systems blindness produce significant negative effects on the climate, natural environment and social well-being.

Systems blindness results from many causes. Human nature, for example, seems predisposed to seek safety and avoid danger and to desire pleasure and shun pain. These traits often manifest themselves in the drive for power, status or material acquisition, and in their worse forms as hatred and violence.

In addition, the human brain has limited capacity. We simply can't think about everything and are best at responding to the familiar. Events that lie outside of our experience are not easily grasped.

'I'm sure glad the hole is not on my end.'

Our Inability to See *Connections Across Boundaries*
in Time & Space

Figure 4.1 *Spatial systems blindness*

Our Inability to See the Full Impacts of Our
Actions Due To _Delays_ In the System

Figure 4.2 *Temporal systems blindness*

Evolutionary biology has shown that humans struggle to imagine events with which we have no history. It is only in the last 150 years or so that humans have developed the technological capacity and sheer numbers to affect the climate, natural environment or other people thousands of kilometres away and well in the future. We have little experience with global or multigenerational impacts. It will likely take generations of repeated practice for humans to develop the innate capacity to naturally consider interconnectedness across time and space and to acknowledge the possibility of delays.

Lacking this ability, we focus only on events that we believe will directly affect us today and dismiss those that may arise elsewhere or at some future time.

In short, our DNA is designed to focus our thinking and behaviour on just our own immediate needs and to ignore the consequences for others or the climate and physical environment. Constant vigilance is needed to overcome these traits.

CHANGE IS POSSIBLE

The desire for status and power won't vanish, nor will greed or hatred. But these traits represent just one side of human nature. Humans are also naturally endowed with positive qualities such as kindness, compassion and a willingness to sacrifice for the common good. If effective change strategies are employed, the destructive qualities of humans can be controlled and positive traits can be mobilized and strengthened. Change is possible.

In Part II of this book we will discuss how you can alter your personal thinking and behaviour, and help the people, teams and organization you work with do the same by adopting a sustainable mind frame.

NOTES

1 Ray Anderson, pers comm, 23 April 2007.
2 This blunder is a variation of a 'systems archetype' described by Kim and Anderson (1998).
3 Rusty Rexius, pers comm, 21 March 2007.
4 Ray Anderson, pers comm, 23 April 2007.
5 Larry Chalfan, pers comm, 23 April 2007.
6 See, for example, *Built to Last* (Collins and Porras, 1994) and *Good to Great* (Collins, 2001).
7 This concept was first used by Barry Oshry (1996) in his book *Seeing Systems*, although it was focused on systems within organizations.

REFERENCES

Collins, J. (2001) *Good to Great*, HarperBusiness, New York
Collins, J. and Porras, J. (1994) *Built to Last*, HarperBusiness, New York
Hardin, G. (1968) 'The tragedy of the commons', *Science*, vol 162, pp1243–1248
Kim, D. and Anderson, V. (1998) *Systems Archetype Basics: From Story to Structure*, Pegasus Communications, Waltham, MA
Kuehr, R. and Williams, E. (eds) (2004) *Computers and the Environment: Understanding and Managing their Impacts*, Kluwer Academic Publishers and United Nations University, Norwell, MA
McDonough, W. and Braungart, M. (2002) *Cradle to Cradle*, North Star Press, New York
Nelson, J. (2006) *Economics for Humans*, University of Chicago Press, Chicago
Oshry, B. (1996) *Seeing Systems: Unlocking the Mysteries of Organizational Life*, Berrett-Koehler Publishers, San Francisco
Stern, N. (2006) *The Stern Review of the Economics of Climate Change*, October, London, www.sternreview.org.uk
Teachout, T. (2003) *The Skeptic: A Life of H. L. Mencken*, Harper Collins, New York
UN (United Nations) (2006) *United Nations Millennium Development Goals Report 2006*, http://mdgs.un.org/unsd/mdg/Resources/Static/Products/Progress2006/MDGReport2006.pdf
US EPA (Environmental Protection Agency) (2006) *Inventory of US Greenhouse Gas Emissions and Sinks: 1990–2005*, www.epa.gov/climatechange/emissions/downloads06/07ES.pdf

Part II The Path Forward

5

How We Think

Our life is what our thoughts make it.
Marcus Aurelius, Meditations, 167 AD

Now that you are aware of the ways in which you may be addicted to myopic unsustainable thinking and blind to the systems you are part of, it is time to learn how to kick the habit. We will start by examining how the mind works.

Human beings think in concepts. The term concept describes any set of closely related ideas that we group together under a single word or image (Gardner, 2006). Concepts allow us to create categories and make distinctions among things. We describe the warmer temperatures caused by the tilt of the Earth's axis towards the sun as the concept of springtime, and the cooler temperatures caused by the Earth's tilt away from the sun as the concept of autumn. We explain the electrons and protons flowing through wires that brighten light bulbs as the concept of electricity, and the liquid molecules flowing through a garden hose as the concept of water. Without an ability to develop concepts and make distinctions, the world would seem opaque and indistinguishable to us.

Some of our concepts are substantive, such as the concept of a refrigerator or a house. Others are more abstract, such as the concept of interdependency, democracy and even climate change. No matter how tangible or intangible they may be, our concepts are merely attempts to describe what we see, sense and experience in the world. Even the term 'ecosystem' is just a concept that humans use to describe homogeneity and stability among certain ecological processes and elements. In reality, it is very difficult to know if or where one ecological process or element ends and another begins. It is only the human need to make distinctions in order to talk about things that leads us to categorize certain natural functions or geographic areas as 'ecosystems'.

This underscores that humans create concepts to serve their personal needs. Just because we name and separate things into different categories does not mean we accurately see or understand them. Because our concepts come about to help us understand the world, we should assume that people or cultures with different needs and goals naturally adopt different concepts to explain the same phenomena we described.

Most of our most important concepts are formed in early childhood as we continually adopt new distinctions in order to make sense of the world around us. When we are children we also learn rules such as 'Don't talk with strangers' and 'Don't stick your finger in electrical sockets' (or, as my wife says, 'Don't lick an ice cube tray'). No formal instruction accompanies this early learning process. It is natural and occurs through trial and error, listening, sensing, observing and undoubtedly genetic influences.

Children combine rules and concepts to form theories of how the world works. Some of these early theories can be accurate. For example, after being bitten, a child may adopt a theory that grabbing small crawling creatures can be painful. Other early theories are inaccurate. Although young children may adopt the theory that their parents are all-knowing, later in life they will find this was not true. Children see only small slivers of the world and have limited capacity to think flexibly, so many of their early theories are wrong.

Most young children continually update their theories as they grow because their concepts are new and not yet embedded in concrete. Children also develop new concepts by observing those of the adults around them, especially their parents. Thus, a child's concepts are influenced by their surroundings.

Rather than reflecting reality, sometimes a child's concepts take on a life of their own. For example, a child may start with the theory that small crawling creatures bite and cause pain, then assume that all small creatures bite, then adopt a belief that all small creatures are dangerous, and, in turn, think that all small creatures should be squashed because they are bad. The rules and concepts that children adopt can gather momentum and, if repeated without challenge, become inflexible, trapping them in their own reality.

Fortunately, as they age, the vast majority of people develop flexible beliefs in most areas of their lives. They learn that certain rules and concepts apply to specific situations and not to others. For example, adults come to understand that not all small crawling creatures bite and that those that do may only be defending themselves against a perceived threat.

However, if our role models, real or imagined early life experiences, or a trauma reinforce distorted notions, some of our early incomplete or flawed rules and concepts may remain fixed as we grow older. Without concerted effort to evaluate whether, on hindsight, our early theories were accurate, and without the capacity to honestly examine how they affect our lives today as adults, rules and concepts can harden in our minds. We become slaves to our concepts and fail to realize that they are not real, but are merely ideas and constructs we established in our heads to make sense of the world. If we aren't careful, we begin to create our own reality and constantly reaffirm the myths and images we already hold.

MENTAL FRAMES

This is how mental frames are formed that produce inflexible, myopic climate-damaging thinking and behaviour. Mental frames are the deeply felt beliefs, assumptions and stories we hold in our minds about the nature of other people, how the world works and our role in it all.

Mental frames have three interlinked elements: core beliefs, core assumptions and automatic thoughts (Beck, 1979). Core beliefs are the deepest level of cognition. They are the unconditional views we hold about the world around us, including the physical environment, other humans and ourselves. Some examples of core beliefs on a personal level may be 'I never get enough ... (love, attention, resources)'; 'I'm inadequate'; or, conversely, 'I'm a good person.' Sample core beliefs about others may include 'People can't be trusted'; 'Everyone is greedy'; or, alternatively, 'People are good inside.'

Sample core beliefs regarding the climate and natural environment may include 'Nature is here for human use'; 'Nature's resources are unlimited'; or 'Nothing I do can harm it.' Sustainable core beliefs may include 'Humans must be stewards of the Earth'; 'Nature's health and beauty matter'; or 'Everything I do has an impact.'

Our core beliefs tend to be absolute – we believe them without reservation. We don't think: 'Some aspects of nature are unlimited.' We simply think: 'Nature's resources are unlimited' (Greenberger and Padesky, 1995).

Take a moment to reflect on your core beliefs about the climate, natural environment and social well-being. Can you describe them in simple sentences?

Our core beliefs lead to basic assumptions about everything we see and experience. Those assumptions take the form of the 'rules' that guide our thinking. The rules become 'self-instructions' that we use to guide what we see around us and how we interpret the information we receive. Our internal rules contain a coding system that we use to determine the meaning of events and to make sense of complex situations. Moreover, our internal rules establish the criteria by which we evaluate our appeal to others and our self-worth. We use these rules to determine our expectations; to guide how we will achieve our goals and achieve pleasure; to protect ourselves from physical or psychological harm; to form and sustain relationships with others; and in other ways to determine how to behave (Beck, 1979).

A prime example of how mental frames influence our behaviour is the experience that my wife and I had when we asked three contractors for bids to install energy-efficient windows in our new house. Our request was straightforward: we wanted a bid to include the purchase and installation of super energy-efficient windows and complete cleanup. One contractor responded angrily, stating that he was not responsible for cleanup or waste removal. He gave us a bid that included extra costs to clean up and haul away the waste (my wife reacted in her typical unflappable way: with nary a word she simply dropped his bid into the 'circular file' on the floor in the corner of the room). The second contractor said little and then gave us the lowest bid, which we initially accepted (as mentioned, we soon learned he did not actually intend to purchase super energy-efficient windows and we luckily dropped him before he installed them). The third accepted our conditions with a smile, gave us the bid we eventually accepted, and went above and beyond the call of duty when he installed the windows (he and my wife immediately hit it off and she thought he was a peach!).

The differences between the responses can be understood by the varying internal mental rules that each contractor used to interpret our request and to guide their behaviour. I can speculate that the first contractor interpreted our bid requirements as an attempt to take advantage of him, so he reacted with suspicion and anger. His general internal rule may have been: 'Extra requirements by customers = taking advantage of me.' His self-instruction may have been: 'I must stick it to people who try to screw me.'

The second contractor probably interpreted our bid requirements as merely 'helpful suggestions', signifying he was not particularly concerned about what we wanted so he tried to slip a fast one by us. His general internal rule may have been: 'Extra requirements by customer = immaterial.' His automatic self-instruction was probably something like: 'I should ignore the request of others and do only what is best for me.'

The third contractor probably interpreted our requirements as legitimate and fair. His general internal rule was likely to have been: 'Reasonable request = reasonable, honest response.' His automatic self-instruction was probably something on the order of: 'When people are reasonable I should respond in kind.'

The point is that our core beliefs lead to assumptions and rules that determine the way in which we interpret and respond to the world around us.

AUTOMATIC THOUGHTS

Most of us are unaware of the private thoughts that steer our behaviour. This is because without realizing it, our reactions to events are shaped by thoughts that simply pop into our minds automatically during the day. Since we are constantly thinking, new images continually arise in our minds. However, we barely notice them. We don't necessarily set out to think and respond in certain predictable ways. Nevertheless, our core beliefs and assumptions about the world and the internal rules that they produce lead to specific types of hidden controlling thoughts (Greenberger and Padesky, 1995). Each of us has many types of automatic thoughts. For our purposes, the thoughts of concern are those that lead to the sustainable thinking blunders and systems blindness.

Automatic thoughts that direct us to take into account the effects of our actions on other people, the climate and the natural environment support sustainable thinking. Automatic thoughts that tell us to discount or ignore the consequences of our actions lead to myopic climate-damaging outcomes.

Automatic thoughts tend to have certain characteristics. They are usually specific and concrete, not general vague notions. The thoughts generally occur not as whole sentences, but as specific words, images, mental pictures or memories that send a distinct message. Most of the time, our automatic thoughts arise without a trigger: they just happen (Beck, 1979).

All too often we unconsciously accept our automatic thoughts without testing their authenticity or logic. We regard them as rational and grounded in reality, even when others clearly see the harm they produce to other people, the environment and ourselves. Without thoughtful self-reflection, no matter how many times our automatic thoughts are invalidated by external experience, we continue to accept them unconditionally.

Spend a minute reflecting on your automatic thoughts. How often are you aware of them? Can you identify the common themes?

Just because automatic thoughts simply happen does not mean we don't monitor our internal thought process. Humans spend much of their time debating their thinking, feelings, desires and behaviours. Plato referred to this process as our 'internal dialogue'. Some individuals fail to monitor their thinking and behaviours adequately, which impedes awareness of the consequences of their actions. Alcoholics, for example, often suspend their self-monitoring to the extent that they loose sight of when their drinking causes harm to themselves or others. Similarly, individuals often suspend their self-monitoring of how their behaviours may affect the climate, natural environment or other people, now or in the future. Lack of self-monitoring is at the heart of many of the sustainability thinking blunders.

Figure 5.1 depicts the hierarchy of core beliefs, assumptions and automatic thoughts – our mental frame. How aware are you of your mental frame about the climate, natural environment and social well-being?

EMOTIONS AND THOUGHTS

Psychologists have long debated the source and importance of human emotions. Although the term has no universally agreed upon definition, the word emotion is a composite of two Latin words: '*motere*', which means to move and create action, and '*e-*' which means outward motion. Thus, at their root, emotions have built-in action tendencies. They are impulses that prepare or cause people to act (Arnold, 1960; Smith, 1991; Goleman, 1995).

My wife and I easily see the link between emotion and action in the deer, wild turkey, fox and other animals that share our property. A noise or movement

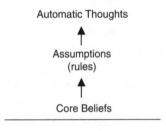

Figure 5.1 *Emotions and thoughts*

Source: adapted from Greenberger and Padesky (1995).

triggers fear that causes instantaneous rapt attention. If the sound is loud or the movement big enough, the animals will immediately flee. It's also easy to see the direct connection between emotions and action in children, who cry when hungry or run to their parent when frightened.

Because of their capacity for rational thought, however, adults are not forced to act on their every emotion. Of all the organisms on Earth, only adult humans have developed the cognitive ability to separate emotions from action by controlling how they view and think through situations.

Despite the potential for adults to control their emotions, all too often our internal impulses still overwhelm and sometimes paralyse our rational thought process. Emotions can produce immediate reactions that seem completely at odds with, or excessive, when compared to the actual situation. Strong emotions can cause us to do things we are ashamed of or are shocked by later when the emotions subside.

Emotions seem to often trump rationality because they are the products of millions of years of evolution. Different emotions evolved by playing distinctive roles in helping our ancestors survive the trials and tribulations of life. Humans who developed skilled emotional reactions to threats and opportunities, and displayed the bonding emotions needed to attract a mate, survived and reproduced. Those with poor emotional repertoires perished.

We are often not aware of our emotions, just as we are usually not conscious of the thoughts that automatically pop into our heads during the day. However, each influences the other. Our automatic thoughts trigger our emotions and our emotions trigger automatic thoughts and behaviours.

Although our emotions produce many of our instantaneous reactions, the rational mind serves as our control panel, managing and moderating our emotions. Thus, although you may not be able to prevent emotions from arising, the way you think is the key to regulating and controlling them. By becoming conscious of and adjusting the thoughts that roll through your mind, you can alter and control your emotions. There is no greater skill in life than the capacity to resist our emotional impulses by altering our thinking. It is the root of all self-control, happiness and maturity in a human.

Of course, some people believe that the right to act on their every emotion constitutes freedom. This, however, is phoney freedom, not real liberty. Whether it is greed, anger or conspicuous consumption, people who demand the right to act on every emotion confuse freedom with control. They cannot harness their internal impulses or their marketing- and advertising-enflamed desires for immediate gratification, so the only freedom they think they can achieve is freedom from the demands of others. People with these beliefs are not free at all. To the contrary, they are rigidly controlled by internal forces that they refuse to acknowledge.

True freedom is responsible freedom. It exists only when people are aware of the internal impulses that drive their thinking and deliberately choose how they will behave, regardless of their conditioning. True freedom exists when people consciously select behaviours that respect the ecological and social systems of which they are part.

Take another moment now, if you would, to contemplate the extent to which you are aware of how your emotions influence your thinking and behaviour about the climate, natural environment and other people.

FALSE FEEDBACK AND SELF-VERIFICATION

Unless people develop what Harvard psychologist Ellen Langer (1989) calls 'mindfulness' skills, they never develop the capacity to honestly examine their automatic thoughts and control their emotional impulses and behaviour. Over time, people who have not developed the capacity for self-reflection come to believe that their mental frames are reality and that this reality is obvious to everyone. They think that their core beliefs and assumptions are based on hard verifiable data, and the data they select are the only valid data. Like a coffee filter that allows liquid to pass, but not the grounds, their mental frames screen out most incoming information that conflicts with their existing concepts and theories. People who lack mindfulness have false feedback mechanisms.

False feedback produces what psychologists call 'self-verification'. People select information to pay attention to and believe only if it reaffirms their existing views about themselves – even if it is negative – and the world around them. Self-verification theory also suggests that individuals are more likely to believe and gravitate towards others who reaffirm the views they already hold about themselves and the world, and discount or ignore people who do not (Swann and Pelham, 2005).

Because our mental frames filter our view of the world, they are, by definition, limited and defective in some manner. Just as children do, adults never actually see the entire picture of the world around them. It takes continued effort to recognize this fact and not get trapped into thinking that our core beliefs, assumptions and automatic thoughts are accurate or all-encompassing.

Recall how important accurate and timely feedback is to any system. When we get false feedback and our mind frame is closed to new concepts, we disregard any experience or information that challenges our theories of the world, and if that does not work, twist them to conform to our existing views. We become increasingly confident, and yet at the same time more and more misguided.

Step back now and reflect on your personal self-verification patterns. How often are you aware that you may be paying attention to information that, or people who, reaffirm your existing views of the world and ignore or discount those that don't?

OUR MENTAL FRAMES SHAPE OUR BEHAVIOURS AND, THUS, POLICIES AND TECHNOLOGIES

It should now be understood that our mental frames direct our thinking and control our emotional and behavioural responses. Mostly unconsciously, our core beliefs and assumptions construct the internal rules that produce our automatic thoughts. In turn, unless we are mindful, our automatic thoughts shape our behaviour. The technologies, policies and procedures that we adopt result from our thinking and behavioural patterns.

As discussed in Chapter 3, the way in which a system is structured shapes its performance. Most of the time, we are unaware of the structures that mould our lives. The daily pressures we face tend to capture most of our attention. But this is just the surface level of reality. If we take a moment to look below the hubbub of daily events, we often find that our current difficulties are part of a long-term pattern. We may discover, for example, that similar situations have arisen numerous times in the past, often in slightly different form. We may also become aware that we responded to each event with a similar response that either failed to solve the problem or sometimes made things worse. This awareness opens the door to new ways of thinking.

If we take the time to dig even deeper, we may realize that the historic patterns of events result from the way in which we design our policies, technologies, decision-making mechanisms and other aspects of our economic and social systems. This awareness engenders deeper understanding and further expands the options available for resolving the problems.

The greatest leverage for understanding and change, however, can be obtained by digging below the way in which our systems are structured, to uncover the core beliefs, assumptions and automatic thoughts that led people to design the structures that way in the first place. This deep level of awareness unveils the greatest number of options for resolving a situation. This is because new thinking, spurred by mindfulness, produces more accurate and effective beliefs and assumptions. Over time, expanded mental frames will lead to new systemic structures that will, after a while, produce different patterns of events that eventually cause people to deal with different types of daily challenges.

Figure 5.2, known as the 'Iceberg' in systems thinking, describes this process.

If our core beliefs and assumptions – our mental frames – are that nature exists solely for the purpose of human use or that the Earth has unlimited resources and an infinite capacity to absorb human-produced greenhouse gases and waste, the internal rules that shape our automatic thoughts and guide our behaviours will be something like: 'There is no need to be concerned about the effects of my actions on the natural environment' or 'I must ignore any suggestion that I should moderate my consumption or waste.' When these types of automatic thoughts dominate, we naturally adopt policies and technologies

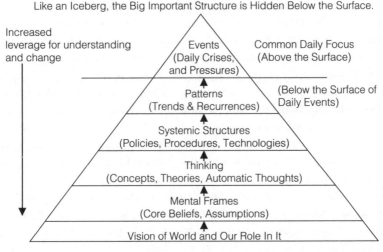

THE ICEBERG
Like an Iceberg, the Big Important Structure is Hidden Below the Surface.

Increased
leverage for understanding
and change

Events
(Daily Crises,
and Pressures)

Common Daily Focus
(Above the Surface)

Patterns
(Trends & Recurrences)

(Below the Surface of
Daily Events)

Systemic Structures
(Policies, Procedures, Technologies)

Thinking
(Concepts, Theories, Automatic Thoughts)

Mental Frames
(Core Beliefs, Assumptions)

Vision of World and Our Role In It

Figure 5.2 *The iceberg*

that foster the continual consumption of resources and generation of greenhouse gas pollutants and waste.

In short, the crises that humanity faces today are very much of our own making. More than anything, climate change and today's other pressing sustainability challenges result from a lack of mindfulness and false feedback mechanisms that produce erroneous and incomplete core beliefs, assumptions and automatic thoughts.

THE POSSIBILITY OF NEW DIRECTIONS

Many people are pessimistic about their personal ability and the capacity of humanity, in general, to make the fundamental shift in thinking and behaviours needed to increase prosperity and security while resolving global warming and other sustainability challenges. Why is this so? One reason may be the influence of professionals. Most individuals change their behaviour on their own and thus do not garner the attention of professionals, whether they are therapists or climate protection and sustainability practitioners. Self-changers also tend to define success in different terms than the concepts and language used by professionals. Thus, it is often the professional's own self-verification mechanisms and resulting rigid concepts that lead them to believe people cannot change.

In addition, people sometimes look at single attempts at change and when they see failure, assume that people can't or won't change. Time and again, however, research has shown that most substantive changes require multiple attempts and persistence over long time periods. Drawing conclusions about the human capacity for change based on the first few attempts is therefore erroneous.

Research on thousands of people in numerous countries has found that the vast majority of smokers, alcoholics, overeaters and others with various addictive behaviours successfully kick their habit (Prochaska et al, 1994). Addicts demonstrate similar defence mechanisms to people who resist the need to change their mental frame about the climate, natural environment and social well-being. A large pool of research has also demonstrated that even those who are most stuck in their ways can change if the right approach is used. Pessimism about the capacity to change is thus greatly misguided and is often itself the single biggest impediment to progress.

Just as ecological systems have built-in self-maintenance and repair mechanisms, human beings have two natural attributes that enhance their resiliency and adaptability and allow them to alter harmful thinking and behaviours. Self-awareness and free will are human traits that are unique to all other organisms on Earth. We have the capacity to act purposely, on our own, to adopt new ways of thinking and behaving that protect the climate, natural environment and social well-being. The greatest changes in human history have occurred when people fundamentally reframed their beliefs, assumptions and thinking and, as a result, designed whole new ways of meeting their needs.

In the next chapter we will investigate how those changes can come about.

REFERENCES

Arnold, M. (1960) *Emotion and Personality: Psychological Aspects, Volume 1*, Columbia University Press, New York

Beck, A. (1979) *Cognitive Therapy and the Emotional Disorders*, Meridian Books, New York

Gardner, H. (2006) *Changing Minds*, Harvard Business School Press, Harvard

Goleman, D. (1995) *Emotional Intelligence*, Bantam Books, New York

Greenberger, D. and Padesky, C. (1995) *Mind over Mood: Change How You Feel by Changing the Way You Think*, Guilford Press, New York

Langer, E. (1989) *Mindfulness*, De Capo Press, Cambridge, MA

Prochaska, J. O., Norcross, J. C. and Diclemente, C. C. (1994) *Changing for Good*, HarperCollins Publishers, New York

Smith, C. A. (1991) 'The self, appraisal, and coping', in C. R. Snyder and D. R. Forsyth (eds) *Handbook of Social and Clinical Psychology: The Health Perspective*, Pergamon Press, Elmsforth, New York

Swann, W. and Pelham, B. (2005) 'The truth about illusions', in C. R. Snyder and D. R. Forsyth (eds) *Handbook of Positive Psychology*, Oxford University Press, Oxford

6
How We Change

The doors we open and close each day decide the lives we lead.
Flora Whittmore, from Koerber, 2004

Now that you have a sense of the basics of how humans think, let's explore how we change. The notion of trying to alter our own thinking and behaviour in any significant way often seems daunting. Trying to motivate other people, teams or organizations to change is even more intimidating. Although many books promote techniques claiming to easily change another person's attitude and behaviour, we all know that reality points in a different direction.

When deciding whether to become a sustainable thinker, it is therefore important to understand that, just as ecological systems constantly adapt to new conditions, humans have an innate capacity to change. By realizing that the key to change is to draw out and mobilize the natural human aptitude for change, and that researchers have identified effective ways of facilitating the process, your prospects for success brighten considerably.

Most people function quite well in life, even when their mental frames and the rote behaviours they produce are flawed or harmful. Not only do the majority of people successfully adapt to new conditions, they also respond to dangerous situations fairly well. From weight loss to smoking, alcohol and drug addictions, we all know of people who, when faced with threats to their well-being, altered their thinking and behaviour.

Change is also not always arduous. In fact, most of the changes we make in life are easy. Our favourite television show goes off the air, so we watch a new one. Our favourite fruit goes out of season, so we switch and eat a different one. We go different places on vacation each year to experience something new. Because they are so routine and effortless, we don't even remember the many changes we regularly make on a daily basis.

By understanding this intrinsic human ability to change, you can avoid actions that may impede the process. Just as importantly, you can help facilitate and speed the change process along.

WHY DON'T PEOPLE CHANGE?

If change is both constant and natural, what prevents people from changing? When you consider the dire condition of the climate and natural environment and the increasing social and political instability around the world today, it would seem obvious that the thinking and behaviour of many people are self-destructive. Why, then, do so many people continually repeat the same harmful patterns?

One reason people stay stuck in destructive patterns is that they do not feel sufficient internal pressure to change. Most people have competing internal goals. The gap between these goals creates tension that humans want to alleviate. On the one hand, because of the way in which our internal psychological, as well as external economic and social, systems are structured, we want to maintain homeostasis and keep doing what we are already doing. On the other hand, most of us have a strong internal desire to set things straight, get a better handle on things, to make a difference and have meaning in our lives. People have a built-in desire to make things right. Humans are competence-seeking organisms (Deci and Ryan, 1995).

It is easy to assume that people who have little interest in change are ignorant, are in denial or are just bullheaded. Often, however, a much simpler explanation exists: *people who resist change simply do not feel a sufficient amount of tension between their current state and an alternative desired condition.*

Self-regulation theory explains this phenomenon (Miller and Rollnick, 2002). This body of cognitive psychology suggests that people monitor their thoughts and emotions much like a thermostat monitors room temperature. When the tension between their deepest desires and their current condition is within an acceptable range of discrepancy, they have little motivation to change: no tension, no change. When the tension between what they really want and their existing state is outside of acceptable levels, people become open to the possibility of change. Tension seeks resolution. Figure 6.1 describes this dynamic.

Feeling sufficient tension, however, is merely half of the change equation. Research on the effects of faith and hope in facilitating change has found that an individual's belief in their ability to change is a strong predictor of their eventual success, a dynamic psychologists call 'self-efficacy' (Bandura, 1986). *If individuals do not believe that they can close the gap between their desired goals and current state, they will often not attempt to change.*

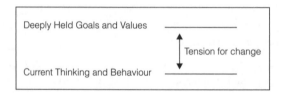

Figure 6.1 *Tension between desired and current conditions*

Self-regulation theory is again pertinent here. If the discrepancy between an individual's current and a desired state is strong enough and they believe they can succeed, they will often pursue change. If, however, people do not have confidence in their ability to successfully make the changes needed to resolve the tension, they are likely to ignore, deny or downplay problems such as climate change, rather than take steps to resolve them.

Sometimes people don't believe they are competent enough to make a change due to lack of understanding. At other times, the problem may be insufficient skill. Social norms that oppose new thinking and behaviour, outright opposition from an individual's social network, or major technical or structural obstacles are other powerful constraints to self-confidence.

So, why don't people change? People often fail to adjust their thinking and behaviour because they do not feel sufficient tension between their existing state and a desired condition, or don't believe they are capable of closing the gap (Miller and Rollnick, 2002).

WHAT MOTIVATES CHANGE?

Let's now spin the question around and investigate the factors that motivate people to change. Despite some popular views, making people feel guilty, shameful or vilifying them rarely succeeds in building motivation for change.[1] People don't change because they have not been castigated enough. To the contrary, these actions usually immobilize humans or cause them to dig in their heels, making change even more difficult.

People also do not fundamentally alter their core beliefs or assumptions merely as a result of rewards and punishments, especially when those incentives are not permanent. The dramatic drop-off in energy efficiency after the US federal tax incentives that promoted them disappeared during the early 1990s offers an example. People altered their behaviour only as long as the incentives lasted. As soon as they ended, people reverted to their old behaviour and efficiency improvements dried up. This shows that rewards and punishments are superficial motivators that rarely, on their own, achieve lasting change in the core beliefs, assumptions or automatic thoughts of adults.

If criticism, reward and punishment are not effective motivators of change, what can build motivation in people to change? As I have continually pointed out, the performance of both ecological and human systems is heavily influenced by their structure. The way in which plants and animals, as well as climate and other natural factors, interrelate shapes the way that ecological systems perform. The way in which physical and social systems that surround humans are structured, and, just as importantly, their perception of those structures, influences how people think and behave.

Recall that the internal psychological structure of a human is composed of core beliefs, assumptions and automatic thoughts, which produce rote behaviours. Unless this structure is altered, people will take extraordinary steps to keep doing what they are already doing, even when those behaviours are self-destructive. As we just discussed, the most powerful force for altering the internal psychological structure of a human is discontinuity between their prevailing thinking and behaviour and some deeply held values and aspirations.[2]

Take a moment to think about some of the big changes you have made in your life. Did this dynamic hold true? Did you feel tension between your current state and a desired goal of some type, and did you need to feel confident that you could close the gap before you took steps to change?

THE 5-D STAGED APPROACH TO CHANGE

If both internal tension and self-confidence are vital, how do these factors combine to produce change? Again, think about your own experience. When you successfully made a significant personal change, did the shift occur instantaneously or, consciously or not, did your thinking and behaviour evolve through a sequence of steps? Although a significant disturbance may occasionally cause you to change on a dime, if you are like most people, change probably occurred through a series of fairly distinct stages.

Although no model of behavioural change is perfect and every model has its critics, one of the best ways I have found to describe the process that people move through when they make a major shift in thinking and behaviour is the 'staged approach' to change. The staged approach is based on the trans-theoretical model of change (TTM) developed by James Prochaska and his colleagues (Prochaska et al, 1994). The TTM model resulted from extensive research that distilled 24 major approaches to cognitive and behavioural change into a single framework.

TTM researchers found that each of the different systems of change implicitly or explicitly agrees on one thing: people go through a series of stages whenever they make a significant change in thinking and behaviour. They also found that cognitive and experiential change methods are most helpful in motivating new thinking and behaviours when people are in the early stages of change, that behavioural change mechanisms have more potency in the later stages, and that humanistic approaches or helping relationships are important throughout the entire change process. TTM therefore incorporates each of these approaches into a comprehensive system that meets the specific needs of people, teams and organizations no matter what stage of change they are in.

TTM researchers have found that a staged approach applies to teams and organizations, as well as individuals. I believe it is a useful model for thinking about broad-scale social change as well. Communications, policy instruments and other forms of change interventions can all benefit from being grounded in the staged approach.

The genesis of the TTM model was health-related behavioural change. Prochaska et al (1994) are, in fact, cancer researchers, and much of the research on the TTM approach has been produced at the University of Rhode Island (URI) Cancer Prevention Research Center. Early in the course of writing this book, I contacted the people at URI and asked if they thought the TTM model would apply to environmental and sustainability-related thinking and behavioural changes. The researchers had already expanded the TTM approach beyond health. However, no one had asked them if it applied to these issues. Numerous emails led to conference calls and meetings. The conclusion turned out to be unequivocally yes. The TTM approach can be a very powerful model when seeking to understand and alter thinking and behaviour that affects the climate, natural environment and social well-being.

TTM APPLIED TO CLIMATE, ENVIRONMENTAL AND SOCIAL WELFARE CHANGE EFFORTS

After a good deal of study and testing, I determined that some of the terms and methods encompassed in the TTM model for health-related behaviours were not sufficient to meet the needs of people, teams and organizations seeking to become sustainable thinkers. I therefore made a number of modifications to the approach. In addition to TTM, the approach offered here and in subsequent chapters incorporates principles and methods from motivational interviewing; appreciative enquiry; the systems change work of Russell Ackoff, Donnella Meadows and others; and my own experience and research in the fields of systems thinking, organizational change for sustainable thinking, sustainable development and global warming.[3] For simplicity purposes I call it the 5-D staged approach to personal, team and organizational change.

If you are interested in changing your own thinking and behaviour about the climate and other sustainability issues, or want to help other people or the teams and organizations with whom you work shift directions, you can use the 5-D staged approach to develop effective change strategies. My research and experience suggests that when people or groups are involved in altering their thinking and behaviours related to the climate, natural environment and social well-being, a useful way to describe the stages of change is as follows. [4]

Stage 1: Disinterest[5]

This is the 'I won't change' stage of the transition to sustainable thinking and behaviour. It constitutes the starting point for most change efforts. People, teams and organizations in this stage have little interest in altering their perspectives or activities regarding the climate, natural environment or social well-being. They either have little awareness of the issues, deny that their behaviour contributes to the problems, believe the effects are inconsequential, have lost hope that they can do anything about the concerns, or don't believe they can alter their longstanding patterns (Levesque et al, 2001, pp139–153).

Although other people can quite clearly see the personal, environmental or social impacts generated by an individual or group's thinking and behaviour, those who are disinterested in change often cannot. They usually lack information about issues such as global warming, and frequently make it a point to remain ignorant at all costs. Many individuals, business and government leaders are disinterested in the true causes, consequences and solutions to global warming, ecological degradation and related social distress. Think of the oil industry executives who for many years have tried to sow doubts about the science of climate change among the public. Despite the fact that thousands of scientists and lay people alike clearly see the ecological and social consequences of climate-damaging thinking and behaviour, disinterested people such as the oil executives cannot.

It is easy to become frustrated with individuals who are not interested in change and write them off as hopeless. People concerned about climate protection and sustainability, however, do so at their peril. Disinterested individuals often have the power to slow or halt climate protection and sustainability efforts. Ignoring them thus threatens everyone.

It's also important not to lump disinterested people into a single group. Many reasons exist for disinterest. In addition, each of us may be disinterested in some problematic personal behaviour, so this is not an uncommon state. My wife often tells me that I am in a state of disinterest regarding my consumption of carbohydrates (I love bagels, pancakes and spaghetti), and my waistline sometimes reflects this. Even though people can seem permanently intransient, by using change mechanisms appropriate for this stage, even the most ardently disinterested people can become sufficiently open to the possibility of new thinking and behaviours that they progress to the next stage of change.

Stage 2: Deliberation

This is the 'I might change' stage of the sustainable thinking transformation process. In this stage, people begin to acknowledge that they might have a problem and start to seriously consider whether to change their thinking and behaviour. They often begin to gather information about global warming and other sustainability issues, for instance, and examine solutions that they can use some time in the distant future. People in the deliberation stage, however, still struggle to understand the nature of global warming, environmental degradation and social distress, see their cause, or identify possible solutions. They don't comprehend, for example, how driving a gas-powered vehicle can possibly contribute to climatic changes occurring at the global scale or how building a 10,000 square foot 'trophy house' can negatively affect the earth's ecological sources and sinks.

Even though people in the deliberation stage are now willing to consider the possibility of a shift in thinking and behaviour and may even have a sense of what it would entail, they continue to overestimate the disadvantages of change and therefore remain ambivalent about making a shift. People go back and forth between wanting and not wanting to sell their SUV, for example, or of giving up the idea of constructing a huge trophy home. Deliberating about whether or not to make a change therefore does not equate to being ready to make the journey. To move to the next stage of change they must decide that the upsides of becoming a sustainable thinker substantially outweigh the downsides.

Stage 3: Design

This is the 'I will change' stage of the shift to sustainable thinking. To reach this stage, people have concluded that the benefits of becoming a sustainable thinker significantly overshadow the costs, so they design a plan for adopting new thinking and behaviours in the near term. In fact, they may have already made a few small changes to see how it feels and to test their ability to succeed. They may tell family, friends and colleagues about their intention to sell their SUV, for example, and check out the prices of hybrids or other fuel-efficient vehicles.

Designing a plan for change does not mean an individual has resolved his or her ambivalence. In the design stage, people often continue to oscillate back and forth between wanting and not wanting to become a sustainable thinker. Oscillation is resolved only when people decide that the pros of change clearly outweigh the cons and then make a firm public commitment to alter their thinking and behaviour.

Stage 4: Doing

This is the 'I am changing' stage of the transition to sustainable thinking. Whereas people, teams and organizations in the design stage are planning to change, in the doing stage they are explicitly taking action to modify thinking and behaviour that affects the climate, natural environment or social well-being. The doing stage is an active time that requires a great deal of commitment because, while the previous stages mostly occurred internally, doing means that overt changes are now visible to others. An individual will actually sell his or her SUV, for instance, and buy a more fuel-efficient vehicle. Family or friends may question such changes. Similarly, a business may purchase renewable power or begin to eliminate toxic substances. Some suppliers or customers may pressure the firm to revert to their old way of doing business because the new approach provokes questions about their own behaviour. Doing therefore puts the doer under the spotlight. To persevere they must remain committed, make structural adjustments and remember that the benefits of change are worth the effort.

Stage 5: Defending

This is the 'I have changed' stage of the sustainable thinking transformation process. After six months to a year of active engagement in sustainable thinking and behaviour, people enter the phase where they seek to fuse together the changes they have made so far and make them stick and grow over the long term. This can be tough work. People must work hard to defend their new approach in the face of resistance from others and the need to continually overcome obstacles and recover from setbacks. Many attempts are often needed because few people, teams or organizations successfully alter longstanding, myopic climate-damaging thought or behavioural patterns on the first try. The inability to deal with the emotional and psychological stress of change and to persevere in the face of social pressure and setbacks are common causes of regress.

THINK ABOUT YOUR OWN LIFE

The stages of change described here represent the normal processes that each of us go through when making a fundamental shift. We are usually unaware of the need to make a change until an event of some type rocks our boat or another person points it out. Sometimes a major disturbance, such as a personal illness or family emergency, causes us to rapidly change. More often than not, however, we spend some time deliberating about whether or not we want to make a change. If we decide a change is warranted, we spend a little time figuring out the best way to proceed. We then take action and, after a while, try to make the new approach become routine. Reflect for a moment on changes you have made in the past. Does this process match your experience?

IS THERE A SIXTH STAGE CALLED 'DONE'?

The ultimate goal for any person, team or organization making a change towards sustainable thinking is for the new patterns to become fully integrated within their mental frame. In this stage individuals would effortlessly think and act in climate-positive sustainable ways. Teams and organizations would fully embed the new approach in their systems and policies. Myopic climate-damaging thinking and behaviours would never return.

Table 6.1 *5-D stages of change for the climate and sustainability*

Disinterest	'I won't change.' No intention of changing. Can't see or won't admit a problem.
Deliberation	'I might change.' Recognition that a problem may exist. Beginning to consider making a change in the distant future.
Design	'I will change.' Committed to taking action in the immediate future and developing an action plan to do so.
Doing	'I am changing.' Making overt changes in thinking and behaviour.
Defending	'I have changed.' Maintaining and expanding upon the change, while defending against resistance, obstacles and backsliding.

This could be considered the 'done' stage of change. However, because our economic system and the social structures established to support it are inherently unsustainable, people will need to defend their new approach for decades to come, if not a lifetime. Sustainable thinking is therefore an ongoing process without an endpoint. For this reason, I don't include a 'done' stage in the framework.

THE FIRST KEY TO SUCCESSFUL CHANGE: KNOW THE STAGE OF CHANGE AND USE APPROPRIATE CHANGE MECHANISMS

Each stage of change can be diagnosed, each is predictable, and successful movement through each requires that a specific set of activities be completed (Prochaska et al, 1994). The first key to successfully altering your own thinking and behaviour regarding the climate, natural environment and social well-being is therefore to know which stage of change you are in and to then use appropriate change mechanisms with each stage. Similarly, the key to helping other people, teams or organizations make the changes necessary to adopt sustainable thinking is to successfully diagnose their stage of change and to use the right change mechanisms in each stage.

When the stage of change is accurately understood, appropriate change mechanisms can be used to help the individual or group complete the necessary activities and progress to the next stage (Prochaska et al, 1994). By change mechanism I mean communications and other processes that help to modify thinking and behaviour about the climate, natural environment and social well-being. It is important not to confuse mechanisms with techniques. For each change mechanism, there are an untold number of possible techniques that can be employed (Prochaska et al, 1994).

Misdiagnosis of the stage of change can lead to the use of change mechanisms better suited for different stages of change. This mistake can delay or irrevocably damage climate protection and sustainability efforts. Using behavioural change mechanisms such as rewards and incentives with people or groups who are in the early change stages of disinterest or deliberation, for example, will usually fail and often cause cynicism and resentment because in those stages people are not ready to actively engage in climate protection or sustainability activities.

This is one of the most common problems I see among climate protection and sustainability advocates. People are not aware of the stages of change, have not taken the time to carefully diagnose which stage they or others are in, or use inappropriate change mechanisms or techniques. Promoters of sustainable thinking themselves are therefore often the cause of delays or activities that fatally wound change efforts.

Progression through the stages of change is by no means a given. Individuals, teams, organizations and society as a whole can get stuck in one stage for a long time or backslide into previous stages. This underscores the importance of knowing the stages of change and using appropriate mechanisms at the right time, in the right sequence.

THE SECOND KEY TO SUCCESSFUL CHANGE: BUILD TENSION FOR CHANGE AND ENHANCE SELF-EFFICACY

To motivate fundamental change, sufficient tension must be established between some deeply held unmet values and aspirations and current conditions. Tension can relate to a potential risk that an individual or group wants to avoid. Action to reduce the risk thus achieves the goals of safety or comfort. Tension can also result from the awareness of important internal or externally established goals or standards that are not being met. Resolving this tension allows people to feel good about themselves, to feel successful, and in other ways to feel high self-esteem.

Tension, however, is not enough. Sufficient confidence must also exist that the changes required to close the gap and reduce the tension can be achieved. Often people see a needed change as too large or too difficult for them to tackle. For example, they may see major technical or structural obstacles in the way and believe they lack the understanding or skills to overcome them. They may also have failed with other changes they have attempted to make in their lives and believe they will fail to become a sustainable thinker as well. Or, they may believe that those with whom they interact or others in their community or place of work do not support sustainable thinking and thus fear social disproval or isolation.

Building self-confidence in the ability to overcome these real or imagined obstacles and making a shift in thinking and behaviour must therefore be an essential element of any successful global warming or sustainability-focused change effort.

THE THIRD KEY TO SUCCESSFUL CHANGE: EMPHASIZE BENEFITS EARLY ON AND DEAL WITH DOWNSIDES IN THE LATER STAGES OF CHANGE

TTM researchers found two very important patterns when investigating the upsides and downsides of change, and the stages of change, seen in people with problem behaviours such as smoking, unprotected sex, lack of sunscreen use and mammography screening for cancer prevention, overeating and lack of exercise leading to weight gain, and trouble with breaking addictions such as cocaine use. First, to advance from the initial stage of disinterest to the advanced stage of doing, an individual's perception of the benefits of new thinking and behaviour must increase by an average of one standard deviation. A standard deviation is sort of the 'mean of the mean'. In other words, for every downside of change people need to see at least two benefits.

Benefits can include the avoidance of harm resulting from awareness of threats to one's personal safety or to the well-being of one's organization or society as a whole. Benefits also include positive gains such as feeling good about oneself or your organization, attaining better physical or emotional health, or getting affection and support from important others. Although some researchers believe that avoiding harm is a more powerful benefit than obtaining a positive gain, my experience suggests this is not always the case. When the issues relate to environmental or social well-being, an individual's perception of the credibility of the options available for steering clear of a threat or attaining a positive benefit influences their decision-making.

Thus, the most important task in the early stages of change is to enhance an individual's perception of the benefits of becoming a sustainable thinker *twice as much* as they decrease their perception of the downsides, while the downsides of change need to shrink by half as much. For this reason, the change mechanisms appropriate for the disinterest and deliberation stages of change are aimed at helping people to increase their perception of the benefits of new patterns.

The second pattern identified by the TTM research is also important. Although emphasis on benefits continues to be important, in the later doing and defending stages of the transition to sustainable thinking the emphasis must be placed on helping people to overcome the downsides of change because of the need people have to deal with resistance and surmount obstacles (Prochaska et al, 1994).

Although the research behind both of these findings focused on health-related thought and behavioural change, I'm confident they hold true for environmental and sustainability-based change efforts as well.

Each of the keys to the successful shift to sustainable thinking is important and different people will respond positively to different factors. The thinking of one person, for example, may be most influenced by their views about the upsides and downsides of the change, while another individual may be primarily influenced by the self-confidence they have about their ability to make the shift. Still others may be influenced by all three factors. This is why it is always important to focus on each of the three keys to change.

CHANGE MECHANISMS

As mentioned, cognitive and experiential approaches are the most important change mechanisms in the early stages of change. Although these two mechanisms remain important throughout the entire process, behavioural change mechanisms become particularly helpful in the later stages of change. Supportive relationships are important in every stage.

Cognitive reframing constitutes the foundation of the entire process of altering personal, team and organizational thinking and behaviours regarding the climate, natural environment and social well-being. Cognitive reframing involves seeing our core beliefs, assumptions and automatic thoughts in a new light, and altering patterns that are dysfunctional or erroneous.

We all know the old saying that knowledge is power. This is particularly true with self-knowledge. Knowledge of our own thought process, which psychologists call 'meta-cognition', and knowledge of our own emotions, which psychologists call 'meta-mood', are the most potent sources of power any human can posses. The term 'meta' means 'about'. Meta-cognition, which is 'thinking about thinking', and meta-mood, which is 'awareness about one's emotions', involve seeing inside your own internal private experiences in a way that allows you to understand, manage and alter how your thought processes function (Flavell, 1979, pp906–911; Sternberg, 1986; Borkowski et al, 1987, pp61–75). These processes enhance the self-knowledge needed to control our thoughts and thus manage our emotional responses and behaviours.

Since at least World War II, Western psychology has focused primarily on pathology: how to remedy human psychological disorders (Seligman, 1990). By studying only pathology, the underlying assumptions of Western psychology have evolved to support a disease model of human nature. People are seen as flawed, brittle, plagued by poor genetics, driven by greed and power, and, consequently, slaves to circumstances that appear beyond their control, such as their economic systems.

In the West, the disease model has led people to accept that the 'normal' mind frame is based on the core belief that the economy is an amoral machine that humans cannot control. As a result, the take–make–waste economic system is seen as natural and 'healthy', even though it is associated with numerous environmental, economic, social and psychological ills (Kasser, 2002).

At its core, Western psychology has a negative, problem orientation. It emphasizes methods of making undesirable mental and emotional conditions go away. Health, however, cannot be defined merely as a lack of disease. Healthy ecological systems are defined by robust feedback, self-maintenance and repair mechanisms that enhance resiliency, not by lack of distress (Seligman, 1990). Similarly, sustainable thinking cannot be defined as merely the absence of environmentally and socially harmful cognitive patterns or behaviours. Sustainable thinking requires the growth of exceptional states of environmental, social and economic awareness, understanding and behaviour.

The cognitive reframing process of thinking about our own thinking and emotions is the key to bringing about the exemplary states of mindfulness needed to think and act in a sustainable manner. The object is deceptively straightforward: identify unsustainable thoughts and behaviours, decide if they allow you, or the team or organization with whom you are involved, to live up to deeply held aspirations and values, and if not replace them with patterns that allow you to do so (Seligman, 1990; Ellis, 2001). Change mechanisms that best facilitate cognitive reframing include disturbances, emotional inspiration, awareness-building, choice expansion, self-appraisal and helping relationships. These mechanisms will be discussed in more detail in subsequent chapters.

After people have decided to engage in sustainable thinking, behavioural change mechanisms become more prominent because they help to reinforce positive behaviours and eliminate influences that prevent the adoption of climate-positive thought and behavioural patterns. Making a firm commitment to change, getting constant reinforcement, substituting factors that elicit unsustainable behaviours with those that trigger sustainable thinking and activity, redesigning the structures around you and forming mentoring relationships are thus the most helpful mechanisms in the doing and defending stages of change.

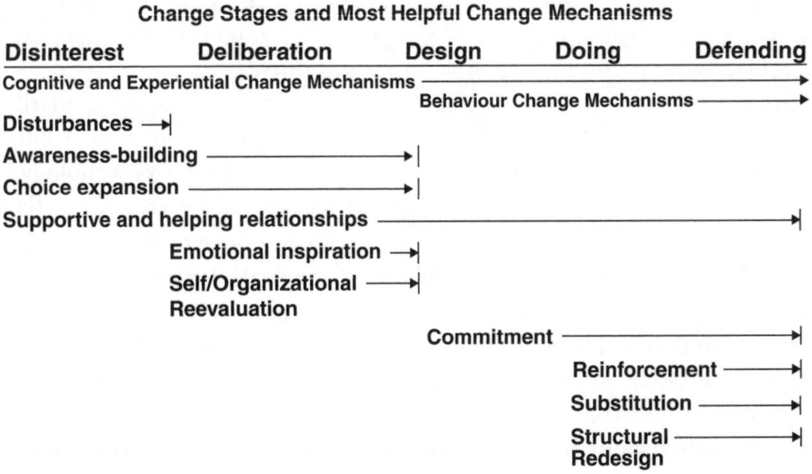

Change Stages and Most Helpful Change Mechanisms

Disinterest	Deliberation	Design	Doing	Defending

Cognitive and Experiential Change Mechanisms ⟶

Behaviour Change Mechanisms ⟶

Disturbances ⟶|

Awareness-building ⟶|

Choice expansion ⟶|

Supportive and helping relationships ⟶|

Emotional inspiration ⟶|

Self/Organizational ⟶|
Reevaluation

Commitment ⟶|

Reinforcement ⟶|

Substitution ⟶|

Structural ⟶|
Redesign

Figure 6.2 *Stages of change and most helpful change mechanisms in the 5-D model*

Source: adapted from Prochaska et al (1994, p54).

CHANGE IS NOT LINEAR

By describing the stages of change in a step-by-step fashion, I don't want to give the impression that the process is linear. Personal, team, organizational and social change is much more like a roller coaster or corkscrew than a straight line. People often make some progress, then backslide to a previous stage, begin again with small incremental changes and then suddenly take huge leaps forward, and in other ways jump back and forth through different stages when altering their thinking and behaviour.[6]

USE THE MODEL TO FOSTER CLIMATE-POSITIVE SUSTAINABLE THINKING AND BEHAVIOUR

By understanding the 5-D staged approach to change, you can create the internal tension and build the self-confidence needed to make the shift to sustainable thinking. The transition to sustainable thinking is likely to produce a number of personal benefits. A good deal of research, for example, shows that increased mindfulness is associated with more ecologically sound behaviours (Kasser, 2002; Brown and Kasser, 2005, pp349–368). The process is also sure to enhance your overall well-being. Ample research, for example, shows that increased self-awareness is associated with greater personal happiness (Brown and Ryan, 2003, pp822–848). The ability to observe your cognitive and emotional patterns enhances your ability to manage the automatic thoughts flowing through your mind and establish more successful ways of seeing and responding to the world.

Through the use of this model you can also help other people and the teams and organizations with whom you associate to make the same type of shift. The more that individuals and organizations adopt sustainable thinking, the greater will be the likelihood of increasing prosperity and security around the world while also resolving climate change and conserving the natural environment.

EVALUATE YOUR STAGE

Use the simple self-assessment that follows to honestly evaluate your personal stage of change regarding the climate, natural environment and social well-being (adapted from Prochaska et al, 1994, p54). You might think you know what stage you are in. Humour me and complete the assessment anyway. You may discover something new.

For the purposes of this questionnaire, taking steps to 'change my thinking and behaviour regarding the climate, natural environment and social well-being' means making explicit efforts to avoid the sustainable thinking blunders and/or actively engaging in activities that protect and restore ecological sources and sinks and enhance social well-being, such as increasing energy efficiency in your home or work, using renewable energy, moving to zero waste, buying Fair Trade-certified products, and other similar actions.[7]

Please answer yes or no to the following four questions:

1   I have taken some steps in the past six months to protect the climate, natural environment and social well-being.
2   I intend to take action in the next month to protect the climate, natural environment and social well-being.
3   I intend to take action in the next six months to protect the climate, natural environment and social well-being.
4   I have been actively involved for more than six months with actions aimed at protecting the climate, natural environment and social well-being.

Scoring (adapted from Prochaska et al, 1994):

•   If you answered no to all statements you are in the disinterest stage of the transition to sustainable thinking.
•   If you answered yes to statement three and no to all of the others, you are in the deliberation stage.
•   If you answered yes to statements two and three and no to the others you are in the design stage.
•   If you answered yes to statement one and no to statement two you are in the doing stage.
•   If you honestly answered yes to statement four, you are in the defending stage.

The next chapter describes how you can personally use the fundamentals of the 5-D change model to become a sustainable thinker.

NOTES

1   I founded and for ten years directed a conservation organization but left distressed, in part, because of the almost universal belief that humiliation, shame and guilt were the primary ways of motivating people to change. Environmentalists saw themselves as the good guys and, implicitly or otherwise, almost always viewed those who failed to walk lock-step with them as evil people. Constant attacks on the credibility and motivation of others was the norm. Amazingly, many environmentalists could not understand why they faced so much resistance to their proposals.
2   For more information see the work on motivational interviewing by William Miller and Stephen Rollnick (2002), *Appreciative Inquiry* by Diana Whitney, Amanda Trosten Bloom and others (2003), and structural tension by Robert Fritz (1999).
3   See Miller and Rollnick (2002); Ackoff (1999); Whitney and Trosten-Bloom (2003); Meadows (1997, pp78–85), as well as many other of her articles and books.

4 The terms 'I won't', 'I might', 'I will', 'I am' and 'I have' used in my description of each stage change are from Reed et al (1997, pp57–66).

5 In *Changing for Good*, James Prochaska and his colleagues (Prochaska et al, 1994) call the stages of change 'pre-contemplation, contemplation, preparation, action and maintenance'. I use the terms 'disinterest, deliberation, design, doing and defending' because I think they more clearly describe the characteristics involved in the stages of change related to climate and sustainability issues.

6 Prochaska et al (1994) call this process 'recycling'.

7 These actions can include, but are not limited to making changes in, personal, avocational or work related to the following:

• transportation patterns (e.g. use of hybrid or biodiesel vehicles, more walking, biking and use of public transportation, less airplane travel);

• energy use (e.g. increased energy efficiency via new appliances, insulation, reduced consumption);

• renewable energy (e.g. shift to wind or solar power);

• food purchasing (e.g. buy local, organic, vegetarian, Fair Trade);

• products and services selection and use (e.g. buy less, use longer, purchase locally made, composed of non-toxic recyclable materials, Fair Trade);

• recycling (e.g. reuse and recycle all spent materials);

• reproduction (e.g. choose to have no more than a replacement number of children); and

• other similar changes.

REFERENCES

Ackoff, R. (1999) *Re-creating the Corporation*, Oxford University Press, New York

Bandura, A. (1986) *Social Foundations of Thought and Action: A Social Cognitive Theory*, Prentice Hall, Englewood Cliffs, NJ

Borkowski, J., Carr, M. and Pressely, M. (1987) '"Spontaneous" strategy use: Perspectives from metacognitive theory', *Intelligence*, vol 11, pp61–75

Brown, K. W. and Ryan. R. M. (2003) 'The benefits of being present: Mindfulness and its role in psychological well-being', *Journal of Personality and Social Psychology*, vol 84, pp822–848

Brown, K. W. and Kasser, T. (2005) 'Are psychological and ecological well-being compatible? The role of values, mindfulness and lifestyle', *Social Indicators Research*, vol 74, pp349–368

Deci, E. L. and Ryan, R. M. (1995) *Intrinsic Motivation and Self Determination in Human Behavior*, Plenum, New York

Ellis, A. (2001) *Overcoming Destructive Beliefs, Feelings and Behaviors: New Directions for Rational Emotive Behavior Therapy*, Prometheus Books, Amherst, New York

Flavell, J. H. (1979) 'Metacognition and cognitive monitoring: A new area of cognitive-developmental inquiry', *American Psychologist*, vol 34, pp906–911

Fritz, R. (1999) *The Path of Least Resistance for Managers*, Berrett-Koehler, San Francisco

Kasser, T. (2002) *The High Price of Materialism*, MIT Press, Cambridge, MA

Koerber, T. (2004) *100 Magical Moments*, Beauty Books, Kingston, WV

Levesque, D. A., Prochaska, J. M., Prochaska, J. O., Dewart, S., Hamby, L. and Weeks, W. (2001) 'Organizational stages and processes of change for continuous quality improvement in health care', *Consulting Psychology Journal: Practice and Research*, vol 53, no 3, pp139–153

Meadows, D. (1997) 'Places to intervene in a system (in increasing order of effectiveness)', *Whole Earth*, winter, pp78–85

Miller, W. and Rollnick, R. (2002) *Motivational Interviewing: Preparing People for Change*, Guilford Press, New York

Prochaska, J. O., Norcross, J. C. and Diclemente, C. C. (1994) *Changing for Good*, HarperCollins Publishers, New York

Reed, G. R., Velicer, W. F., Prochaska, J. O., Rossi, J. S. and Marcus, B. H. (1997) 'What makes a good staging algorithm: Examples from regular exercise', *Methods, Issues, and Results in Evaluation and Research: American Journal of Health Promotion*, September/October, vol 12, no 1, pp57–66

Seligman, M. E. P. (1990) *Learned Optimism*, Vintage Books, New York

Sternberg, R. J. (1986) *Intelligence Applied*, Harcourt Brace Jovanovich, New York

Whitney, D. and Trosten-Bloom, A. (2003) *The Power of Appreciative Inquiry: A Practical Guide to Positive Change*, Berrett-Koehler, San Francisco

7

Transforming Your Personal Thinking and Behaviour

The difficulty lies not in the new ideas, but in escaping the old ones, which ramify for those brought up as most of us have been, into every corner of our minds.

John Maynard Keynes, 1935

For decades, Rusty Rexius, third-generation family member and current co-president of Rexius Company, thought of himself as 'traditionally aligned with the timber business'. Although he realized that without a healthy forest his company would not have trees to make their products from, Rusty and the other family members who ran the company 'never thought about sustainability'. In fact, he said: 'The term "environmentalism" was sort of a swear word in the company.'[1] Global warming and other sustainability issues were simply not spoken about or acknowledged.

Around 2003, however, Rusty began to feel some internal tension about his company's future due to changes occurring in the timber industry, as well as the increased attention he saw in the media about peak oil, climate change and other issues of sustainability. This discomfort caused Rusty and other family members to wonder if the next generation could survive with the type of thinking and company operations that had worked well in the past. Rusty eventually concluded: 'We needed to do our business differently because the world was changing.'[2]

At the same time that Rexius was pondering the future, one of his employees told him that because the company made mulch from forest by-products, they were actually recyclers and therefore already in the business of sustainability. 'We never really thought of ourselves in this way', said Rexius. 'We just thought we were using local timber products. This new concept turned on a light. It dawned on us to ask what else are we doing regarding sustainability.'[3]

By coincidence, at that same time Rusty and his company were beginning to consider a new approach, he was invited to join the Lane Clean Fuel Coalition, a local group focused on finding ways of reducing emissions from trucks. The idea of using biodiesel that produces much fewer greenhouse emissions than regular diesel truck fuel was born. This new concept led to even further enquiry. Rusty and others in the company started to ask what else they could do to become more sustainable.

This question led Rusty to re-examine his own thinking and behaviour. For instance, he began to 'think about the environmental footprint I leave all the time'. He ended up selling his personal SUV, buying a diesel pickup and running it on biodiesel, reducing his travel, and continually looking for areas of his life where he asked himself: 'Is this is the right thing to do – the sustainable thing to do?' This deep-seated personal transformation, in turn, drove his efforts to make over his company.

Incremental changes were initially pursued within the business because Rusty was still debating the pros and cons of becoming a sustainable thinker. For example, they devised a small erosion-control project using what eventually came to be known as EcoBlanket to replace hydro-seeding and the use of seed or straw to control erosion in sensitive waterways. Sometime afterwards, they 'stumbled' onto using a product they now call EcoBerm as an alternative to the use of silt fencing for erosion control.[4] These became highly successful products.

Each success reinforced his perception of the benefits of the new approach and emboldened him to take further steps. Eventually, Rusty and his partners decided that the benefits of sustainable thinking far outweighed the downsides, so they designed a plan to reorient the entire company around sustainability. A new logo was developed and the company even adopted a new tag line. Today, company vehicles can be seen all over town promoting their use of biodiesel with 'Rexius Sustainable Solutions' proudly displayed on the side. As a result of a deep-rooted shift in his beliefs and thought patterns, Rusty successfully transformed himself and his company into a local leader in the sustainability field.

The transition Rusty Rexius experienced highlights the basic stages people move through when making a fundamental change in their personal thinking and behaviour about the climate, natural environment and social well-being. Most people start in a state of *disinterest*. They are unaware of or don't acknowledge that a problem exists, and minimize, or rationalize away, the harmful consequences of their thinking and behaviour. To move beyond disinterest, their level of awareness must rise and their defences must be relaxed enough to consider the possibility that new thinking and behaviour would prove beneficial. When this occurs they begin to *deliberate* over whether or not to make a change, with the deciding factor usually being whether their current thinking and behaviour allows them to live up to some deeply held aspirations and values. If they conclude that a change in thinking and behaviour would be beneficial, they *design* a plan to do so. Once enough design work is completed, they firm up their commitment and begin to act. Numerous obstacles usually arise during the *doing* stage. For this reason, people must *defend* their new approach against resistance from others and other impediments for quite some time until it sticks and becomes routine.

It's important to note that Rusty Rexius could not have helped his employees understand the issues or make the transition towards sustainable thinking until he had first made the transition himself. You can't help others change until you are aware of the need to change yourself. The first and most important step you can take to expand climate-positive sustainable thinking is therefore to alter your own mind frame.

This chapter offers a step-wise method you can use to personally progress through the five stages of the sustainable thinking transformation process, much as Rusty Rexius did. By using the 5-D staged-approach, you can make the transition consciously rather than by chance. All that is needed to allow this process to succeed is openness to new concepts, persistence and a willingness to learn.

THE DISINTEREST STAGE OF CHANGE

CHANGE MECHANISMS FOR DISINTEREST

- Disturbances
- Awareness-building
- Choice expansion
- Supportive relationships

This is the 'not ready to change' stage of the transition to sustainable thinking and where change begins for most people. One of the most perplexing aspects of people who are disinterested in altering their thinking and behaviour about the climate and other sustainability issues is that they stay stuck here even when the downsides of their current patterns are obvious to other people. In fact, people often work hard to stay mired in disinterest.

It seems almost too obvious to say, but change is more likely to occur if a person sees it as important. For disinterested people, however, change is not a priority. They refuse to acknowledge problems and reject attempts by others to point them out. Because it often takes effort to maintain disinterest, people who are in this stage often need help from others to progress beyond it. Strategies for motivating others to change are discussed in Chapter 9.

What's important here is to realize that people stay rooted in disinterest for different reasons, which can be summarized as the four Rs: reluctance, rebellion, resignation and rationalization.[5] Often, a combination of these defence mechanisms is at play.

People are sometimes *reluctant* to change due to inertia, fear or, perhaps, comfort with their current condition. Individuals with this form of disinterest do not allow information about the causes and effects of global warming or other sustainability issues to permeate their minds. As a result, their disinterest is usually passive, meaning they don't have much investment in their existing thinking or behaviour. My 87-year-old father-in-law is not strongly opposed to reducing emissions by improving the energy efficiency of his 100-year-old house;

but he nevertheless remains disinterested because he is reluctant to disrupt his daily routine (a posture my wife is hesitant to mess with).

Rebellious individuals are often very knowledgeable and extremely invested in their harmful patterns. They insist on making their own decisions and will not let others tell them they need to change. Their rebellion may be the result of prolonged adolescence, overcompensation caused by lack of self-confidence, or fear of lost opportunities such as profits made from environmentally or socially harmful activities. Again, think of the many auto and oil industry executives who rebelliously deny the reality of global warming. No matter what the roots, a rebellious individual has a lot of energy tied up in their myopic climate-damaging mental frame and will often be antagonistic towards anyone suggesting that they change.

In contrast to rebellious individuals who have lots of vigour, people who feel *resigned* to their current condition typically lack drive. As a rule, they seem overwhelmed by issues such as global warming, ecological degradation and growing social inequity, have given up hope that the issues can be resolved, or lack confidence in their ability to alter thinking and behaviours that contribute to the problems. They may have tried to make a change in the past but failed, felt foolish or defeated, and gave up.

One individual I know, for example, purchased compact florescent lights for his house but failed to realize that both his dining room and bedroom had dimmer switches, which the compact fluorescents would not work with. Not only did he feel he had wasted money on the new bulbs, he also decided that whatever he did to reduce his greenhouse gas emissions would fail because he was incompetent.

While the resigned individual has few answers, *rationalizers* think they know it all. They don't consider becoming a sustainable thinker because they believe they are immune from harm caused by global warming and other sustainability crises or can figure out how to avoid it. When they can't find a way to explain away risks, rationalizers tend to assign responsibility for their problem behaviour to other people or to forces over which they have no control. They may have convinced themselves, for example, that global warming won't have an effect until well into the next century after they are dead, or that it will actually benefit them.

A former senior city administrator in my hometown often said that global warming would be good for the local area because it would mean more warmer days (despite the fact that rising temperatures would also bring more forest fires, drought, heat waves and disease). He was a rationalizer (and was eventually transferred out of his position in large part due to this type of thinking on many issues).

MOVING BEYOND DISINTEREST

If you want to move beyond disinterest you must begin to reframe your thinking. As discussed in Chapter 6, cognitive reframing is important throughout the entire sustainable thinking transformation process. However, it's especially important here.

Cognitive reframing involves surfacing and recognizing your current perspectives and the behaviours that they generate, consciously challenging illogical, distorted or maladaptive beliefs and thought patters, and then adopting new perspectives that are more helpful.

Four basic change mechanisms contribute to the cognitive reframing process: disturbances, awareness-building, choice expansion and supportive relationships.

CHANGE MECHANISM 1: DISTURBANCES

Just as a major fire, drought or other incident opens an ecological system to change, some type of disturbance event in our lives is often needed to trigger the cognitive reframing process. Disturbances can rip away our blinders and expose the flaws in our current thinking and behaviour about the climate, natural environment and social well-being.

Oil and gas price shocks or major shifts in the industry you work in, such as those that Rusty Rexius experienced, sometimes serve as mind-changing disturbances.

Milestones can also disrupt business as usual. The first time one of my wife's colleagues asked about global warming was after the birth of her first child. Life-changing events such as this often force us to think deeply about how our existing thought and behavioural patterns may affect the child's future.

Action by the Portland City Council committing the city to sustainability was the disturbance that launched Sue Klobertanz's engagement in the change process. Klobertanz is the former head of purchasing for the City of Portland, Oregon. As a self-described 'bottom-line' person, Klobertanz was initially sceptical about environmental concerns and 'green' products. She knew, for example, that 'she was not supposed to pour oil into the sewer system', but she was 'ambivalent' about the risk that chemicals posed to the environment. The city council's commitment to sustainability, however, led Klobertanz to attend workshops and seminars on the issue. The more she learned, the more she warmed to the idea. Under her leadership, her department eventually adopted the city's first sustainable purchasing plan.

One of the most common forms of disturbance is pressure from others. Sometimes it's pressure from our close confidants. For many years I travelled extensively, teaching and consulting. Much of the travel was by air. My wife kept urging me to cut down on my air travel because she felt I was being hypocritical given the large amounts of greenhouse gases that the air travel produced. I rebuffed her efforts to increase my awareness, however, by saying that my travel was necessary to help others implement climate protection and sustainability plans and to generate an income for us. I was firmly caught in the grips of the 'all for one, none for all' and 'my actions don't matter' sustainability thinking blunders.

It was not until my wife finally convinced me to calculate my travel-related greenhouse gas emissions (and I decided that a happy wife is a good thing!) that I realized I was merely justifying my problem behaviour. This awareness led me to substantially reduce my travel.

As a side benefit, by reducing my travel I was also able to eat better, get myself in shape, spend more time with my family and, in general, feel healthier.

The more aware you are of such disturbances, large or small, the greater the likelihood that you can use them as catalysts to question if your current thinking and behaviours are appropriate, accurate and effective. Ask yourself, for example, if your use of straight-line, quick-fix or any of the other sustainability thinking blunders may have led to or exacerbated the disturbance. Ponder how effective your current mental frame may be if a disturbance caught you by surprise. Determine if your current thinking and behaviours will allow you to successfully adapt to changing circumstances created by the disturbance.

This type of introspection requires some soul-searching. If you knew, for example, that you were contributing to the catastrophic breakdown of the climate, natural environment or social well-being, would you continue your current thought and behavioural patterns? Is that how you want to live your life? Is that how you want to be remembered? Ask yourself these tough questions.

CHANGE MECHANISM 2: AWARENESS-BUILDING

Although a disturbance is often helpful in 'unfreezing' your thinking, the process is essentially reactive. You can also take proactive steps to move beyond disinterest. This can be achieved by asking yourself questions such as: 'How aware am I of how my thinking and activities affect the climate, natural environment and social well-being?' and 'Am I a climate-positive sustainable thinker or do I employ one or more of the sustainability thinking blunders and have a myopic take–make–waste mental frame?' If you are not sure how to answer these questions, you may benefit by increasing your understanding of global warming and other issues of sustainability.

Get informed

Numerous books and magazine articles offer information about global warming, ecological degradation and related social and political distress. You can also surf the web for information, see movies such as Al Gore's *An Inconvenient Truth*, talk with knowledgeable people such as scientists, attend lectures, watch TV shows, or listen to the radio.

I first learned about global warming many years ago by reading scientific literature when I was managing the production of a 'state of the environment report' for the State of Oregon. I needed to know the basics in order to produce a good report. My interest was sufficiently piqued, however, to cause me to read more, attend conferences and speak to climate scientists. Slowly but surely I increased my understanding of the issue. The education also helped me to understand how my own behaviour, including my home energy use, travel, consumption patterns and waste, contributed to the problem.

Pick a topic

You may not want to take the same types of steps I did to become more informed about global warming, but there are many ways in which you can increase your understanding. Start by choosing one or two areas to investigate. You might want to begin, for example, by learning about how your home energy use or personal transportation patterns contribute to global warming. Then, search the web, read magazine articles and in other ways learn more about those issues. After you have a basic understanding, allow yourself to examine your common thought and behavioural patterns in relation to the issue to determine if they are sustainable. Examine the extent to which you use sustainability thinking blunders rather than sustainable thinking patterns. Move on to other topics when you feel ready.

Identify the benefits of sustainable thinking

As you become more knowledgeable about climate change and other issues of sustainability, you may begin to feel at least a wee bit concerned about their potential consequences for yourself and others. You may also be concerned, however, that the effort and costs of doing something about the problems may be much larger than any positive benefit you get from adopting new thinking and behaviours. If this is the case, it often helps to see if this perspective is accurate by identifying some of the benefits you might get from becoming a sustainable thinker.

A sample list of benefits is provided in Box 7.1, which I initially developed when I considered changing my travel patterns.

BOX 7.1 BENEFITS OF REDUCING TRAVEL

- I will feel good about myself for making the decision to reduce my air travel.
- I will get more exercise.
- I will eat better.
- I might learn new ways of communicating with my clients.
- My wife will appreciate that I am home more often and am walking the talk.

Take a moment now to make a list for yourself of the potential benefits of altering your thinking and behaviour regarding the climate, natural environment or social well-being. Be honest and try to identify as many benefits as you can.

CHANGE MECHANISM 3: CHOICE EXPANSION

When we are disinterested in the causes and consequences of and solutions to global warming or other sustainability issues, and our possible role in propagating them, we often think that the changes required to resolve the problems are too big or too complicated for us to handle. We think to ourselves, for example: 'How can I possibly reduce my greenhouse gas emissions by 80 per cent?'

I felt this way when my wife first raised questions about my travel. Not meeting personally with my clients seemed like a huge change and I feared losing substantial income. Once again my wife came to the rescue. She simply said: 'Why don't you try to hold a few conference calls and see how it goes?' The realization that I did not have to go whole hog right away and could, instead, take small steps dissipated my fear of change.

There is an old saying: 'The journey of a thousand miles starts with the first step.' All sorts of small steps are available for testing out how to engage in sustainable thinking. Take the time to identify some of these measures. After you take one step, you can decide if you want to take another. For example, walk rather than drive to the grocery store just one time to reduce fuel use and see if you want to do it again. Turn down the temperature of your home hot water heater for just a few days to save energy and see how your family feels about permanently keeping it lower. After some testing, I found that about one third to one half of the meetings I previously travelled to could be effectively done by conference call or email. Expanding upon the choices available for making a change can be very liberating.

Search the web, read books and magazine articles and in other ways identify bite-size steps that you can take to protect the climate and support sustainability. For example, you can check out my organization's website for information from our Climate Masters Program about small changes you can make to reduce greenhouse gas emissions in your home, lawn and garden, food consumption and personal transportation patterns (see http://climlead.uoregon.edu). Many other avenues are available for expanding your awareness of the options that are available for starting down the path of becoming a sustainable thinker.

CHANGE MECHANISM 4: SUPPORTIVE RELATIONSHIPS

Considering a change can be stressful. One of the most helpful steps that you can take as you begin to consider becoming a sustainable thinker is therefore to find someone to support your efforts and help you come to believe that change is possible. My wife served as a close supporter when I began to examine my travel patterns. One of my close personal friends also helped out.

Ask others for help

Share any concerns you may have about your current thinking and behaviour with your supporter and seek their advice about the potential benefits of becoming a sustainable thinker. Having someone who can provide you with non-judgemental feedback and who expects you to make a shift is extremely helpful.

Identify your defences

One of the most important things your supporter can assist with is to help you become aware of your defence mechanisms. If you find yourself unwilling to increase your knowledge about climate change or other issues of sustainability, or to identify some of the benefits of sustainable thinking, examining your defences can help.

We are often unaware of the defences we use to justify our longstanding patterns. Although we believe our defences are convincing to others, it is usually only ourselves who end up being deceived. When we are defensive we employ false feedback mechanisms. We select information that supports our existing perspectives and ignore data that could produce a different view. It is very difficult to make good decisions without credible information.

Because of our defences we tend to overemphasize the downsides of becoming a sustainable thinker and underestimate the benefits. The rationalizations I used to justify my continued air travel, for example, initially convinced me that there was absolutely no way I could do my job without constant face-to-face contact.

Making a list of our defences helps us to acknowledge the ways in which we justify our current thinking and behaviours. Six common defence mechanisms are included in Table 7.1, along with the list I developed for myself during the process of considering a change in my travel. Use the categories to make a list specifically focused on the defences you use.

It is usually beneficial to identify the defences you employ in relation to specific issues. For example, list the defences you use to prevent yourself from learning about the climatic and social effects of your transportation patterns, or to ignore the potential benefits of turning down your home hot water. Examine the defences you employ to deflect introspection about your use of sustainability thinking blunders. Think hard and be as honest as you can be as you make the list. Ask your supporter to review it and give you honest feedback.

Are you willing to consider a change?

The use of one of more of these change mechanisms may cause you to become aware of the potential risks of the status quo and the benefits of engaging in

Table 7.1 *Sample list of defences used to justify my continued travel*

Defence	Travel and greenhouse gases
Denial (Ignoring evidence)	My travel doesn't add much greenhouse gas to the atmosphere.
Reluctance (I don't know enough)	I don't see how I can reduce my travel and be effective.
Resignation (I am powerless)	There is no other way to do my work.
Rebelliousness (Don't tell me what to do)	I'll make a change only when I decide it's worth it.
Rationalization (Explain away the problem)	Helping others to reduce emissions is more important than reducing my own.
Projection (Blaming others)	My clients demand that I meet with them personally.

activities that help protect the climate, natural environment or social well-being. If so, you are ready to progress to the next stage of the sustainable thinking process.

If you don't feel this way, that's all right as well. Set aside your lists of the risks and benefits of change and pick them back up when you feel ready.

THE DELIBERATION STAGE OF CHANGE

CHANGE MECHANISMS FOR DELIBERATION

- Continued awareness-building
- Continued choice expansion
- Continued supportive relationships
- Emotional inspiration
- Self-appraisal

This is the 'I might change' stage of the sustainable thinking transformation process. It's likely you now have some awareness, however small, of the risks that global warming, ecological degradation and related social distress poses to your family, others or yourself, and your possible role in perpetuating the problems. If you are like others, your curiosity may be growing and you may even be excited about this new awareness and the possibility of engaging in sustainable thinking.

It's also probable, however, that you are still unclear about the causes of climate change and the other issues of sustainability or what's involved with doing your part to resolve the matters. You may wonder, for example, if steps that you take will actually make a difference. And you may naturally be pondering what you will have to give up to engage in new thinking and behaviours. Because of these concerns you are probably oscillating back and forth between whether or not you want to alter your thinking and behaviour. Oscillation could go on for quite some time.

You might become stuck in deliberation if you suffer from one or more of the 4 Rs previously discussed in the disinterest stage. For instance, you might want a guarantee that before doing anything to protect the climate, every detail about global warming is fully understood. Alternatively, you may be hoping that some new technological solution will resolve the problem or that some new scientific discovery will dismiss the notion of global warming without you having to do much of anything. Humans have an enormous capacity for wishful thinking.

If any of these perspectives dominate your thinking, you run the risk of becoming a chronic deliberator. The use of specific change mechanisms, however, can help you to resolve your concerns and move to the next stage of change.

Change mechanisms

Despite the potential risks of deliberation, it's important to spend some time internally debating the pros and cons of becoming a sustainable thinker before moving to the design stage. Your primary task here is to determine if the benefits of adopting climate-positive thought and behaviour outweigh the costs. If you do not eventually conclude that the advantages are substantially greater than the disadvantages, you won't move beyond deliberation. The change mechanisms that are particularly helpful in making this decision include continued awareness-building, choice expansion and supportive relationships. Emotional inspiration and self-appraisal also become important at this stage.

Continued awareness-building

In order to see that the upsides of sustainable thinking and behaviour warrant a change, continue to increase your awareness of the causes and consequences of global warming, ecological degradation and social distress. You also need to enhance your understanding of how your thought and behaviours contribute to these troubles. For example, as before, try to identify how often you make one or more of the sustainability thinking blunders. Consider the extent to which you make sustainable ethical or unethical decisions discussed in Chapter 8. A basic level of understanding of the problems and solutions is needed before engaging in action (DiClemente and Velasquez, 2002).

This point warrants closer examination. If you don't know when or why your thinking and behaviour are problematic and are unsure if new patterns can help to resolve global warming or other issues, you are not likely to make or stick with change for long. Almost every psychological and sociological approach to change emphasizes that some degree of awareness must come before change. This is why cognitive and emotive approaches are so important here and behavioural change mechanisms, which do not focus on increased awareness, are best suited for the later stages of change. Changing behaviour without first developing some level of increased awareness is not likely to lead to fundamental change.

Ask evocative questions

I'm not suggesting that long drawn-out periods of deliberation are needed here. The length and intensity of your debate should correlate to the frequency and intensity of your use of sustainability thinking blunders and the extent of change needed. A week or two may be all that's needed, depending upon the thinking or behaviour that is subject to change. No matter how much time it takes, the key is to be clear about what you want to know and what you are striving to achieve through the change process.

Here are some sample questions you can use to guide your investigation:

- How much greenhouse gases do I personally, my family or my business generate annually?
- What are the primary sources of my greenhouse gas emissions?
- How do my emissions compare with other people in my community, the nation as a whole or other industrialized nations?
- How might global warming affect my family, my business, local community, the region in which I live or other parts of the nation and even the world?
- What actions can I take to reduce my emissions and how can I know they will actually work?

Use a similar set of questions to explore your affects on other environmental and social welfare issues.

Goal setting

Implicit in these types of questions is setting goals (see Prochaska et al, 1994). To raise awareness you must set some initial goals for yourself to help guide your information-gathering process. You might, for example, select the initial goal of learning about home energy use and leave transportation, consumption patterns or waste for another time. You might also choose a goal of learning how to prevent yourself from employing one of the sustainability thinking blunders. If you decide to go the latter route, ask your personal supporter to give you feedback on when, why and how often you employ the sustainability thinking blunder and the common outcomes.

Data collection

Once you have established your goals, it's important to collect appropriate data (see Prochaska et al, 1994). If you decide to learn about home energy use, for example, understanding the extent and effects of your greenhouse gas emissions will be possible only if you collect data on your average home monthly and annual energy usage, the type of fuels used to produce your energy (e.g. gas, coal, hydroelectricity, nuclear) and their 'greenhouse gas equivalents'. Your local power utility should have this information.

Continued choice expansion and supportive relationships

To enhance the awareness-building process, it's usually helpful to continue to explore a range of options available for engaging in sustainable thinking and behaviours. Both small and large changes can be investigated. The more choices at hand, the more likely it is that you can test out small changes without much risk.

Maintaining the close communication and non-judgemental feedback provided by supportive relationships is also important. Keep asking for input from your confidant about your thinking, behaviours and the defence mechanisms you use to discount or deflect away information about global warming and other issues of sustainability. The more conscious you can become of your defences, the more likely it is that you can overcome them.

CHANGE MECHANISM 5: EMOTIONAL INSPIRATION

The power of being emotionally inspired to alter your thinking and behaviour should not be underestimated. Often, the negative emotions that are associated with seeing or imagining the effects of global warming, environmental degradation and related social distress or the sense of relief that comes from doing your part to resolve the issues provide a potent stimulus for change (see Prochaska et al, 1994).

A strong emotional reaction to a unique event shook Reverend Richard Cizik out of disinterest and altered the course of his life. Reverend Cizik is vice president of governmental affairs for the National Association of Evangelicals (NAE) based in Washington, DC, one of the most politically powerful religious advocacy organizations in the US (Little, 2005). Reverend Cizik was always personally sensitive to the environment due to his agricultural roots growing up on a farm in eastern Washington. However, he went off to seminary school in Colorado where he 'became entombed in the evangelical world' and in spite of his natural concern for the environment, 'for many years he was never encouraged to act on these issues'. Thirty years went by, to be exact, without 'any motivational incentive to work on environmental issues'. Acknowledgment of global warming or other environmental problems was essentially taboo.

Around 2002, however, Reverend Cizik was persuaded by a friend to attend a presentation by Sir John Houghton, an evangelical British scientist who is a leading member of the Intergovernmental Panel on Climate Change (IPCC). The dramatic information he heard, as well as other experiences, produced an emotional reaction that shook him to his roots. He came to realize that 'climate change was a phenomena of truly biblical proportions'. He also realized that God was calling him out to change his own thinking and to engage the evangelical community in combating global warming.[6] You will learn more about the change process employed by Reverend Cizik later in the book.

It's helpful to continually look for opportunities to become emotionally inspired by the tragedies or opportunities afforded by rising global temperatures and other issues of sustainability. For instance, as in the disinterest stage of change, you can read books and magazine articles, see movies such as Al Gore's *An Inconvenient Truth*, attend lectures, watch TV shows or listen to the radio. You can also use your imagination and develop a mental picture of what a future of uncontrolled climate change may mean for you, those around you and the world as a whole. No matter what method you use, putting yourself in situations that emotionally inspire you to reconsider your current perspectives and adopt new ones can be very potent.

CHANGE MECHANISM 6: SELF-APPRAISAL

Perhaps the most important change mechanism in the deliberation stage is self-appraisal (Prochaska et al, 1994). This involves deciding if your current thinking and behaviour patterns allow you to be the person you really want to be. To answer this question you must identify your automatic thoughts and the behaviours they produce, and then do an honest appraisal to determine if they allow you to live up to the aspirations and values you hold dear. If the answer is no, that you do not feel good about yourself given your current perspectives and activities regarding the climate, natural environment or social well-being, you can make a decision to change and move on to the design stage of the change process.

Identify and challenge your automatic thoughts

Here is a three-step method you can use to identify and challenge your automatic thoughts.

First, learn to recognize the emotional and behavioural responses, as well as the automatic thoughts, that quickly fly through your mind whenever you are about to make a decision or take action. For example, one time I arrived home bone-tired after a long day at work. It was hot and humid outside and I looked forward to settling into my favourite chair in the cool of our living room. However, I was in a rush when I left in the morning and forgot to turn our old inefficient heat pump to 'auto'. It consequently failed to kick on when the temperature rose, so the house was blistering hot.

My emotional response was anger, irritation and urgency. My behavioural response was to immediately crank up the air conditioning as high as it could go, which used a tremendous amount of energy and certainly generated a large amount of greenhouse gas emissions. In other words, I quickly fell into the pattern of 'quick-fix, short-term' and 'my actions don't matter' thinking.

I have now learned to recognize that right after events like this when I feel angry and irritated, I usually say to myself something like: 'Typical Bob, you're so lazy' and 'The darn (not the actual word I used) heat pump never works. Why should I suffer because it is not designed to start on its own when it gets hot?' The more I learned how to become aware of my automatic thoughts and associated emotions, the more chances I had of controlling my responses and avoiding the STBs.

Second, learn to explicitly dispute your automatic thoughts by gathering credible contrary evidence. After I realized the thoughts that immediately popped into my mind, I made a conscious effort to determine if they were true. Was I really lazy? I remembered, for example, that I had worked a nine-hour day, helped three staff members to resolve complicated matters, taught a class and had also stopped on my way home from work to grocery shop. I was far from lazy. I also sought to determine if it was really so hot that I needed to turn the heat pump on high, or if it was my emotional state that caused me to feel so overheated? Upon reflection, I realized that the house temperature was only in the mid 20°C (mid 70s°F), which is far from blazing. By focusing on evidence that contradicted my automatic thoughts, I was able to determine if they were accurate.

Third, learn to give different explanations, which are called replacement thoughts, and use them to dispute your automatic thoughts and emotional responses when they arise. I learned to say, for example: 'I'm forgetful in the morning when I am rushed to get to work.' This is a much more accurate explanation for my behaviour than: 'I'm lazy.' I also learned to say: 'Be aware of my tendency to catastrophize. It's a little warm; but after I sit and calm down, I will cool off.'

Replacement thoughts can be used to interrupt your automatic thoughts and emotional reactions when they arise and to produce a different way of explaining a situation. Different explanations will lead to new behavioural responses.

Box 7.2 offers a different example of how to identify and challenge your automatic thoughts.

BOX 7.2 EXAMPLE OF HOW TO IDENTIFY AND
CHALLENGE YOUR AUTOMATIC
THOUGHTS

- *Situation*: Jill is at the garden store, has just a few minutes available to shop before she has to leave to pick up her kids, and needs to make a decision about whether to use petrochemicals or organic fertilizer and natural pest controls on her lawn and garden.
- *Emotional reaction*: irritation at having to make a decision and impatience with the time it takes to sort through the issues.
- *Automatic thoughts*: 'Chemical fertilizers and pest controls will be easier and quicker to use. I don't believe all the hype about the negative effects of (petrochemical) fertilizers.
- 'It takes too much time and effort to know which of these products is better and safer to use.'
- *Behavioural reaction*: buy the cheapest fertilizer available and leave quickly.
- *Replacement thoughts*:
  - I have a tendency to jump to quick conclusions. Take a deep breath, relax and before drawing a conclusion find out if organic products are really more difficult to use and less effective than petrochemical products.
  - The hype about the risks of petrochemical fertilizers may not be all nonsense, so I should check out the pros and cons of the various products.
  - My kids are my first priority so I should take whatever time is needed to make sure I am buying products that are safe for them and their environment.

Determine what's really important to you

After assessing your automatic thoughts and the behaviours that they produce, the next step is to determine if your current thinking and behaviour allow you to be the person you want to be. You can start by asking yourself what goals and values are *truly important to you* (see Prochaska et al, 1994). Although simple, this question is often difficult to answer because most of us do not know want we really want. At best, all we can do is to state what we don't want.

Box 7.3 offers examples of questions that can be asked to elicit your most important goals and values. No matter how you phrase the question, the key is to delve deeply by asking it over and over again. Box 7.4 includes an example of how I used the 'downward arrow' technique to dig deep and answer this question regarding my travel. Make a similar list for yourself now.

BOX 7.3 QUESTIONS TO ELICIT YOUR DEEPLY HELD ASPIRATIONS AND VALUES

- How do I ideally want to live my life regarding the climate, natural environment and social well-being?
- What values are most important to me and how might caring for the climate, natural environment and communities fit in with those values?
- If I could have the ideal world today, without constraints, how would I treat the climate, natural environment, or communities?
- What type of climate, natural environment and social well-being do I want to leave my children and grandchildren?

BOX 7.4 DOWNWARD ARROW TECHNIQUE FOR IDENTIFYING WHAT'S REALLY IMPORTANT

Situation: I need to make a decision about whether to reduce my travel to cut my greenhouse gas (GHG) emissions or to continue to travel in order to help others reduce their emissions and generate an income.

Question: What is really important to me?

↓

'I want to walk the talk and be a role model of how to reduce GHG emissions.'
(What is really important to me?)

↓

'I want to feel good about myself by doing my part to reduce GHG emissions.'
(What is really important to me?)

↓

(Continue)

What do you have to give up?

Determining what you ideally want is only half the equation. You must also identify what you have to *give up* in order to alter myopic climate-damaging thinking and behaviour (see Prochaska et al, 1994). Often this question is much more difficult. Every thought and behaviour pattern we hold provides some type of advantage to us or we would not use it.

Sometimes you may believe you must give up tangible things such as money. I feared reducing my travel would cut our income. At other times, we must give up part of our self-image in order to make a change. I always liked to think of myself as a person who would help others whenever they called. By reducing my travel I assumed I would no longer be able to see myself this way. No matter what's involved, in order to determine if the benefits of change outweigh the costs, you must honestly identify what you think you will need to give up if you shift gears.

BOX 7.5 DOWNWARD ARROW TECHNIQUE FOR IDENTIFYING WHAT YOU NEED TO GIVE UP

Situation: I need to make a decision about whether to reduce my travel to cut my greenhouse gas emissions or to continue to travel to help others reduce their emissions and generate income.

Question: What do I have to give up by reducing my travel?
Answer: 'I have to give up some personal interaction with clients.'
(What do I have to give up by reducing my travel?)

↓

'I have to give up some income.'
(What do I have to give up by reducing my travel?)

↓

'I have to give up the image of myself as a person whom others can count on to come to their assistance whenever they need me.'

↓

(Continue)

Use the downward arrow technique again to uncover what you might have to give up if you abandon your unsustainable thinking and behaviour. Box 7.5 includes my example.

Minimize the downsides of change

As mentioned in Chapter 6, to progress from disinterest to the doing stage of change, the benefits you get from becoming a sustainable thinker must substantially outweigh the downsides. One way of making this happen is to keep adding to the list of benefits of new issues and behaviours that you developed in the previous stage, as illustrated in Box 7.1 regarding my travel.

It is also helpful, however, to try to shrink your perception of the drawbacks of becoming a sustainable thinker (see Prochaska et al, 1994). Start by making a complete list of the downsides of change. Box 7.6 includes a list of the downsides

---

BOX 7.6 DOWNSIDES OF REDUCING TRAVEL

- I will have to give up personal contact with clients.
- My family may have to give up some income.
- I will no longer be able to see myself as someone who responds quickly to others in need.
- My colleagues will think I am crazy for giving up my clients and income.

---

that I identified in reducing my travel. They included giving up personal contact with clients, reduced income, giving up part of my self-image and being criticized by my colleagues.

Now examine your list to determine how many of the downsides are actually permanent. Most of the time the disadvantages of new thinking and behaviours are temporary; but we think they are permanent and consequently give them much greater weight than they deserve.

Upon review, I found that none of the downsides in my list were permanent. I realized, for example, that if I lost clients after a transition period, I could find others closer to my home with whom I could work without the need for flying. I would therefore be able to have face-to-face contact, would not lose income over the long haul and could still respond to people quickly. My colleagues were also likely to eventually envy the new approach I took rather than think I was nuts. This assessment helped me to see that the downsides of reducing my travel were, at worst, short term and may actually turn out to be beneficial for me.

Table 7.2 outlines how I reframed the cons on my list. Take a moment to reframe the downsides of adopting sustainable thinking on your list.

Table 7.2 *Reframing downsides of reducing my travel*

Downsides	Reframed view
I will have to give up personal contact with clients.	I can find other clients closer to my home.
My family may have to give up some income.	New clients mean no lost income after the transition period.
I will no longer be able to see myself as someone who quickly responds to others in need.	I can respond quickly (maybe even more quickly) to clients who are close by.
My colleagues will think I am crazy for giving up clients and income.	Colleagues are likely to eventually envy me.

Compare the pros and cons

Now let's put the work you have done so far together in one place and compare the upsides and downsides of becoming a sustainable thinker. A 'decision balance scale' can be helpful here. The scale should address four types of outcomes. The first two represent practical issues, and the later two categories represent non-utilitarian issues such as self-esteem, social approval and other personal issues (Bandura, 1982, pp122–147; Velicer and DiClemente, 1985, pp1279–1289):

1　the consequences of becoming a sustainable thinker for yourself;
2　the consequences of becoming a sustainable thinker for others;
3　your reactions to becoming a sustainable thinker;
4　the reactions of others to you becoming a sustainable thinker.

The upsides and downsides of becoming a sustainable thinker can be listed next to each of the four categories. Careful thought and a good deal of honesty are needed to complete this analysis. Try to be as comprehensive as possible when making the list. Go over it numerous times to flesh out the pros and cons. Notice that I have added a number of additional benefits to the list of pros that I initially developed.

In addition, make sure you focus as much or more on the positive as you do on the negative aspects of change. As we just discovered, most negative issues have positive elements if you take the time to think about them. A decision balance scale related to my dilemma about reducing my travel is included in Table 7.3.

Make a choice

Now that you have identified your most cherished goals and values and analysed the pros and cons of becoming a sustainable thinker, it's time to make a choice. If you decide you are ready to make the shift, you are ready for the design stage. The positive aspects of reducing my travel outweighed the negatives on my list by a two to one ratio, so I decided to cut back on my air travel.

It is perfectly fine to decide you are not ready to move on. If this is the case, take a break and when you feel up to it re-examine the processes we discussed. At some time in the future, you may reach a different conclusion and be ready to move to the next stage.

Faster is slower – slower is faster

If you have decided to move on to the design stage, you might be tempted to quickly start making changes. Try to resist this urge. Premature action often leads to the sustainable thinking blunders. This is a common problem. People decide

Table 7.3 *Decision balance scale for reducing my travel*

	Benefits		Disadvantages	
Personal consequences	1	I will feel good about making the decision to change.	1	I will have to give up personal interaction with clients.
	2	I will get more exercise.	2	I will need to give up my image of myself as someone who quickly responds to others in need.
	3	I will eat better.		
	4	I will spend less time away from my family.		
	5	I might learn new ways of communicating and interacting with clients.		
Consequences for others	6	My wife will feel good that we cared about the environment.	3	My family may have to give up some income.
	7	My wife will be proud of me for walking the talk, even if it means reduced income.		
Reaction of self	8	I will feel more congruent and less hypocritical.	4	I'll be disappointed if I lose some clients and income.
Reactions of others	9	My colleagues may decide to make similar decisions.	5	Colleagues may think I'm crazy for giving up income.
	10	Some entrepreneurs may be spurred to invent better ways of communicating.		

to make a change and quickly rush off and spend time and money to demonstrate to themselves or others that they are beginning to think and act sustainably.

Unfortunately, because their thinking has not yet really changed and because they did not design a thoughtful plan of attack, premature action often backfires. Feeling discouraged or burned, people regress back to the deliberation stage or abandon the sustainable thinking effort altogether. Instead of rapidly jumping off the high dive, take a little time to design a plan for change.

THE DESIGN STAGE OF CHANGE

CHANGE MECHANISMS FOR DESIGN

- Continued self-appraisal
- Continued helping relationships
- Commitment

This is the 'I will change' stage of the shift to sustainable thinking. It involves designing a plan to alter your thinking and behaviour. The design stage is an important, though often overlooked, step in the change process. Without a carefully designed plan to implement climate-positive sustainable thinking and behaviour, you will be ill-equipped for the challenges that lie ahead. A well-designed strategy, however, can provide you with ways to overcome obstacles and to monitor and measure your progress.

The experience of Sue Klobertanz, former head of the City of Portland procurement department, underscores the importance of the design stage. She had tested 'green' cleaning and garden products at her home and often found their performance to be lacking, especially when compared to their costs. So when the Portland City Council voted to engage the city in sustainability, Klobertanz knew she had to craft a careful step-wise plan to transition to sustainable purchasing or risk spotty performance, wasted resources and, possibly, public backlash.

Psychologists have developed an approach for better goal attainment called an 'implementation intention' (Gollwitzer and Brandstatter, 1997, pp186–199). What this means is that planning in advance when, where and how you will complete a self-assigned goal produces greater success. Studies have found that implementation intentions will help you to work towards goals and, over time, allow the process to feel automatic. This is especially true for goals that are especially hard to complete. Making specific goals for yourself in the sense of 'I intend to achieve x' is a powerful way of implementing specific changes in your thinking and behaviour, and achieving specific outcomes even when difficulties arise.

Change mechanisms

The benefit of setting specific goals underscores that the most important change mechanism in the design stage is commitment (Prochaska et al, 1994). Making a firm pledge to adopt sustainable thinking and behaviour involves developing a positive vision of how you want to think and treat the climate, natural environment and other people now and in the future. Other important change mechanisms in the design stage include continued self-appraisal and supportive relationships.

The design stage does not need to be long. However, it needs to be thorough enough to give you a good sense of the initial steps you will take to engage in sustainable thinking. It should also prepare you with options to use when things go haywire, as some are sure to do.

Keep the plan fluid. Action plans are best used to guide, not to dictate. Focus on the mind and behavioural change process you have learned, not on rigidly following the plan or attaining specific results.

Continued self-appraisal

You would not be in the design stage unless the processes you have gone through so far led you to conclude that adopting sustainable thinking and behaviour is more desirable than the status quo. At this point you want to solidify your decision to adopt new patterns. Whenever you attempt to change your thinking and behaviour, there will be positive and negative aspects. If you want to lose weight, you know there will be times when you crave chocolate; but you also know that you must refrain from indulging. You will also undoubtedly feel physical pangs of hunger as your body adjusts to less food intake. To succeed in these circumstances, you need to clearly imagine the positive aspects of making the change. If you can see yourself looking and feeling better and having more energy, you have a greater chance of success. Envisioning yourself in a new way allows you to begin to let go of the old image you hold of yourself as overweight and tired.

Keep focused on the benefits of sustainable thinking

Holding steady a positive vision of the new you that will emerge after you become a sustainable thinker is one of the most effective ways of shoring up your commitment to change. The list of the benefits of change you developed, as I illustrated in Table 7.3, reinforces the benefits of making the shift to sustainable thinking. It should be kept front and centre at all times. Pin it on your bathroom mirror or refrigerator so you can regularly glance at it. Make it a point to continually update and expand the list.

When I first decided to reduce my travel, I called a number of the people with whom I worked and asked them what they thought about doing some of our work by conference call and email, rather than in person. A few people had negative reactions. One said that I must no longer be interested in their business. Another thought it had something to do with not liking them personally (which was actually true, but not the reason for the proposed change). To stay motivated given the resistance I encountered, I had to keep telling myself how much better I would feel about myself, how my diet would improve and how I would get more exercise while I reduced my emissions by travelling less.

This points out how important it is in the design stage to keep your focus on an image of yourself as a climate-positive sustainable thinker and leave the old you behind. Unsustainable thinking and behaviours are habit forming and like many bad habits, we get benefits or we would not repeat them. I had to give up the image of myself as a super helper – a person who would immediately drop everything and hop on a plane to help out a client. Establishing and holding a new image of yourself as a sustainable thinker is essential for staying focused on the future and relinquishing the past.

CHANGE MECHANISM 7: MAKE A FIRM AND PUBLIC COMMITMENT TO CHANGE

You undoubtedly have many tasks on your plate. Even though you might now feel like you want to change your thinking and behaviour, without a firm commitment it will be easy to let other issues take precedent and for the shift to sustainable thinking to move to the back burner. You may also still be oscillating back and forth over whether you really want to change your thinking and behaviour. Making a firm commitment to change settles these issues for you. You can leave indecision behind and orient yourself to the future.

Make your commitment public

Initially, your commitment is likely to be internal and private. It's a decision you make in your head. For a commitment to be most helpful, however, it should be made public. The more people who know about your commitment, the more likely you are to follow through (Prochaska et al, 1994). This was the approach Rusty Rexius took. He and the other senior executives decided that if they were going to meaningfully engage in sustainability, they would go all out and broadcast it to their employees, suppliers and customers. When I decided to reduce my travel, I quickly told my wife about my decision. Not only did this make her proud of me (remember my view that a happy wife is a good thing), verbalizing my commitment increased my desire to make the change.

Set a date

It's also helpful to include specific due dates in the plan. Many of us put off action until a deadline. That's certainly been my method of operation since my college days – why do today what I can put off until tomorrow? (This, by the way, is a trait my wife wishes I would alter.) If no deadlines exist, however, there is nothing to force you to act. Establishing a definitive starting point is therefore very helpful in preventing procrastination. It can also work in the reverse. If you know you will act by a specific date, you can ward off tendencies towards premature action.

Identify your expectations

When designing a plan it is often helpful to write down what you expect to learn from each step you take and then, after you have taken a step, note what actually occurred. This process clarifies how much your expectations conform to reality.

Design an action plan

The act of designing a change plan helps to orient your thinking towards the future. Start by identifying some relatively safe steps that you can take. The phone calls I made to clients to determine their reactions to more conference calls and email exchanges were small steps I could make without much risk. Identify similar actions applicable to your situation and then design a step-wise implementation plan.

Included in your action plan should be mechanisms to signify when you are about to fall prey to a sustainability thinking blunder (STB). Perhaps you can post the ten STBs in front of your desk or on your bedroom mirror and make an agreement with yourself that you will vet decisions you make with the list prior to acting on them. Or, maybe you can ask your supportive helper to ask if you considered the STBs prior to engaging in various activities.

Also included in your action plan should be a way of considering the ethical and moral dimensions of your activities from a sustainability perspective. Chapter 8 provides a method for accomplishing this.

The possible troubles you may encounter as you march down the path, and predetermined techniques for responding to them, can also be included in your sustainable thinking action plan. I expected a few clients to balk at the idea of working by phone and email, so I decided that I would be prepared to immediately tell them that if they did not like the proposed change, I would stay with our current approach.

Table 7.4 includes a sample sustainable thinking action plan with a little information about how I planned to reduce my personal travel.

HELPING RELATIONSHIPS

Just as it's important to continue with the self-appraisal process in the design stage, it is important to maintain your supportive relationships. Any deep-rooted change in your thinking and behaviour will be felt by your family, friends, fellow workers and others. Some of these people may not like the fact that you are engaging in sustainable thinking. If you change your ways, their own myopic climate-damaging thinking and behaviour may become visibly apparent and make them look bad or feel guilty.

Table 7.4 *Sample sustainable thinking action plan for reducing my travel*

Action	Begin	Predicted results	Possible troubles	Methods of overcoming troubles	Results	Comparison of predicted and actual results
Call five clients to determine how they feel about more conference call and emails.	1 June	Most say OK; one or two have concerns or say no.	Irritate a few clients and possibly lose them.	Assure them that if they don't want to shift to conference calls and emails, I will continue to visit them regularly.	Two were very sceptical; but all clients said they were willing to try out the new approach.	I was wrong about the level of acceptance.
Establish an interactive website to facilitate information-sharing with my clients.	1 July	Most people will use it, but some will baulk or forget.	People may have technical problems and I may forget to check this.	Send a query to my clients once a week to see what they think Set a tickler in my scheduler to remind me to check this.	A few clients initially did not use it or had difficulty; but we quickly worked through the problem.	Approximately what I expected; but it worked out.

Your change plan is also certain to run head long into numerous technical and structural obstacles. Even though I can reduce my travel by using conference calls and email, for example, these tools are not the same as face-to-face contact. Sometimes I therefore still need to see clients and thus cannot yet completely eliminate my travel-related greenhouse gases. For these reasons, as you design your plan, it's important to continue to have someone in whom to confide. You will benefit by having someone to support your efforts, bounce ideas off, keep your spirits up when you hit an obstacle and tell you how proud they are about the changes you are making.

THE DOING STAGE OF CHANGE

CHANGE MECHANISMS FOR DOING

- Commitment
- Continued helping relationships
- Continued reinforcement
- Substitution
- Structural redesign

This is the 'I am changing' stage of the sustainable thinking transformation process. It involves implementing the steps outlined in your action plan. Thinking sustainably is hard work. It won't happen on its own. Effort must be made. Doing, however, is also exciting. As you begin to see changes occurring, your spirits will lift and your energy level will rise.

Keep in mind that because systems are structured to resist change, as you begin to act, resistance from others as well as technical and logistical barriers are certain to emerge. Because people tend to avoid situations that cause unease, to prevent yourself from procrastinating or backing away you need to be armed with specific strategies for responding to obstacles of all kinds.

The importance of a positive orientation

Human evolution has taken place over thousands of years of constant adjustments to localized short-term climatic changes, environmental hardships, disease, predators and human-caused disruptions, such as wars. People who were good at worrying about immediate threats survived – those who were not, perished. A pessimistic problem-solving approach to life is therefore, in many ways, hardwired into our psyches (Seligman, 1990).

It is always important to see reality clearly. However, it is equally important to know that reality is just as much, or more, a function of our perspectives than it is related to tangible circumstances. Our sense of reality usually changes when we alter our mind frame.

This is why it is so important to keep a positive orientation when implementing your change plan. Researchers have called the way an individual habitually explains the causes of events that happen to them as their 'explanatory style' (see Seligman, 1990; and Peterson and Steen, 2005). If you believe that the problems and unpleasant conditions that occur to you are permanent, all encompassing and due mostly to deep-rooted personal failings, your explanatory style is likely to be pessimistic. You are likely to struggle to successfully overcome obstacles if you hold a pessimistic orientation.

On the other hand, if you see unpleasant conditions as temporary, limited to specific circumstances and caused by factors other than fundamental personal flaws, your explanatory style is likely to be optimistic. You are much more likely to succeed in identifying ways of overcoming obstacles if you hold an optimistic orientation. Ample research and experience shows that people can adopt an optimistic orientation if they choose to do so (Seligman, 1990).

Change mechanisms

In order to maintain a positive orientation during the doing stage of the sustainable thinking change process, you need to continue to keep your commitment high. Because of the need to overcome resistance and obstacles at this point, behaviour change mechanisms such as reinforcement, substitution and structural redesign become especially important.

CHANGE MECHANISM 8: REINFORCEMENT

Much as the constant barrage of obstacles often tempted my wife and I to go the quick, easy and unsustainable route desired by the contractors when we were rebuilding our new house, you will occasionally get exhausted and feel down in the dumps as you implement your sustainable thinking change plan. The longer this goes on, the harder it will be to keep your commitment high. Reinforcement helps to lift your spirits. Recognizing accomplishments and receiving rewards reinforces your new sustainable thinking and behaviours.

I don't just mean awards given by organizations to which you belong, such as the Rotary, although this type of public acknowledgement can recharge your batteries. You can also establish your own reward system. For example, you can consciously decide to give yourself a reward whenever you catch yourself before you behave in an unsustainable manner or when you realize that you acted in a climate-positive manner. Self-administered rewards will not only serve to counter your unsustainable thinking patters, they will, over time, strengthen your new belief system.

I decided to give myself a reward every time I stopped myself from immediately saying yes when a client asked me to fly to their facility to discuss their sustainability efforts. One time I took myself out to lunch at my favourite lunch spot, something I love to do but rarely get time for. Another time I allowed myself to leave work an hour early, under the justification that I would have been gone for much longer than an hour had I flown off to the client's location.

Reinforcement is also important when you achieve a milestone in your action plan. I bought myself a bottle of nice wine after I had called five clients to query them about altering the way in which we worked together. This was a way of saying: 'Nice going, Bob.' If self-administered rewards help to reinforce sustainable thinking and behaviour, is the opposite true: does punishment deter bad behaviour? The answer is unequivocally no. Psychologists have long known that punishment does not alter thinking or behaviour in the long run. The primary reason is that it does not offer a positive substitute behaviour. Berating yourself when you fail will not have the same effect as rewarding yourself when you succeed.

Perhaps you are uncomfortable giving yourself reinforcement. An alternative approach is to ask the individual serving as your supporter to acknowledge your successes and reward you for accomplishments. You can ask your spouse, for example, to say something positive whenever you stop yourself from behaving in a myopic climate-damaging manner, such as leaving the lights on when no one is in the room, which wastes energy and produces greenhouse gases. You can also ask your helper to praise you whenever you do something positive, such as make a conscious decision to reduce your consumption or change your transportation patterns.

The bottom line is to establish explicit mechanisms to get acknowledgement and reinforcement whenever you successfully prevent yourself from acting unsustainably *and* when you act in a climate-positive manner. The more reinforcement you get, the more likely that your commitment to change will remain high and you will be able to persevere when obstacles arise.

CHANGE MECHANISM 9: SUBSTITUTION

Climate-damaging unsustainable thinking and behaviours offer benefits or you would not repeat them. They are often easy to pursue, cheaper than sustainable alternatives (because the full costs have been externalized), do not conflict with standard customs and therefore do not produce social or political tension, and offer other advantages. Trying to eliminate unsustainable patterns without substituting climate-positive ones in their place that provide their own benefits is certain to produce frustration and failure. For this reason, explicit effort should be made to substitute sustainable factors in place of those that elicit climate-damaging unsustainable thinking and behaviour. Psychologists call this counter-conditioning.

Substitute behaviours

For example, you might need new paint for a house project and without thinking drive to the local hardware store to buy the least expensive paint they have without checking whether it is a low volatile organic compound (VOC) emissions paint. Substituting climate-positive responses for unsustainable ones can help you to avoid these slip-ups.

The most effective substitution is active and straightforward. Identifying stores ahead of time that sell environmentally sound 'zero VOC' or 'low VOC' paints and then going to those locations when you need paint is an example of direct substitution. Another example is to make a date with a friend, see a movie or engage in other diversionary activities whenever you have the urge to go on a shopping spree that leads to unnecessary consumption. When you begin to implement your action plan, consider behaviours, places or situations that are likely to draw you into myopic climate-damaging thinking and behaviour and prepare substitute sustainable options to counter those tendencies.

Substitute thoughts

Certain situations are likely to trigger your old habitual climate-damaging thinking and behavioural patterns. The more you can become aware of what triggers unsustainable thinking, the more likelihood that you can adopt ways of preventing those factors from causing harm.

An ABCD approach can be used for these purposes (Prochaska et al, 1994). This is a different version of the method previously discussed for identifying and challenging your automatic thoughts. The idea is to identify (A) *activating* events or situations, that trigger (B) certain climate-damaging unsustainable *behaviours* and their (C) ecological, social or personal *consequences*. Table 7.5 includes an example of an ABC analysis I did for my travel patterns. Take a moment to make a list of some of your ABCs.

After you become aware of your inclinations, identify (D) *disruptions* that can alter the patterns. In the examples provided in Table 7.5, my disruptions included

Table 7.5 *Sample ABCDs for my travel dilemma*

A Activating events	B Behaviours	C Consequences	D Disruptions
A client calls and says that their climate initiative is facing a crisis. I now know that I will be on the road to meet with the client.	I immediately say that I will hop on a plane and meet with the client. I plan meetings with other clients in the same region.	Time away from home, no time to exercise, and more greenhouse gases generated.	Make no quick decisions. Plan only one meeting per trip. Call clients more frequently.

making a conscious effort to not make a quick decision when someone calls to ask me to fly out to their location and to, instead, take a day to consider my response. I also made an explicit decision to book only one client per trip to cut down on my time away. Finally, I decided to make up for reduced client contact with additional phone calls and email exchanges. Reflect for a moment on how you can use the ABCD approach to substitute climate-positive for unsustainable thinking and behavioural patterns.

CHANGE MECHANISM 10: STRUCTURAL REDESIGN

Redesigning the structure of your family, work, spiritual and recreational life will be important to help you persevere through the many obstacles you face as you implement your change plan. As discussed throughout this book, your thinking and behaviour is heavily influenced by the structure of the systems within which you live.

Sometimes your physical environment shapes your thinking. For instance, you may live outside of an urban area where few public transportation options exist to your place of work in the downtown core. Your long commute therefore leads you to believe that a large vehicle such as an SUV and more highways are best, even though they lead to more vehicle use, increased congestion and higher greenhouse gas emissions.

Your perception of the structure, however, is as much or more important than the actual physical context itself. If you open yourself to alternative ideas about work and transportation, many new ways to meet your needs may become evident. Following our example, you may find it possible to work at home part or full time, carpool to work with others from your neighbourhood, move closer to your downtown place of employment, or conversely find a job closer to your current home.

Once you begin to apply your new thinking, it is important to redesign the environment around you as much as possible so that it supports and reinforces your new approach to sustainable thinking. Here are a few suggestions for redesigning your external structures.

Start at home

If you want to change a complex system, the place to start is where you are located. Because each component of a system is affected by, and affects, other components, starting where you are often produces ripple effects that may eventually alter the entire system.

Your home life centres you most immediately, and it is also the place where you have the most direct control and responsibility. Your home environment is therefore a logical place to start redesigning the structures that surround you. You can begin to redesign your home life tonight. You can talk with your family about your new approach to sustainable thinking and the vision you have of a climate-positive sustainable household. Then, you can begin to redesign the way in which your household is structured to avoid or eliminate unsustainable influences.

For example, you can systematically analyse the way in which your family makes purchasing decisions, uses energy and water, or plans vacations to avoid making sustainable thinking blunders. In addition, you may not be able, by yourself, to alter your community's transportation system or eliminate its landfill; but you can, on your own, alter your personal transportation patterns and seek to become waste free. You can also begin to use renewable energy if your local utility sells green power or you have the funds available to install a solar hot water heater, photovoltaic or small-scale hydropower system.

As mentioned, both Rusty Rexius and Richard Cizik sold their SUVs, and made other personal changes as a starting point of their effort to redesign the structure of their home lives. Larry Chalfan also sold his SUV and made other changes in his personal life and eventually made the bold decision to devote his entire life to sustainability work. He left the private sector and formed a non-profit called The Zero Waste Alliance.

Seek stair-stepped successes

Designing a stair-stepped approach is usually best when first engaging in sustainable thinking. Try to hit singles and doubles, rather than triples and home runs, right off the bat.

When Rusty Rexius started to implement his new sustainability action plan he did not quickly dive into the deep end by suggesting big changes. Instead, he took a very measured approach. 'Internally we were really very careful', says Rexius.[7] He first shared his new thinking with people around him. He then shared his new ideas with members of the management team. Although he got some resistance, it was not overwhelming, so he took a few additional steps. Slowly but surely Rexius and his team became more comfortable with the new way of thinking and behaving. Rexius also found that his new approach was infectious. By initially treading softly, he avoided triggering the defence mechanisms of people. This allowed others to carefully consider the new ideas and eventually think along similar lines.

Richard Cizik, Ray Anderson, Larry Chalfan and Sue Klobertanz followed a similar path. They first discussed their new thinking with their inner circle, then expanded it to other key people and then continued to expand outward.

Redesign your social systems

Just as stair-stepped successes are important, taking steps to *avoid* people who reinforce your use of the sustainability thinking blunders and undermine your success is also imperative. Your efforts to alter your mental frame will undoubtedly be met with resistance from some family members, friends or fellow workers. If, after a little interaction, it becomes clear that the individuals exerting pressure on you will not desist, you may need to find a way to avoid them. This may require developing new friends, moving to another work unit, changing your work schedule, or taking other steps to defend yourself against social pressure aimed at getting you to revert to your old climate-damaging ways of thinking and acting.

Continued helping relationships

A key aspect of redesigning the conditions around you is to continue to associate with people who can help you to expand your new sustainable thinking and behaviour. I'm using helping relationships here, however, in a slightly different context than the supportive relationships that are so important in the earlier stages of change. A trusted confidant is very important when you need to share personal angst about whether or not to become a sustainable thinker. After you commit to change and enter the doing stage, however, a different type of relationship is needed. At this point you need to link up with people involved with similar experiences. This type of helper provides a role model and someone you can learn from who has experienced situations that you are likely to encounter. The people who supported you in the early stages of change can fill this role, but only if they are engaged in changes similar to the type you are now experiencing. If they are not, you probably need to find different people.

One way to develop helping relationships is to join a climate protection or sustainability support network. These groups help you to learn from others and allow you to confide in people struggling with similar issues. The Oregon Natural Step Network[8] and Natural Step Canada are examples of such support groups for business leaders. Many other informal support networks exist in Europe and elsewhere around the globe.

One of the primary roles your helper can play is to monitor your change plan. Put it in writing and ask them to keep tabs on your progress. Written agreements, complete with goals, actions, expected outcomes and due dates, hold your feet to the fire. Set up formal check-in times that do not overburden your helper. Perhaps lunch once a month will do. As discussed in a few moments, your helpers can also be asked to acknowledge and reward you when you take positive steps.

Turn about is fair play

Just as helping relationships are important to you, serving as a helper for *others* seeking to become sustainable thinkers can be extremely satisfying. Ironically, one of the best ways to feel supported *and* at the same time intimately learn a subject is to teach. The act of forcing ideas and concepts out of your head into the public arena demands that you learn the subject extremely well. Teaching climate protection or sustainability classes at the local community college or during brown bag lunch talks with colleagues at work can be a wonderful way of nourishing others and yourself.

The defending stage of change

> ### Change mechanisms for defending
>
> - Continued commitment
> - Continued helping relationships
> - Continued reinforcement
> - Continued substitution
> - Advanced structural design

This is the 'I have changed' stage of the transition to sustainable thinking. After about six months or so of actively pursuing climate-positive activities, your task shifts to learning how to make the new patterns grow, stick and become routine over the long haul. This is not easy. Resistance from others and numerous obstacles are likely to continue to pop up as you trek down the path. You must therefore continually defend your new thinking and behaviour until they become as automatic as your former climate-damaging thoughts and behaviour once were.

One of the most important points to remember when implementing your change plan is that *action is not the same as change* (Prochaska et al, 1994). Just because you start to make a few short-term changes does not mean your core beliefs, assumptions and automatic thoughts have fundamentally changed. It takes a long time for new thinking to become embedded in the core of your being. The defending stage of the shift to sustainable thinking may last for years – and, more than likely, a lifetime.

Even though I am involved with research and teach climate change and sustainability courses, for instance, the effort needed to continually fend off resistance from others and to surmount obstacles often causes me to consider falling back into unsustainable thinking and behaviour patterns (my wife is kind enough to frequently point this out). The defending stage of change is therefore the most arduous stage. It can also, however, be the most enjoyable part of the change process.

Change mechanisms

The same change mechanisms that you used in the doing stage are important when defending your new thinking and behaviour. What's different in this stage is the emphasis on long-term commitment and on major structural redesign.

Use reinforcement to keep commitment high

To defend your new sustainable thinking and behaviour against resistance and obstacles you must make a decision to stick with it over the long haul, no matter what impediments arise or how many setbacks you experience. Keeping your commitment high is key to successful change. One way of doing this is to write down the difficulties you experience, how you responded to them and the results. Every so often, review your list. You are likely to find that the type, frequency and intensity of the challenges you have faced decline over time. This can give you an emotional boost.

As in the doing stage, you should also make it a point to explicitly acknowledge and take credit for each of your accomplishments. There will undoubtedly be numerous times when you feel defeated. Acknowledging your successes alone or with others will help balance the down times with positive feelings and give you a shot of energy. You might want to pick specific days or events to celebrate. The first of each month, major holidays and other special times can be chosen. No matter what day you choose, recognize your accomplishments regularly.

Finally, reward yourself for accomplishments. You can, for example, establish a pattern of taking yourself out for dinner at your favourite restaurant, seeing a new movie or taking a day off just for yourself each time you hit a major milestone. You can also ask your supportive helper to provide you with rewards on special occasions. One approach is to give them some money, say US$50, and ask them to give back US$5 as a reward each time you achieve a major accomplishment. Don't underestimate the power of this type of reinforcement. It can be extremely powerful in keeping your energy level high and helping you to stay the course.

Advanced structural redesign

Any architect will tell you that the way in which a building is designed determines its long-term comfort and performance. Similarly, the way in which you design your personal, work and leisure time will determine your capacity to maintain your new sustainable thinking and behaviour over the long term. We'll say more about how to motivate others to adopt sustainable thinking in Chapter 9. Here I will provide some suggestions for redesigning your personal situation so that factors that elicit unsustainable thinking and behaviours are removed and new ones become prevalent that reinforce your new thought and behavioural patterns.

Keep your vision front and centre
Keeping your eye on the deeply held goals and values you want to achieve is the most important step you can take at this point. Rather than allowing yourself to

get bogged down in all the minutia of the problems you experience, keep thinking about and verbalizing your vision of how you ideally want to live your life, and what it means for you to think and act in a sustainable manner.

Don't be deterred by the size of the obstacles

Our society is designed to promote climate-damaging thinking and behaviour. The vast majority of products and services, as well as their production processes and energy systems, are based on the take–make–waste model. Just as importantly, the structure of most organizations serves to undermine climate protection and sustainability. The more you practise changing your thinking and behaviour, the more you will notice the unsustainable nature of our society.

Don't let the size of obstacles scare you off. Take small steps, one at a time. Each successful step will increase your knowledge and enhance your self-confidence. Over time, you will be able to take bigger steps.

Seek opportunities to change systems and structures

In the doing stage, you began to alter your social systems to reduce the influence of people who persistently elicit or reinforce unsustainable thinking and behaviour. At this point it is important to go further and seek ways of altering entire systems and structures. For example, look for ways to redesign your house, lawn and garden, food purchasing and transportation patterns in order to dramatically reduce greenhouse gases, protect the natural environment and support social equity. This may include remodelling to include more passive solar heat, the installation of solar hot water or PV systems, shifting to public transportation and other steps. If your job requires you to think and act unsustainably, talk with your co-workers and supervisors about changing it. If that isn't successful, try to motivate the people with whom you work to make a shift to sustainable thinking. As a last resort, you may need to find a new job.

Create, don't problem solve

When an obstacle pops up, avoid the tendency to problem solve. Two ways exist of approaching a situation: problem-solving and creating. These outlooks constitute fundamentally different ways of approaching the world. Problem-solving seeks to make something unpleasant go away. The vision is negative, focused on elimination. Creating, on the other hand, strives to bring something new into existence. The vision is positive, focused on innovation and invention.

When your mental frame is oriented towards solving problems, the basic question you ask is: 'How do I make this obstacle or negative situation go away?' You begin with a canvas already full with shapes, figures and conundrums. Your thinking focuses on devising intricate ways of characterizing the obstacles, identifying alternative ways out of your difficulties and applying the most efficient 'solutions'. If you are lucky, the problem you have targeted may disappear.

However, as we have discussed, eliminating what you don't want rarely gets you closer to what you do want. Often, you end up with something as bad as or worse than your original problem. Furthermore, the exertion demanded by problem-solving deflects our attention away from what you really want. After one problem is 'solved' another appears, leaving you running as fast as you can but rarely getting anywhere because you forgot where you ideally wanted to go.

Most efforts to resolve global warming and other social and economic challenges today are focused on making bad things go away, such as greenhouse gas emissions. However, negative visions excite no one. It should be no surprise that despite all of the exceptionally talented people and billions of dollars going towards solving the world's problems, conditions rarely seem to improve. You simply can't resolve most troubles through problem-solving.

Creating involves a positive orientation and brings out positive qualities in people. To create, start by envisioning what you ideally desire and remain focused on achieving that end throughout the process. The key question in a creative process is: 'What do I really want to bring into being?' Painters begin with a blank canvas and writers begin with a blank sheet of paper. Similarly, creating starts not by thinking about how to remove impediments or reduce greenhouse gas emissions by 10 per cent, but by imagining how an ideal outcome or situation would look when you produce no emissions, absent of the constraints imposed by existing structures. Hindrances are merely challenges from which to learn and improve. Current reality is important, but only as a way to know how far you are from your desired end.

Even with his success, Rusty Rexius hit a number of stumbling blocks. For example, Rexius told me that one day: 'We were sitting in a meeting beating our chests about all the good things we were doing and then someone pointed out that right behind us was a stack of Styrofoam cups. I realized then my thinking still had some holes in it.'[9] However, Rexius did not let this setback deflate his effort. He realized the presence of Styrofoam cups indicated that his company's purchasing department had not yet embraced the new way of thinking. He therefore spent time helping them to understand the purpose and benefits of the new thinking and envisioning what success would mean for their department. In this way, Rexius helped his employees to move towards a new vision.

Develop a 'structural change' action plan

Write down your approach for altering the structures around you. This helps to keep the plan front and centre. The same type of action plan can be used as you are employed in the design phase (see Table 7.6).

Table 7.6 *Developing a structural change action plan*

Action	Begin	Predicted Results	Possible troubles	Methods of overcoming troubles	Results	Comparison of predicted and actual results

Remember: Setbacks do not mean failure!

When you look at people who are deeply engaged in climate-positive sustainable thinking, you may believe they have their act together and that you fail to match up. What you need to recognize is that each of the people whom you observe has undoubtedly invested a great deal of time learning about the issue, taking small and large steps, making mistakes, learning from them and trying again. The Rexius Styrofoam cup example shows that humans learn primarily through mistakes. Setbacks therefore do not mean failure. To the contrary, they provide our best opportunities to learn and improve. If you remain focused on learning rather than constant success, you can begin again after a setback. Little by little, you will succeed.

Continual learning is especially important because no one today actually knows how to reduce global greenhouse gas emissions by the 80 per cent or more needed to stabilize the climate. No one knows all of the steps necessary to restore biodiversity and the natural environment to self-sustaining levels. A great deal of uncertainty exists about the best way of equalizing global and regional income disparities and of reducing global social unrest. The ability to free the mind of old rigid concepts and to constantly learn is the most important skill any human can possess today. Master the art and skill of continual learning and the results will follow.

Achieving integration

The willingness to honestly examine and challenge your current thought and behavioural patterns, hold steady a vision of how you really want to live your life, and reorient your perspective towards respecting the systems within which you are enmeshed are the keys to embedding sustainable thinking in your mind frame. Continued dedication and persistence will be vital. Over time, sustainable thinking and behaviour will become routine. When this occurs, you will not be tempted to fall back into unsustainable patterns.

Even with enhanced personal awareness and thinking skills, however, complex situations are certain to arise during your journey towards sustainable thinking that will be difficult to navigate. Some will involve moral and ethical issues. The next chapter explores how to make ethical and moral decisions that support climate protection and sustainability.

Notes

1 Rusty Rexius, pers comm, 21 March 2007.
2 Rusty Rexius, pers comm, 21 March 2007.
3 Rusty Rexius, pers comm, 21 March 2007.
4 Rusty Rexius, pers email comm, 17 April 2007.
5 These terms and the discussion to follow is from DiClemente and Velasquez (2002).
6 Richard Cizik, pers comm, 21March 2007.
7 Rusty Rexius, pers comm, 21 March 2007.
8 See Oregon Natural Step Network at www.ortns.org/.
9 Rusty Rexius, pers comm, 21 March 2007.

References

Bandura, A. (1982) 'A. Self-efficacy: Mechanisms in human agency', *American Psychologist*, vol 37, pp122–147

DiClemente, C. C. and Velasquez, M. M. (2002) 'Motivational interviewing and the stages of change', in W. R. Miller and S. Rollnick (eds) *Motivational Interviewing*, The Guilford Press, New York and London

Gollwitzer, P. M. and Brandstatter, V. (1997) 'Implementation intentions and effective goal pursuit', *Journal of Personality and Social Psychology*, vol 73, pp186–199

Greenberger, D. and Padesky, C. (1995) *Mind over Mood: Change How You Feel by Changing the Way You Think*, The Guilford Press, New York

Little, A. (2005) 'Cizik matters: An interview with green evangelical leader Richard Cizik', *Grist Environmental News and Commentary*, October, www.grist.org/news/maindish/2005/10/05/cizik

Maynard Keynes, J. (1935) *The General Theory of Employment, Interest and Money*, Harcourt, Brace and Co, New York

Peterson, C. and Steen, T. (2005) 'Optimistic explanatory style', in C. R. Snyder and S. J. Lopez (eds) *Handbook of Positive Psychology*, Oxford University Press, New York

Prochaska, J. O., Norcross, J. C. and DiClemente, C. C. (1994) *Changing for Good*, HarperCollins Publishers, New York

Seligman, M. E. P. (1990) *Learned Optimism*, Vintage Books, New York

Velicer, W. E. and DiClemente, C. (1985) 'Decision balance measures for assessing and predicting smoking status', *Journal of Personality and Social Psychology*, vol 48, no 5, pp1279–1289

8

The Ethics of Sustainable Thinking

Things which matter the most must never be at the mercy of things which matter least.

Goethe

Food is a particularly challenging issue for my wife and me. We like to eat organic fruit and vegetables. They taste better than conventionally grown produce and organic farming is better for the environment and for our personal health. In the winter, however, the availability of organic produce in our neck of the woods is dependent upon shipments from southern California, Mexico and South America. The greenhouse gases generated by the 2400km (1500 miles), on average, that food travels from the farm to grocery, along with other impacts associated with packaging and refrigeration likely counterbalance the environmental benefits of organic production. We consequently question whether is makes sense to buy organic produce when it is out of season locally.

We are also torn about the social effects of our purchasing decisions. We know, for example, that the production of organic produce helps to expand environmentally sound farming in economically depressed regions of the world, such as Mexico. If we stop purchasing organic produce from those countries, we would likely impair the opportunity for those businesses to grow, while shifting our money to domestic conventional industrial farm operations.

These dilemmas symbolize the tough choices you will face when you adopt a sustainable mind frame. The road towards climate protection and sustainability is laden with quandaries that often have no clear-cut, right-versus-wrong answers. Until this point, you have probably ignored the finer points of these predicaments. Now that you have started to become a sustainable thinker, your awareness of these dilemmas will expand, and the choices you faced are likely to become much more complicated.

This chapter provides a framework for making ethical and moral choices that support the climate and sustainability fundamentals of endurance, cleanliness and community and help you to avoid the thinking blunders that undermine them. I am indebted to Rushworth Kidder for allowing me to modify some of the methods discussed in his wonderful book *How Good People Make Tough Choices* (Kidder, 1995) in the following discussion.[1]

THE ROLE OF ETHICS

The term 'ethics' often conjures up images of philosophical discourses that have little application to real life. Ethics are also easily dismissed because people believe they are context dependent, meaning they apply only to a specific group or situation and are not universal. To many people, the term 'morality' has even worse connotations, suggesting puritanical edicts intended to impose one group's religious views on another.

When we consider that all life on Earth today, human and otherwise, is at grave risk due to global warming, environmental degradation and associated social turmoil, it becomes obvious that these views are erroneous. Every production, consumption and reproduction decision we make now has moral implications. All ethics worthy of the name are not dependent upon religion and must help to guide everyday decision-making and behaviour.

Thinking and behaving ethically today means that the interests of each individual, team, organization and nation cannot count for more than the interests of others because every action has an effect on other people and the climate and natural environment upon which we all depend for life. Similarly, the actions of others affect us and the systems upon which our survival depends. Thus, at the most fundamental level, sustainable ethics describes the range of acceptable behaviours required to ensure that all of us living today, and those who follow, can endure in the future.

Although thinkers much greater than I have argued about the differences for centuries, for the purposes of this discussion I will use the terms ethics and morals interchangeably.

LAWS, FREE WILL AND ETHICS

How do ethics differ from laws? What is the role of ethics when one considers free will? From a climate and sustainability perspective, what does it mean to live ethically? Rush Kidder explains that early 20th-century English jurist John Fletcher Moulton coined a phrase that provides one of the most useful definitions of ethics ever devised: 'obedience to the unenforceable' (Kidder, 1995). Moulton distinguished 'three great domains of human action': positive laws, free choice and manners, by which he meant ethics. Positive laws are 'laws binding upon us which must be obeyed', which essentially means laws that are enforceable with punishment. At the other end of the scale lies free choice, which is the area where 'spontaneity, originality and energy are born' and where we 'claim and enjoy complete freedom'. Between positive law and free will lies a large area that cannot be regulated and yet where the freedom to 'choose as we would' also does not apply. This is the realm of ethics, where man is the 'enforcer of the law upon himself' and where humans 'obey self-imposed law'.

The middle ground of the 'domain of obedience to the unenforceable' is always at risk of intrusion from both sides. Some people will try to impose more laws and regulations, while others will try to expand the area where humans are free to do whatever they want. However, according to Moulton, the true worth of a people lies in the extent to which they understand the need for, and impose on themselves, the proper balance of ethical standards of behaviour.

Scholars have noted that Moulton wrote these words in a time much like ours today, when people felt a desperate need for ethical codes to guide personal, team and organizational behaviour (Kidder, 1995). They were published in the *Atlantic Monthly* just six years after World War I ended, at a time when fascism was already on the rise in Europe and the US was in social turmoil due to political scandals, the introduction of mechanization by Henry Ford that triggered deep-seated changes in the economy, and other social upheavals. Today's political, social and environmental instability similarly suggest a pressing need for the adoption of new ethical codes of behaviour.

Moulton's statements have direct bearing on the climate and sustainability. Laws can be adopted to regulate some activities that threaten the fundamentals of endurance, cleanliness and community. For example, energy producers and manufacturing plants that generate large amounts of greenhouse gas pollutants can be regulated. Tailpipe emission standards can be established for cars and trucks. Minimum wage, health and safety standards can be established to protect workers. Laws lead to relatively easy decisions between what Rush Kidder (1995) calls 'right versus wrong' options. In principle, if it is illegal, it's wrong.

It is not possible, however, for government to regulate every activity that might undermine the climate and sustainability fundamentals of endurance, cleanliness and community. The issues are too complex and fast changing, and the capacity of government is too limited for this to ever be a realistic option. It would also frighten most of us to death to think that government would intrude into our lives so much that every action that might affect the environment or other humans is regulated.

At the same time, many people in Western societies today believe that anything not prohibited by law is acceptable. Despite the fact that very few toxic substances are ever tested to determine their full effects on the natural environment or public health, if a hazardous substance is not restricted by law, it is deemed acceptable for use. Even though gas-guzzling SUVs produce more greenhouse gases than smaller, more efficient vehicles, and are more dangerous to drive, people can buy them because they are legal. Global warming and the other crises that humanity faces today, however, underscore that the licence to do whatever one wants short of violating the law has brought us to the precipice of calamity. The expanse of 'free will' described by Moulton has grown too large.

As Moulton pointed out, something in the middle between laws and unbridled individualism is urgently needed to guide society towards climate protection and sustainability. This middle alternative must help people to choose between 'right versus wrong' options and to guide decision-making for what Rush Kidder calls 'right versus right' dilemmas. Many decisions that affect the climate, natural environment and social welfare fall into the difficult and confusing 'right versus right' category. This middle ground demands new ethical codes of behaviour.

What, then, do sustainable ethics involve? The essence of these moral codes is the self-regulation of personal, team and organizational behaviours that degrade the Earth's climate, natural environment and communities. Sustainable ethics is the self-imposition of prohibitions on activities that fail to take into account the impacts of our actions on the Earth's sources, sinks and people, now and in the future.

The road to sustainable ethics starts with the recognition of need. Your willingness to read this book, I would contend, suggests that you recognize the need. As with other forms of sustainable thinking, however, in order to fully embrace sustainable ethics, your awareness of their benefits must come to significantly outweigh the downsides of ignoring them.

CLIMATE AND SUSTAINABILITY ETHICAL DILEMMAS

The organic food dilemma discussed at the beginning of this chapter illustrates that it is often not easy to decide exactly what type of decisions do and do not support sustainable ethics. Sometimes a choice is easy to make because something is so obviously bad for the environment or communities that we know we should not do it. These are 'right versus wrong' decisions. It would have been clearly wrong for my wife and me to violate local building codes or land-use policies when we reconstructed our junker house. The production and use of banned toxic carcinogenic substances such as DDT are clearly wrong. The release into the environment of radioactive material from nuclear plants is clearly wrong.

Rush Kidder (1995) suggests that right-versus-wrong decisions are 'moral temptations'. Only those without moral fibre would conclude that pursing the wrong choice is appropriate and upright. For most people, a moment of sober reflection is all that is required to recognize a moral temptation and to make the proper decision (Kidder, 1995).

More often than not, however, decisions are much less straightforward because the options on the table all seem to have good qualities, or pit one right perspective against another. In our example, my wife and I were confronted with the decision about whether to reduce out indirect greenhouse gas emissions by not buying out-of-season organic produce and to put jobs at risk in the infant organic foods industry in Latin and South America, or to support the nascent foreign industries and knowingly add more emissions to the atmosphere. Because of their complexity, these right-versus-right conundrums don't lend themselves to easy answers.

From a climate and sustainability perspective, I believe that the most common right-versus-right dilemmas tend to fall into six categories, most of which have been discussed in some form in this book already.[2] The roots of each dilemma can be found in the sustainability thinking blunders (STBs) and systems blindness:

- individual versus community;
- global versus local;
- laws versus truth;
- short term versus long term;
- toxic versus non-toxic;
- justice versus mercy.

A brief description is provided of each of these dilemmas below. Summarize how you usually resolve these issues by recording your answers in the sustainable ethics evaluation chart provided at the end of the chapter (see Table 8.1).

Individual versus community

As someone with fond memories of driving his SUV whenever and wherever he wants to, a good friend of mine named Peter is loath to think that he should give up his individual desires and rights for the benefit of the broader community. Many other SUV drivers feel the same way, as does President George W. Bush, who apparently believes that the US should not take the risk of straining its economy by limiting its greenhouse gas emissions to prevent catastrophic global warming, which would affect the entire world. Choosing between an individual's right to do as they please versus the rights of the larger community is what this ethical dilemma entails.

The dilemma of choosing between the individual and the community takes numerous forms. It is sometimes expressed as 'us versus them' – for example, large industrial greenhouse gas emitters such as the US versus smaller individual emitters such as non-industrial developing nations. It can also be stated as 'self versus others', which describes my friend Peter's situation. Still another version is 'smaller versus larger group' (Kidder, 1995) – for example, when corporate retail giants such as Wal-Mart or Barnes and Noble move into a community and wipe out small retailers. At the most basic level, this ethical dilemma pits the rights of individual players to do as they please against the rights and well-being of the larger community of people and other organisms.

Take a moment to reflect on how often you find yourself favouring individual rights over the rights and well-being of the larger community.

Global versus local

Economic globalization has become a hot button issue across the world. There are plenty of people who claim that the results have been positive and just as many who say the effects have been negative. Do the pros outweigh the cons? Is an emphasis on global best from a climatic and sustainability perspective, or is a local focus better? These questions lie at the heart of the global versus local ethical dilemma.

Globalization has created jobs in low-income regions of the world. Industries that benefit workers and the local environment, such as organic farming discussed at the beginning of this chapter, have sprung up in non-industrial nations to meet growing demand in Western markets. Consumers in industrialized nations also benefit by paying low prices for goods produced in foreign nations. The internet has allowed people to communicate and even design goods and services instantaneously from all over the world, thus breaking down all sorts of longstanding cultural, political and economic barriers. These are positive outcomes of globalization.

At the same time, ample data shows that globalization has not reduced poverty. To the contrary, the gap between the rich and the poor globally is growing. The richest 1 per cent of adults, most of whom live in Europe and the US, now own 40 per cent of the global assets. By contrast, the bottom 50 per cent of the world's adults, who mostly live in non-industrial nations, barely own 1 per cent of the world's wealth.[3]

Moreover, energy consumption, greenhouse gas emissions and other environmental and social impacts associated with long-distance shipping of goods and the explosion of electronic equipment needed for global web-based communication are immense. Globalization has also uprooted indigenous cultures, forced peasant farmers off their land, and put enormous downward pressure on local environmental, public health and worker health and safety laws.

Local production, on the other hand, reduces the need to transport goods long distances and therefore cuts down greenhouse gas emissions. In general, a dollar spent locally generates twice as much income for the local economy as a dollar spent outside of the local area. Local firms can also be held to high environmental standards and worker health and safety laws can be enforced.

Economies that shun trade and depend primarily upon locally produced goods, however, are rarely very vibrant. Consumer demand in a 'closed economy' is usually not sufficient to trigger the level of competition needed to spur innovation. Regions that are not actively interacting with others through trade also invariably end up lacking intellectual and creative know-how.

The global-versus-local ethical dilemma obviously does not lend itself to easy answers. However, a thoughtful assessment of the pros and cons of this dilemma helps to prioritize and weigh the most important considerations.

How often do you find yourself choosing global over local production and consumption?

Laws versus truth

Despite ample scientific evidence showing what the environmental effects would be, from the late 1960s through the early 1990s, federal law allowed – indeed, promoted – excessive clear-cutting of ancient forests in the US Pacific Northwest. As scientists predicted, ecological keystone species such as the northern spotted owl and Pacific salmon were driven to the brink of extinction.

Although protests have erupted across the world, many biotechnology companies today not only lawfully engage in dubious experiments on plants and animals and patent all forms of life that rightly belong to the public, they also cause a dramatic reduction in biodiversity due to the depletion of plant species.

There are numerous other examples of laws and regulations that undermine the climate and sustainability fundamentals of endurance, cleanliness and community even when ample evidence shows their harmful effects.

On the other hand, the US National Environmental Policy Act, Endangered Species Act, Clean Air and Clean Water acts and similar policies in Europe and other nations and states represent some of the most progressive environmental laws ever written. Social Security, Medicare and minimum wage laws are some of the most far-thinking social policies in existence. A society that abandons the rule of laws collapses into chaos.

Should laws that clearly violate the sustainability fundamentals of endurance, cleanliness and community be followed, or should they be opposed and even purposefully disobeyed? If you disobey them, where do you draw the line? Which laws do you decide to follow and which laws do you ignore? How can you expect anyone to follow the law if you pick and choose those that you will obey? The ethical dilemma of 'laws versus truth' pits an allegiance to laws and regulations against empirical evidence that shows the laws to be ecologically and socially harmful or unjust.

How often do you find yourself choosing allegiance to laws and regulations over empirical evidence that shows the laws to be detrimental or unfair?

Short term versus long term

Looking back at his thinking before he became engaged in sustainability in the early 1990s, Ray Anderson from Interface realized that meeting quarterly financial targets was more important than any long-term effect his company's activities had on the environment or other people. He always chose the short term over the long term. This ethical dilemma typically pits the desire for short-term gain against our long-term well-being and that of other people and future generations. It is a mirror of the 'quick-fix' sustainability thinking blunder.

There are many good arguments to be made for a short-term focus. Sometimes problems are critical and must be resolved immediately in order to contain damage or prevent problems from snowballing. Reducing greenhouse gases now, for example, will prevent large-scale catastrophe in the future. Experimentation today is also needed to invent the new energy sources that will power society in the future. Some economists argue that no one can guarantee that the future will even exist, so we have little reason to take it into account when planning (this is the justification given for setting low 'discount' rates).

Other people say it makes no sense to deprive the present generation of access to the Earth's resources because we have no way of knowing the type of energy or raw materials that future generations will need or may invent.

The focus on the short term, however, is exactly what has produced global warming and most of today's other pressing ecological, social and economic problems. Despite the academic arguments about the unknown future, on a practical level every parent visibly sees the future in their children and grandchildren. A brief moment of reflection makes obvious that each of us exists today only because of our ancestors. Thinking and acting in ways that ensure ample options for future generations is therefore a real-time, down-to-earth issue.

So there are good arguments to be made for both short- and long-term perspectives. Which option should we choose? This is the ethical dilemma of short term versus long term.

How often do you find yourself choosing short term over long term?

Toxic versus non-toxic

This may seem like an odd issue to place within a suite of ethical dilemmas. What type of moral quandary could possibly be associated with whether people choose toxic or non-toxic materials? Actually, the choices people make today about this issue will determine how global warming unfolds, the extent to which the world's agricultural soils become contaminated, and the trajectory of many cancers and other human health problems. Each of these is a life and death issue. Few issues have greater moral implications today than the dilemma of whether we choose to produce and use toxic or non-toxic materials and substances.

Fossil fuels power much of the world's economy today. Because it will not be possible to scale up renewables fast enough to meet global demand, fossil fuels are certain to remain a major source of energy around the globe for many years to come. Heavy metals such as mercury, lead, iron, copper, magnesium and zinc serve important functions in many of the electronic products and other goods produced by industry today. Even most soils normally contain low background levels of heavy metals.

Fossil fuels, however, are toxic to people and the environment. Carbon dioxide produced by burning fossil fuels is also a major contributor to global warming. Although living organisms require trace amounts of some heavy metals, excessive levels can be hazardous to humans, animals and plants. Nature's sinks are not designed to absorb and break down most synthetic toxic substances, so they accumulate in the soil, plants and animals, and in human tissue as well.

Non-toxic materials, on the other hand, are not harmful to living organisms and do not contribute to global warming. Organic fertilizers, for example, regenerate the soil while fossil fuel-based fertilizers (which are derived from natural gas) and pesticides (which are derived from oil) deplete it.

There are real questions, however, about whether sufficient quantities of non-toxic natural substances exist to meet the needs of today's burgeoning population. For instance, there is simply not enough natural rubber available to make tires for all of the vehicles on the road today. Biofuels and consumer bio-products compete for agricultural land against food production needed to feed the world's population. Even if you want to use only non-toxic materials, it takes tremendous effort to examine every item you purchase, and frequently it is impossible to know what goes into most products.

The use of toxic versus non-toxic materials and substances thus poses a major dilemma for us. Toxic substances provide many benefits, yet their use degrades the environment and can kill people. From a climate perspective, the choices we make about the type of substances we produce and how they are handled will determine the future of the entire planet.

How often do you find yourself choosing toxic over non-toxic substances and products?

Justice versus mercy

After he began to practise sustainable thinking, Rusty Rexius became increasingly aware of the ways in which his choices affected the climate and natural environment, as well as other people. He quickly began to make different decisions that reduced his impacts. Reverend Richard Cizik, Ray Anderson, Sue Klobertanz and Larry Chalfan did the same. Most people would say that it is right to be merciful and compassionate towards people who make mistakes out of ignorance, but rapidly change after they learn the errors of their ways.

Some people, however, knowingly continue destructive activities even after having numerous opportunities to learn about the problem and to clean up their act. A number of corporate executives, for example, think repeated fines for polluting the air or water is just part of the cost of doing business. Wal-Mart, for example, has a long history of violating environmental law. In 2004, the company was hit with a US$3.1 million penalty for violating the US Clean Water Act and paid US$400,000 to settle violations of the Clean Air Act. But then in August 2005, Wal-Mart again agreed to pay US$1.5 million in penalties in Connecticut for storm water violations.[4]

Wal-Mart and other similar corporations, however, employ hundreds of thousands of people and provide goods at low prices to consumers, thus providing benefits to communities.

Is it right to be merciful to people who knowingly cause harm, or should the full force of justice be enforced through fines, dismissal, jail time or other means? This is the question that must be answered in the justice-versus-mercy ethical dilemma.

How often do you find yourself choosing justice over mercy?

Decision-making for sustainable ethics

Sorting through these moral dilemmas and making choices that support the climate and sustainability fundamentals of endurance, cleanliness and community can be difficult. However, just as a systematic methodology can be helpful when seeking to make the transition to sustainable thinking, a systematic – but not necessarily simple – process can be used to resolve global warming and sustainability-related ethical dilemmas. The method involves assessing the pros and cons of situations from the perspective of three principles that have been at the core of human ethics for hundreds of years. They can be described through three simple common expressions (Kidder, 1995):

1   'Do what's best for the greatest number of people.' This can be called *ends-based* thinking.
2   'Act in accordance with whatever law we would want everyone else to follow in similar situations.' This can be called *rule-based* thinking.
3   'Do what you want others to do to you.' This can be considered *care-based* thinking.

Let's explore what these principles mean and how they can be used to resolve sustainability ethical dilemmas.

Ends-based thinking

In the field of ethics, this principle is known as 'utilitarianism'. It asks us to think about the greatest good for the greatest number of people. Rush Kidder (1995) calls this ends-based thinking because it relies on evaluating the end result or consequence of an action. The term utilitarianism was coined by John Stuart Mill in 1861, who said that: 'The happiness which forms the utilitarian standard of what is right in conduct … is not the agent's own happiness, but that of all concerned' (cited in Kidder, 1995, pp156–157).

Rather than focusing on the motives behind an action or specific rules to guide behaviour, utilitarian or ends-based thinking focuses on the outcomes of a choice. Two broad decision-making categories have evolved from this way of thinking: *act utilitarianism*, which means to take whatever action derives the greatest good for the greatest number of people, and *rule utilitarianism*, which means follow whatever rule will maximize the overall good (Kidder, 1995, p157).

Democracy is based on the utilitarian principle. The most fundamental question asked by most policy-makers when considering new laws relate to which options will provide the greatest good for the greatest number of people. To answer this question two issues must be analysed: the size of the population that may benefit, and the breadth and scope of the benefit a proposed policy may provide in the future.

Critics of the utilitarian principle often say ends-based thinking should not be used because humans are not very good at speculating about the future, and special interest groups that loudly proclaim they are the people that policies should benefit can easily sway the calculation.

There are practical reasons, as well, for why this principle can be difficult to apply. When this precept is pushed to its extreme, for example, it can become the tyranny of the majority. To gain modest climate protections, an isolated economically depressed community may be forced to abandon its small gas-fired power plant and pay exorbitant rates to some far-off source for renewable energy. All Muslims might be banned from Western nations to prevent a few who are terrorists from causing harm.

Despite its imperfections, from a climate and sustainability perspective, ends-based thinking has a number of benefits. The process of asking about the greatest good for the greatest number of people helps you to overcome systems blindness and many sustainability thinking blunders. You must, for example, consider the impacts of your actions over time and space, as well as the possibility that delays may cause the impacts of your actions to show later rather than sooner.

Ends-based thinking forces us to ask questions such as: 'Is it in the best interests of the greatest number of people to clear-cut forests, drive fish to extinction through over-fishing or use so much water that aquifers run dry?' and 'Is it in the best interests of the greatest number of people for the US and other industrial nations to generate massive amounts of greenhouse pollutants that undermine food production and living conditions around the world?' These are very important considerations.

Rule-based thinking

Rule-based thinking is a different way to describe the 'categorical imperative' proposed by 18th-century German Philosopher Immanuel Kant. It says that our behaviour should conform to certain universal principles of action, which means we should 'act in accordance with whatever law we would like everyone else in the world to follow in relevant circumstances' (cited in Kidder, 1995).

One way to think of this axiom is to ask: 'What if everyone else in the world did as I am about to do?' If the answer to this question is positive, your decision or action would meet the rules-based test. If you realize that unacceptable negative consequences would result if everyone did as you are proposing to do, then your action would fail the test (Sherwin, 1998). In this way, rules-based thinking is 'the fullest expression of the adage that we should always live and act according to our highest principles' (Kidder, 1995).

The criticisms of rules-based thinking are typically associated with the rigidity that it seems to impose. It would seem to preclude, for example, allowing one entity from performing a risky experiment to produce new sources of energy because to allow one would mean allowing anyone to perform such experimentation. Rules-based thinking also seems to demand that if you make a commitment it can never be broken or changed. If you commit to a rule that allocates specific limits on greenhouse gas emissions among energy-producing utilities to achieve an overall emission cap, does this unequivocally mean that a utility cannot go above this cap when drought caused by climate change eliminates their clean sources of hydropower?

Although there are limits to the situations in which rule-based thinking can be applied, this approach can offer numerous insights into climate and sustainability ethical dilemmas. Asking the question: 'What if everyone else in the world did as I am about to do?' forces us to think about systems effects.

For instance, the average household in the US produces about 10,400kg (22,960lbs) of carbon dioxide each year for lighting, heating and other internal operations. When personal transportation, food production and processing, transporting goods and equipment, and the decay of household wastes in landfills are added, the average American household produces the equivalent of 66,580kg (146,800lbs) of carbon dioxide per year (www.epa.gov/climatechange/emissions/usgginventory.html). Would it be acceptable if every household in the world produced the same amount of greenhouse gases as the average American household does?

Considering our actions as the basis of a universal rule also expands our thinking beyond short-term immediate benefits. Buying products made with polyvinylchloride (vinyl, or PVC), one of the most toxic plastics in use today, may be cheaper in the short run; but if everyone in the world used these products, would the long-term effects on ecological and human health be acceptable?

While not perfect, in combination with the other moral principles, rule-based thinking can force us to consider the pros and cons of our actions in a larger context.

Care-based thinking

Whereas the test of rightness or wrongness of ends-based and rule-based thinking requires you to imagine yourself as the agent of an action, care-based thinking asks you to consider how you would feel if you were the object of an act. The third moral principle urges us to do to others what we want others to do to us, or, conversely, avoid doing to others what we don't want done to us. This is universally known as the Golden Rule. Although it is typically thought of as a Christian maxim, Confucius wrote about the Golden Rule in 500 BC and it also appears in the Jewish *Talmud* and in Islam. The basic message is: 'Love thy neighbour as thyself.' Rush Kidder (1995) calls this 'care-based thinking' because, unlike the other two moral precepts, it asks us to 'care enough about the others involved to put ourselves in their shoes' (Kidder, 1995).

Numerous scholars have pointed out that the Golden Rule not only sets limits on our actions, it encourages us to advocate for the interests of others (Kidder, 1995). Care-based thinking prevents us from applying double standards, making arbitrary exceptions and judging people with similar situations or skills differently. It requires us to give the same weight to the interests of others as we give to our own interests.

Philosopher John Rawls constructed what he called the 'veil of ignorance' to demonstrate the power of the Golden Rule. Imagine, he said, that decision-makers are 'situated behind a veil of ignorance' where they have access to all relevant information about contemporary society, but do not have any knowledge about how they differ from anyone else. This means that the decision-makers don't know their class, social status, where they are from, who their parents are or even their level of wealth. Consequently, they don't know how the decisions they make will affect them personally because they don't know who they are. Rawls asks what principles the decision-makers would use to guide their choices in this situation? His answer is the Golden Rule because all others might work against the decision makers (Rawls, 1971).

Critics of care-based thinking, including Immanuel Kant, contend that the rule is too simplistic to be a moral precept. For instance, it does not offer a way of distinguishing between good and bad when all the options appear to be negative. It would seem to approve of the US removing every restriction on the generation of its greenhouse gases as long as other nations know that they are free to do likewise. The principle also provides no guidance as to who the appropriate 'others' are in whose shoes you are to walk. Must you consider everyone in the world all the time? What about people whose situations are fundamentally different from our own?

Despite the limitations, care-based thinking has many implications for the climate and sustainability. Expanding upon Rawls's construction into the future, for example, the Golden Rule asks those of us who live in industrial societies to decide if the unrestrained emission of greenhouse gases would be permitted if we knew we would end up being born in Africa or in the Arctic region? It asks us to determine how we would feel if large foreign corporations moved into our community, took control of huge swaths of prime agricultural land, and then paid us slave wages to produce agricultural goods for foreign markets.

By applying care-based thinking, the upsides and downsides of decisions or actions based can be considered based on how they would affect us.

APPLICATIONS

Let's now turn to the question of how you can apply the three moral precepts in a systematic way. The key is to follow a five-step process (Kidder, 1995).

1: Recognize the existence of a sustainable ethics issue

This is an important step from a climate and sustainability perspective. Too often, people dismiss the possibility that their choices and activities may have ethical implications. However, the links between the precarious condition of the Earth's sources and sinks and growing income disparities and social distress mean that every production and consumption decision you make today has moral implications. Your first step is to recognize this possibility.

2: Test for right versus wrong issues

If you have decided that the issue you are concerned about has ethical overtones, the next step is to determine if the situation involves 'right versus wrong' issues. These are the simplest and easiest questions to answer because they deal with violations of the law. Ask yourself: 'Would the decision violate legal mandates?' and 'Would this violate any reasonable human rights or social justice standards?'

Sometimes a decision does not violate the law; but you still wonder if it is the morally right thing to do because somehow it just feels yucky. In this case, you can use a *gut check* to indicate your course of action. Dig deep and ask yourself: 'Does the decision feel right to me?' You can also use the *front-page* test. Ask yourself: 'How would I feel if the decision I am about to make turned up on the cover of tomorrow's newspaper?' The *mother test* is another option you can use. Ask yourself: 'If I were my mother (or rabbi, wife or best friend), what would I do?' These three questions, which are similar to the three moral tests already discussed, offer ways of determining if a decision is right or wrong.

3: Test for 'right versus right' issues

If you have determined that the issue at hand is murkier than a clear-cut right versus wrong dilemma, testing for right versus right issues is the next step. Many climate and sustainability issues fall into this category. Your task at this point is to determine if the issue you are struggling with pertains to:

- individual versus community – the rights of individuals to do as they want versus the rights and well-being of the larger community;
- global versus local – global versus local production and consumption;
- short term versus long term – immediate benefits versus long-term well-being;
- toxic versus non-toxic – the production and use of natural and human-made synthetic toxic substances versus non-toxic substances and materials;
- laws versus truth – allegiance to laws and regulations versus empirical evidence and truth.
- justice versus mercy – showing mercy to those who knowingly harm the climate, natural environment or other people versus applying the full force of the law.

4: Apply the three ethical principles of decision-making

After you have determined the right versus right ethical dilemma that your issue is associated with, the next step is to apply the three moral principles we discussed and to identify the arguments that seem most pertinent and convincing to you. Sometimes the dilemmas may fall into more than one category. For example, short-term versus long-term dilemmas may also involve global versus local questions. When this occurs, start with the dilemma that seems to have the most power or energy behind it. Applying the three moral precepts to these situations helps you to make ethical choices that support the climate and sustainability fundamentals of endurance, cleanliness and community.

To refresh your memory, the three moral precepts are:

1   ends-based thinking (do what's best for the greatest number of people);
2   rule-based thinking (if everyone in the world followed the rule of action I am following, what would be the result?);
3   care-based thinking (act as I would want others to treat me).

5: Make a decision, act, evaluate, learn and improve

Don't stop with this analysis. Sustainable ethics is not an academic exercise. It requires that you engage in the world. Choices must be made and actions taken. Your final step is therefore to make a decision and act. As you move forward, however, keep in mind the need to monitor the effects. The more you can observe the outcomes of your decisions, reflect on whether or not the results are what you desired, and make adjustments when they are not, the more skilled you will become at living a life consistent with sustainability.

FIVE ETHICAL COMMITMENTS FOR A CARBON CONSTRAINED WORLD

Until now, I have focused on the principles and methods of making ethical decisions that support sustainability ethics and avoided offering my personal recommendations about what you should choose. I am now going to take the liberty of shifting gears and briefly offer suggestions for resolving the five ethical dilemmas just discussed.

If humanity is to successfully stabilize the climate and adopt a path towards a sustainable future, most of us will need to make deep-seated changes in our mental frames. This will not be easy. A new sustainable worldview will, of necessity, require us to make difficult decisions about many fundamental questions. Are we willing to come to grips with the fact that the Earth is a finite system and, as such, the continued growth of population, resource consumption, greenhouse gases and other forms of waste and environmental degradation are simply not possible without widespread devastation? Are we willing to give up our longstanding views of how the economy works and accept a new perspective that ensures that it serves all of humanity while restoring the climate, natural environment and social well-being?

Are we willing to do what is needed to ensure that future generations live in a world as abundant and healthy as the one passed on to us by our ancestors?

Sustainable ethics provides an important part of the equation for answering these questions. The degraded conditions of the climate and natural environment, scale of the global economy and size of the world's population mean that decisions made by businesses, governments and consumers today have far-ranging and possibly irreversible affects on human health, as well as the survival of living organisms everywhere. All questions related to production, consumption and population growth are therefore deeply moral issues.

Moral questions demand ethical solutions. Humanity must decide on the rules of behaviour that we all will choose to live by once we realize that living together on the planet we call Earth depends upon sustaining the climate and physical environment and caring for all living beings, now and in the future.

Although some people may argue with me on a few of these points, given the precarious condition of the world today, I believe the ethical and moral rules of behaviour must be heavily weighted to the following dictums. When compelled to choose between:

- the individual or the community, *choose community*;
- the global or local, *choose local*;
- short term or long term, *choose long term*;
- laws or truth, *choose truth*;
- toxic or non-toxic, *choose non-toxic*;
- justice or mercy, *choose justice*.

I believe the balance of evidence overwhelmingly points to the need for personal, team and organizational decisions today to prioritize the broader community of humankind over individual rights and freedom; local over global economic activities (at least until the energy demand and greenhouse gases associated with long-distance shipping are resolved); a long-term perspective over short term; allegiance to the truth about the condition of the climate, natural environment and social welfare over existing laws; the production and use of non-toxic rather than toxic materials and substances; and the application of justice for those who knowingly violate these precepts over showing them mercy.

APPLICATIONS

My wife and I used this process to resolve our dilemma about whether or not to purchase organic produce from foreign countries when it is out of season locally. Due to the profound implications for the Earth's sources and sinks as well as its communities, we first recognized that this was, without a doubt, a moral issue.

We then decided that the issue was not one of 'right versus wrong' because no laws or human rights issues that we knew of were being violated. It was, however, a 'right versus right' ethical dilemma involving questions related primarily to 'local versus global' and 'toxic versus non-toxic' (organic versus non-organic and more greenhouse gas emissions versus less or none). We then applied the three ethical principles.

Our ends-based thinking considerations. This moral principle asks what the greatest good is for the greatest number of people. Using this precept, my wife and I considered that the shift to organic farming was important to preserve soil health and, thus, agricultural productivity for people around the world. Expanding an organic farming industry in Mexico and South America would also help lift many people out of poverty, while also improving overall physical health.

On the other hand, we considered that even in developing nations, comparatively few people work in agriculture today. We also realized that the climate represents a 'good' that is vital to the health and well-being of every economic sector and that agriculture depends upon sufficient rainfall, temperatures and other conditions provided by a stable climate.

Considering our dilemma from an ends-based perspective in this way allowed us to weigh the evidence and draw thoughtful conclusions.

Our rule-based thinking considerations. This moral principle asks us to imagine that whatever we propose to do will become a universal law or standard that everyone else will follow. The questions my wife and I had to ask included: 'What if everyone else in the world purchased organic produce as we are proposing to do?' and 'What rule would we like to see universally applied?'

With these questions in mind, we realized that if everyone in the world purchased organic produce from far-off places when it was out of season locally, the organic produce industry would boom worldwide. On the other hand, transportation-related greenhouse gas emissions would likely soar as well, which would counter the environmental benefits of organic.

One approach to the universal rule that we considered was that 'absolute proof is needed before we make any changes in our behaviour'. For example, no absolute proof exists that reducing transportation-related greenhouse gas emissions would make a significant difference in future global climatic conditions. We realized, however, that this rule would lead to numerous problems. No one would ever listen to the recommendations of their doctor, for example, who may not have proof of an ailment but could make a good diagnosis based on symptoms. This suggested to us that a more appropriate universal rule would be: 'Take precautions when there may be risks.' This rule would lead us to err on the side of caution by not buying organic produce grown outside of our local area until we more clearly understand the effects of long-distance transportation on the climate.

As with the process we used in ends-based thinking, rule-based thinking gave us far greater clarity about the pros and cons of all sides of the issue.

Our care-based thinking considerations. The Golden Rule asks us to put ourselves in the shoes of another and to consider how we would want them to treat us. One of the first acts when taking this principle into consideration is to determine whom the 'others' are.

My wife and I decided that in this case, the most important others were the farmers in Mexico and South America who were producing organic produce, consumers in the US Pacific Northwest, and future generations who will be affected by dangerous climate change if emissions are not controlled. Putting ourselves in the shoes of the foreign farmers, we realized we could be convinced that the emissions produced by the transport of their produce to the US was small in comparison to larger sources of emissions, such as coal-fired power plants in the US or China, while the economic benefits to them were large. From the perspective of US consumers, we could see that ample supplies of organic produce in the winter months were better for their health and having access to the produce was better than having no produce at all. On the other hand, when we took the viewpoint of future generations, we realized that any unnecessary emissions were unacceptable when greenhouse gas concentrations are already at hazardous levels.

Our conclusions. When we took the three moral precepts into account, my wife and I concluded that the negative consequences of buying out-of-season organic produce from foreign countries far outweighed the benefits. We decided that the well-being of people worldwide and of future generations was more important than the welfare of a small number of organic farmers in Latin and South America. We were particularly struck by the implications of rule-based thinking. We were concerned that if everyone in the world purchased organic produce from foreign sources, transportation-related greenhouse gas emissions would skyrocket and cause everyone to suffer today and in the future.

Our decisions. These considerations led my wife and me to specific decisions. We first decided that we would continue to buy organic food, even in the winter. We did not want to contribute to the market for conventional food produced with toxic substances because toxics are a serious problem worldwide. We chose non-toxic over toxic.

We then decided that it was important to support local farmers whenever we could. Although we wanted to support the growing organic food industry in Latin and South America, we felt it was more essential to support local organic farmers who were trying to make a go of it against increasingly large obstacles, such as the Wal-Marts of the world that are moving into the field primarily by purchasing cheap organic food from China.

We also decided to invest in ourselves, which we thought was as local as we could get. Because we want to continue to eat organic produce in the winter, we put up a small greenhouse that could grow lettuce and other cold-weather organic produce. We chose local over global.

In summary, the interlinked nature of global warming, environmental degradation and social and political distress found worldwide means that every production and consumption activity today has ethical and moral implications. At your disposal now is a method that can be used to sort through these complex moral issues and make ethical decisions that support the climate and sustainability conditions of endurance, cleanliness and community.

Table 8.1 *Sustainable ethics evaluation chart*

On a scale of 1 to 5, with 1 being never and 5 being always, how often do you find yourself choosing one approach over another?				
Individual rights over community rights and well-being	1	2	3	4	5
Global over local	1	2	3	4	5
Laws over truth	1	2	3	4	5
Short term over long term	1	2	3	4	5
Toxic over non-toxic	1	2	3	4	5
Justice over mercy	1	2	3	4	5
Totals	—	—	—	—	—
				= Total score

Changing your perspectives and behaviour and making ethical decisions are vital steps in the shift to sustainable thinking. Once you have mastered these activities, however, you may want to encourage other people to take similar steps. The next chapter discusses how this can be achieved.

NOTES

1 The discussion of Mouton's term is taken from Kidder (1995, p66).
2 I am indebted to Rush Kidder for allowing me to modify his four categories, which are truth versus loyalty; individual versus community; short term versus long term; and justice versus mercy.
3 Derived from World Institute for Economics Research, Helsinki, Finland, December 2006.
4 Derived from *Forbes Magazine*, 15 August 2005.

REFERENCES

Kidder, R. (1995) *How Good People Make Tough Choices*, HarperCollins Publishers, New York

Rawls, J. (1971) *A Theory of Justice*, The Belknap Press of Harvard University Press, Boston, MA

Sherwin B. (1998) *Why Be Good*, Daybreak Books, New York

9

Motivating Others To Think and Act Sustainably

The only thing necessary for the triumph of evil is for good men to do nothing.

Edmund Burke

Four days a week I play basketball with a group of (old, slow) guys at the local YMCA. One day as I was dressing after my workout, I watched the business news on the locker room TV and realized that not one speaker had mentioned the risks that global warming posed for the markets. To the contrary, expert after expert prattled on about how this and that stock was set for continued growth. They seemed completely oblivious to the fact that left unchecked, global warming would severely impact most, if not all, of the so-called growth sectors they were raving about in the not-too-distant future. Disinterest was palpable. Once again, I was struck by how difficult it is to motivate people to think sustainably.

This chapter explores the fundamentals of motivating others to alter their thinking and behaviour to protect the climate, natural environment and social well-being. The mechanisms used to motivate others are similar to the ones used in Chapter 7 to transform your own thinking and behaviour. This chapter therefore focuses on the role of the change agent in using those mechanisms to motivate people to change.[1] Motivating others to become sustainable thinkers is important because unless those of you who are beginning to think and act sustainably encourage others do the same, society will struggle to resolve climate change and adopt a path towards sustainability.

RECAP OF CHANGE DRIVERS

In Chapter 6 I pointed out that human beings have a natural propensity to change. Those of us alive today exist only because our ancestors successfully adapted to changing conditions. And each of us constantly adapts to changing circumstances, even if we are often not conscious of the adjustments we make.

I also discussed the fact that at least three factors must be present for an individual to change his or her thinking and behaviour: sufficient tension must exist between their existing state and some important unmet values and aspirations; the benefits of altering their thinking and behaviour to attain the desired goals must be seen to significantly outweigh the downsides; and they must have adequate confidence in their ability to close the gap and resolve the tension.

It turns out that change agents play a particularly important role in helping people to experience and resolve internal tension, weigh the benefits and downsides of change, and build self-confidence in the ability to make the shift. By change agent I mean someone with the specific goal of helping others to make a positive shift in their thinking and behaviour.

In almost any type of helping relationship, certain characteristics, including the degree of empathy shown by a change agent and the way in which they interact with people, go a long way toward determining an individual's willingness to change. When a change agent fails to demonstrate these traits or to express faith in the ability of others to change, the self-confidence of those individuals to make a shift inevitably suffers.

Psychologists have learned that how a person talks about change is a strong indicator of their ability to adjust. Give a survey to people in the early stages of change asking them to predict their chances of making a shift, and their answers typically provide a good indication of what will eventually happen. Thus, the way in which people *think and talk about change* is a critical indicator of success.

Not surprisingly, a change agent's way of relating to another person and the confidence they exude in the ability of others to make a shift significantly influence that individual's change talk (Miller and Rollnick, 2002).

My wife and I found out how true these principles were when working with the contractors whom we hired to help rebuild our rundown house. After we shared the type of practices and products we wanted them to use, a few said that, although the methods were new to them, they thought they could meet our needs. Others, however, voiced reservations. My wife had an uncanny ability to predict who would work out (it must be her southern US upbringing). Invariably, the contractors who voiced confidence in their ability to apply the new practices successfully did so, and those who voiced scepticism did not. And the contractors with whom we developed good relationships tended to be the ones who went on to voice confidence in their ability to go the sustainable route, while those with whom we did not develop good relationships voiced doubt.

Role of the change agent

This information underscores that the most important role of a change agent in the initial stages of the transition to sustainable thinking is to build and then help the individual to resolve tension between their current state and desired goals and values. This must be closely linked with steps to help the individual increase self-confidence in the ability to successfully make the shift.

This was Reverend Richard Cizik's strategy. Living up to God's vision is the highest aspiration of evangelicals. He first made it clear that evangelicals were failing because they were not conforming to God's vision for the climate and the natural environment. He then made it clear that evangelicals had the capacity to make the needed changes.

Sue Klobertanz, former director of purchasing for the City of Portland, took a similar route. Her employees defined success as purchasing quality products for the city at the lowest possible cost and providing contract opportunities for minority-owned companies. She linked the need to adopt green purchasing methods with her employee's desire to achieve cost savings and support minority-owned firms. Klobertanz then instituted measures that helped people to see that they could successfully adopt the new approach.

In contrast to the initial focus of developing tension for change and building self-confidence, a change agent's primary role in the later stages of change is to continually reinforce positive action and to help keep commitment levels high.

At the most fundamental level, then, motivating people to become sustainable thinkers involves tapping into their deep-seated desire to achieve something they intrinsically value and building confidence in their ability to make the shift. Let's now apply these concepts to a stage-based approach to change and discuss the ways in which change agents can mobilize people to become sustainable thinkers.

Assess readiness for change

One of the first steps that a change agent should take is to assess the readiness of the individual or group they are working with to make a shift to sustainable thinking. This involves determining their current stage of change and their confidence level in the ability to adopt sustainable thinking. If a formal approach is possible, electronic or written surveys can be used. When a change agent is working in a more informal setting, readiness for change can be determined by casually asking the set of simple questions described below.

It's best to be as specific as possible when describing the thinking and behaviours that are the subject of change when measuring readiness for change. In a business setting, for example, this could range from the willingness to consider the carbon footprint of a purchasing decision to thinking about the long-term costs and benefits of a specific purchase, not just immediate needs. It could also include small actions, such the willingness to turn off computers and lights when not in use, and much more. In a home setting, the thinking and behaviours could include, for example, the willingness to install monitors that allow residents to observe their energy use in real time, to reducing energy use from 'plug loads', which is utility speak for lighting and electrical outlet usage that can be directly controlled by individuals. The more specific and easy to understand the definition and criteria are for measuring the cognitive or behavioural changes of interest, the easier it is to determine readiness for change. When using formal surveys, simple true/false or a five-choice response format (e.g. 1 to 5 scale, with 1 being never and 5 being always) are helpful for soliciting clear responses to questions (Reed et al, 1997, pp57–66).

At the beginning of a sustainable thinking change effort, however, the desired cognitive and behavioural changes are not always known. In this case, focus on the issues of interest, such as energy efficiency, renewable energy, food purchasing and the like, and try to be as specific as you can when asking the questions.

An individual or group can often be in a different stage of readiness on different climate and sustainability issues. They might, for example, be in the doing stage on recycling, but still be disinterested in altering their mode of transportation to reduce their greenhouse gas emissions. One way of addressing this issue is to repeat the questions discussed below for each of the behaviours that is of interest.

Given the many causes of global warming and other sustainability issues, however, it's likely that the shift to sustainable thinking will often involve multiple cognitive and behavioural changes. An alternative approach is therefore to develop a 'construct', which is a word or phrase that can be used to incorporate a number of activities under one umbrella, and then to ask people about their readiness for change in relation to the construct. 'Pro-climate' or 'carbon neutral', for example, could be used as constructs to describe a suite of specific cognitive and behavioural activities aimed at planning long term, considering full life-cycle effects, increasing energy efficiency, shifting to renewable energy, and taking other steps to become climate positive.

Make sure that the specific activities that a construct describes are internally consistent. For example, activities encapsulated under the construct of 'waste free' should all relate to eliminating gaseous, solid or hazardous waste. If the specific cognitive or behavioural elements of an overall construct are described to an individual prior to asking about their readiness for change, they can usually provide credible responses.

The questions listed at the close of Chapter 6 can form the basis of a simple climate and sustainability change readiness analysis. Tailor them to your situation. Each question asks about a time frame. Although more detailed information about the frequency and intensity of the use of new thinking and behaviour is always helpful, this points out that one way of making an initial determination of readiness for change is to find out how long into the future an individual or group expects that it will take before they actively engage in sustainable thinking, or the length of time that they have already been engaged.

For example, if people say that they have taken no steps in the past six months to engage in the specific activities of interest and have no plans to do so in the next six months, they can be considered to be in the disinterest stage of change. If people say that they intend to take action within six months, they can be classified as being in the deliberation stage of change. If they intend to take action within the next month or so, they can be placed in the design stage of change. If people say that they have taken some steps within the past six months, they can be considered to be in the doing stage. And if they have been engaged in activities for longer than six months, it's probably safe to assume that they are in the defending stage of change.

Understanding the readiness for change of an individual or group allows a change agent to focus their efforts on the change mechanisms that are best suited for the stages people are in. Thus, if the individual or group with whom you are working is in the stage of disinterest, begin with the change mechanisms appropriate for this stage. If most are in the design phase, however, don't mess with the processes involved with previous stages. Instead, start with the mechanisms that are most helpful when people are designing an action plan for change.

Let's now explore the role of a change agent in each of the stages involved with the 5-D staged approach to sustainable thinking. Each of the change techniques discussed in the following section were discussed in Chapter 6. I will therefore not repeat all of the details here. Refer to Chapter 6 for more detail as needed.

THE DISINTEREST STAGE OF CHANGE

CHANGE MECHANISMS FOR DISINTEREST

- Disturbances
- Awareness-building
- Choice expansion
- Supportive relationships

Recall that disinterested people are in the 'I won't change' stage of the transition to sustainable thinking. They often lack information about climate change and other issues of sustainability, as well as their own personal contribution to the problems, and do their best to remain uninformed.

Why do people remain disinterested? One reason is that it seems safe. Maintaining a state of disinterest means that they can't fail, nor do they have to expend energy. People are also free of guilt because if they don't acknowledge environmentally or socially harmful practices, they have nothing to feel guilty about. In addition, people who are disinterested are free from social pressure to think and act differently. After rebuffing others a few times, they will often give up and leave you alone (Prochaska et al, 1994).

Rather than feeling discouraged or irritated with disinterested people, a change agent should remember that the individual is merely in the very early stage of change. The change agent's challenge is to learn why the individual may be disinterested and then use mechanisms that address their concerns in a constructive manner. Recall that at least four types of defence mechanisms reinforce disinterest, which in Chapter 7 were summarized as the four Rs: reluctance, rebellion, resignation and rationalization (Miller and Rollnick, 2002). As a change agent your job is to diffuse resistance to change by matching the change mechanisms that are most beneficial in this stage with the primary defence mechanisms employed by the individual or group.

Role of the change agent

The key change mechanisms in this stage include the use of disturbances to demonstrate the risks of existing thought and behavioural patterns, building awareness of the benefits of climate-positive sustainable thinking, expanding knowledge of the wide range of choices available for engaging in sustainable thinking, and developing supportive relationships. Through these processes the change agent's primary goal at this stage is to help people acknowledge the desirability and benefits of new ways of perceiving and responding to the world.

Recall that individuals who are *reluctantly* disinterested in adopting climate-positive sustainable thinking and behaviours usually lack knowledge of the causes, risks or solutions to global warming and other issues of sustainability, fear change, or are content with their current situation. As previously mentioned, my father-in-law falls into this category.

The development of a supportive relationship usually forms the starting point for helping the reluctant individual. They need someone to share their concerns with, listen to them, and make them believe that change is possible without great discomfort. Pointing out the risks that an individual faces which a major disturbance may have unveiled, sharing information to build awareness of the causes and solutions to sustainability challenges, and expanding awareness of a variety of small steps that can be taken to reduce those risks can then be used to build tension between their current state and a different future. These mechanisms can help move reluctant individuals out of their comfort zones towards change.

Although a reluctant individual may sometimes quickly move to the deliberation stage of change after experiencing these change mechanisms, more often than not reluctant people change very slowly (Miller and Rollnick, 2002). Although my wife and I have talked about the likely impacts of climate change with my father-in-law, for example, he has taken no action to improve the energy consumption of his house or in other ways reduce his emissions. Be patient and don't push too hard too fast.

Rebellious disinterested individuals often have a good deal of knowledge about global warming and other issues of sustainability and even about how they may be contributing to the problems. However, they are usually very emotionally invested in their current behaviours and therefore resist all suggestions that a change may be beneficial. For example, much as US auto executives often do when they oppose raising fuel efficiency standards, rebellious individuals frequently provide a list of reasons why instigating a change does not make sense.

It's usually best for change agents to allow rebellious individuals to vent their feelings and then try to direct their energy in a constructive direction. Using disturbances to help them see the risks of maintaining their current approaches, and encouraging them to explore a variety of small steps that they can take to make the shift towards climate protection and sustainability, are some of the best ways in which to engage rebellious individuals.

If a rebellious individual decides to shift direction, they often throw the full weight of their energy behind their effort and make a good deal of progress (Miller and Rollnick, 2002). Can you imagine the tremendous forces that would be mobilized, for instance, if US auto executives turned a new leaf and directed their efforts towards producing only super-high-mileage hybrids, electric, biodiesel or hydrogen vehicles (or, even better, developing altogether new ways to move people and goods around)?

People who are disinterested in change because they are *resigned* to their fate have given up hope that they can make the shift to sustainable thinking or are overwhelmed by climate change and other sustainability challenges. Resigned individuals often say that climate protection efforts should focus on other people, such as youth, because it is too late for them to make a change. People in this state of mind need hope and increased confidence in their ability to succeed (Miller and Rollnick, 2002). The friend of mine who felt defeated after he failed to realize that the compact fluorescent light bulbs he purchased would not work with dimmer switches falls into this category.

Exploring the barriers to change often helps resigned individuals to see that although the downsides may be difficult to overcome, they are not insurmountable. For example, change agents can point out that multiple attempts are usually required before people successfully make a change, so setbacks do not mean failure. Sharing a wide range of options and encouraging the resigned individual to take small steps, such as turning the temperature down slightly on their hot water heater or shifting to (the right type of) compact fluorescent or light-emitting diode (LED) light bulbs, can help to build their confidence one step at a time. Soliciting from the individual examples of difficulties that they overcame in the past and pointing out that their past success indicates they have the capacity to succeed again in the future is also helpful.

Disinterested *rationalizing* individuals resist change because they believe they have figured out how to avoid harm caused by global warming, ecological degradation and related social distress, or they blame other people for the problems. Because it is their thinking that they are invested in, rationalizers usually come across as having all of the answers and will often debate change point by point. The senior government official in my community who believed global warming would be a good thing symbolizes this type of individual. He constantly challenged every concern people raised about climate change with arguments obviously taken from the websites of climate sceptics. For this reason, rational arguments are usually not the best approach with rationalizers because they will simply turn them upside down and use facts and figures to strengthen their own position.

Instead, the best approach for working with rationalizers is normally to keep an eye out for disturbances that can be used to help them see the flaws in their thinking. Decision balance scales, such as the one discussed in Chapter 7, can also be helpful here. Talking about the benefits of their current thinking and behaviour often makes rationalizers more willing to admit that downsides also exist. When using decision balance scales, however, the change agent needs to avoid any hint of implicitly trying to emphasize the downsides of the rationalizers' thinking and behaviour. Let the individual reach his or her own conclusion (Miller and Rollnick, 2002).

When working with people who exhibit any of these defence mechanisms, remember that the faith that a change agent demonstrates in the ability of others to change will influence the confidence level of those individuals to make a shift. No matter how intransient they may seem, change agents should therefore always exude confidence in the ability of others to become sustainable thinkers.

Tips for change agents

As a change agent, you can be an important source of support and motivation for people as they consider whether or not to alter their current thought and behavioural patterns. You can also be instrumental in encouraging them to partner with someone whom they trust to share their concerns and decide if moving towards sustainable thinking may be something they want to consider. Here are some tips for change agents as they seek to motivate people to consider engaging in sustainable thinking.

Motivate, don't advocate

Each of the approaches just discussed involves intensifying the tension required for people to become motivated to alter their thinking and behaviour. This does not mean, however, that a change agent should argue for adopting sustainable thinking. Many people who want to help others become sustainable thinkers have a built-in desire to make the world a better place. That's important because it takes passion to bring about change. This drive, however, can also cause change agents to become overly zealous with people who are not ready to make a shift.

Take extra caution not to impose your own agenda on others, come across as the expert, take sides, label, blame or purport to know what others should do. Each of these behaviours is likely to enflame resistance mechanisms. The harder you push, the harder others will push back.

Instead, change agents should seek to diffuse the defences that people hold, tap into their instinctive internal desire to make things right, and help them begin to voice their own arguments for change.

Be constantly empathetic

Anyone who desires to motivate others to change their thinking and behaviour about the climate and other issues of sustainability must accept people as they are.

Acceptance does not mean concurrence or consent. It means having compassion for others. The belief in the economy as an amoral machine has been drummed into people since childhood. Cultural forces, advertising and the media reinforce iron-cage thinking and make the myopic unsustainable take–make–waste economic model seem like the only viable option.

It is very important for change agents to genuinely accept that people have done the best they can, given the structures they live within and their perception of these structures. Ironically, accepting people as they are tends to free them to change, while implicitly or explicitly suggesting that they are stupid or ignorant tends to freeze them in their existing condition.

Listen appreciatively

Appreciative listening, also called reflective listening, is one of the most important skills that can be used at this stage – and throughout every stage of the change process. Appreciative listening does not involve interpreting, analysing, questioning, probing, sympathizing or reassuring others. The essential ingredient of appreciative listening is simply to serve as a mirror for the speaker.

Paraphrasing, which is a concise response to a speaker that summarizes the essence of their substantive comments in the listener's own words, is an important tool in appreciative listening. People have a certain meaning or intent behind the words and phrases they use. Often the significance is encoded and people don't say exactly what they mean. An appreciative listener must hear the words, try to decipher the intent, and then feed back to the speaker a statement that summarizes a best guess as to their meaning in a way that makes it clear you want to know if you have understood them correctly.

Appreciative summary statements are not questions. They are statements of understanding. After listening to an individual share his or her views on climate change, you might respond with the reflective statement: 'You are not convinced that global warming is a problem.' This is very different than: 'So, you are not convinced that global warming is real?' The statement allows the speaker to affirm or clarify what they mean, and then continue on. The question, on the other hand, is likely to produce defensiveness. The difference is in the inflection of your voice. Appreciative listening statements help a speaker to know that they are being understood and encourage them to continue on and go deeper. They do not create roadblocks (Rodgers, 1961).

Breaking through defences

If a change agent has skilfully employed the mechanisms described here, the individual or group with whom they are working may begin to feel sufficiently concerned about their current thinking and behaviour that they are willing to at least consider alternatives. When this occurs, the individual has progressed to the deliberation stage of change.

THE DELIBERATION STAGE OF CHANGE

CHANGE MECHANISMS FOR DELIBERATION

- Continued awareness-building
- Continued choice expansion
- Continued supportive relationships
- Emotional inspiration
- Self-appraisal

This is the 'I might change' stage of the transition to sustainable thinking. Individuals in this stage acknowledge the possibility that their old thinking and behavioural patterns may no longer be effective or sufficient. They therefore deliberate over whether or not to adopt a new approach. However, they are not ready to make a change. Because their awareness is just beginning to grow, people in deliberation still have a difficult time understanding the causes, risks or steps they can take to address global warming and other issues of sustainability. Oscillation consequently occurs, which means they go back and forth between wanting and not wanting to alter their thinking and behaviour in order to protect the climate, natural environment and social well-being.

It is important to note that even though people may not make overt changes in the deliberation stage, many subtle internal changes may be occurring. Their level of awareness may be growing, for instance, and they may be making subtle changes in their thinking. These adjustments provide a platform for progress to the next stage of change. A change agent's role is therefore to help the individual enhance these internal changes and resolve their oscillation.

Oscillation

One of the most important skills that a change agent can develop is the capacity to work with oscillation. Remember, it is the gap between an individual's existing condition and a desired state that produces the tension needed to stimulate change. Without this tension, no motivation will exist. Oscillation is therefore a natural process. It is often verbalized as 'Yes, but ...' statements. Who amongst us has not felt drawn to a change, then become nervous and backed away? People who are not considering a change have no reason to oscillate back and forth about whether or not to do so. This type of approach–withdrawal behaviour is therefore usually a good sign because it means an individual is considering the possibility of making a change.

People oscillate because they have not yet decided if the costs of inaction outweigh the benefits. This means that when in the midst of deliberation, people may be filled with contradictions such as: 'I know I should sell my SUV, but I'm not sure it's the right time.' Oscillation often comes across as resistance; but this is not necessarily what is going on. It is more directly associated with the process of considering the pros and cons of a change.

People can live in a state of oscillation for quite some time. Helping an individual to resolve this is therefore a primary goal of change agents. Sometimes, just a little nudge pushes an individual off the dime and enables them to decide to change. More often, a larger effort is needed.

Role of the change agent

A change agent should use the change mechanisms best suited for this stage to assist a deliberating individual to consider the risks associated with their current thinking and behaviour, and the potential benefits of sustainable thinking: awareness-building, choice expansion, supportive relationships, emotional inspiration and self-appraisal. The underlying goal is to help the deliberator identify their most cherished goals and values and determine if their current thought and behavioural patterns will allow them to attain those aspirations. This process creates the tension needed to mobilize change. At the same time, change agents must build confidence that steps can be taken to successfully resolve the tension.

In order to help the individual or group make this determination, change agents should continue to encourage them to obtain accurate information about how global warming and other issues of sustainability are likely to affect their family, community and themselves. It is also important to provide feedback about how their use of one or more of the sustainability thinking blunders, or the lack of sustainable ethical decisions may come back to haunt them, their families and others whom they care about in the future. This type of feedback can be very powerful.

Emotional inspiration

Also important is the use of emotional inspiration. Change agents should continue to encourage the individual or group with whom they are working to experience the stress of seeing first hand, or at least imagining, the negative effects of global warming and other sustainability crises on their family, friends, children or themselves. Similarly, people should be encouraged to experience the positive feelings associated with taking steps to resolve the issues.

Self-appraisal

As discussed in Chapter 7, perhaps the most important change mechanism in the deliberation stage of change is self-appraisal. The people or group with whom a change agent is working should be helped to decide whether their current thinking and behaviour allow them to live in accordance with their highest values and achieve their most important goals. This can be accomplished by asking evocative questions. The techniques described in Chapter 7 can be used for these purposes.

Identify the benefits of sustainable thinking

Remember that people continue to oscillate back and forth between wanting and not wanting to engage in sustainable thinking because the benefits and downsides of doing so seem relatively equal in their minds. Whenever a change agent helps people to acknowledge that a gap exists between their deepest aspirations and current patterns, they should also help them to surface and understand the benefits of new patterns. The job of the change agent is therefore to assist deliberating people in resolving oscillation by building up the benefits of sustainable thinking until they see the pros as significantly greater than the cons. As mentioned, this usually requires a two-to-one ratio where the individual sees twice as many benefits to sustainable thinking for every downside. Making a list of benefits, as outlined in Chapter 7, is a good way to start the process.

Build confidence in the ability to change

At the same time, a change agent must take explicit steps to instil in people the belief that they can make the changes needed to relieve the tension between their desired way of thinking and behaving and their current patterns (Miller and Rollnick, 2002). For example, change agents can help people to see that the obstacles to adopting sustainable thinking which may appear overwhelming to them now are mostly temporary and may even have upsides that they have not considered. Making a list of the perceived obstacles, in the form of the downsides of adopting sustainable thinking, using techniques to reframe them in positive ways, and using the decision balance scale exercise described in Chapter 7 can be very effective at this stage. In addition, change agents can help the individual or group to become aware of the qualities that allowed them to successfully work through previous problems and then point out that those attributes are the same ones needed to make the shift to sustainable thinking.

Encourage responsibility and making a choice

After the individual or group has identified their most cherished goals and values, compared them with their current condition, and analysed the pros and cons of becoming a sustainable thinker, they should be encouraged to make a choice. If they decide that they want to become a climate-positive sustainable thinker, they are ready to move to the design stage. If the individual is not ready to make the shift, change agents should make sure that the individual knows this is OK. In fact, they should understand that oscillation is perfectly natural. Some people need a long time to think about making a major change before they are ready to act. Be understanding and empathetic. Share an example of a time when you were not ready for change to show them that you understand how they feel. Encourage the individual to step back and take a break. Then, ask them to review their list of pros and cons sometime in the future and see if additional benefits of becoming a sustainable thinker come to mind.

Tips for change agents

Listen for change talk

I have already said that the way in which people think and talk about change goes a long way towards determining their success. Throughout the processes just described, change agents should communicate in a way that brings forth the individual's own reasons for becoming a sustainable thinker. Four types of change talk are common (Miller and Rollnick, 2002).

- *Disadvantages of their existing thinking and behaviour*
  This type of change statement acknowledges that the status quo no longer seems acceptable. Comments such as: 'The use of my SUV may be a problem' or 'Using this much energy in our home is not representative of the type of person I want to be' symbolizes this type of talk. Although they may not explicitly acknowledge that a problem exists, the individual will voice discomfort with their current state.
- *Advantages of sustainable thinking and behaviour*
  The flip side of the previous form of change talk occurs when an individual starts to mention the potential benefits of making a change. 'Buying a hybrid vehicle may turn out better for me than I thought' illustrates this type of language.
- *Confidence in the ability to change*
  These types of comments demonstrate that an individual is confident they can make a change. 'Cutting my household energy use does not seem that hard' or 'I'm sure I can walk or bike to work once a week' are the type of comments you might hear when someone feels optimistic about their chances of becoming a sustainable thinker.
- *Intention to change*
  As motivation for change builds in people, they often begin to talk about their goals and desire to address global warming and other issues of sustainability, or describe what sustainable thinking would be like for them. No matter if the commitment level is modest or strong, when an individual begins to voice the intention to change, things are looking up.

When people begin to voice these types of messages, they are in the process of considering a change to sustainable thinking.

Elicit change talk

Change agents can help people voice their internal thoughts about their interest in becoming a sustainable thinker through the use of several techniques (Miller and Rollnick, 2002).

- *Ask open-ended questions*
  The most straightforward way of eliciting change talk is to ask open-ended questions. Sample questions for conjuring up each of the four types of change talk are offered in Box 9.1. Simply asking these questions, however, is not enough. Once a response is given, you must be empathetic and skilfully use your appreciative listening to allow the speaker to explore their thoughts and feelings.
- *Ask about worst-case scenarios*
  Asking an individual to describe the worst and best possible outcomes of their current thinking and activities can also trigger change talk. Questions such as: 'What concerns you the most about the effects of your behaviour on the climate, natural environment or communities?' and 'What might be the best results of your current behaviour on the climate, natural environment or communities?' can engage an individual in deliberative reflection and dialogue about their current situation.
- *Looking backward and forward*
  It can be helpful to ask an individual what their thought patterns were in the past when they made decisions that benefited the climate, environment or social well-being. Questions such as: 'How is it that you decided to buy a small fuel-efficient car rather than an SUV two years ago?' Looking back in time can create awareness of thought processes or values that individuals relied on to make sustainable decisions. Similarly, asking an individual to imagine what their thinking and behaviour might be like in the future if it were sustainable or, conversely, if it remained unsustainable can spur change talk. Questions such as: 'If you were going to adopt climate-positive thinking, how might you see your actions being different in the future?' or 'If you continue your existing patterns, what do you imagine your life or that of your children will be like ten years from now?' can provoke introspection and elicit change talk.

When an individual begins to voice change statements of this type, they are either beginning to resolve or have resolved their oscillation and are ready to move to the design stage of change. The more that a change agent can use open-ended

BOX 9.1 EXAMPLES OF OPEN-ENDED QUESTIONS TO ELICIT CHANGE TALK

Disadvantages of the status quo

- What worries you about the effects of your current way of thinking and behaviour regarding the climate, natural environment and social well-being?
- Why do you think you need to do something about the greenhouse gases your activities produce?
- What is it about your lifestyle's effect on the climate, natural environment or social well-being that you or other people might see as being of concern?
- What do you think will happen to the climate, natural environment or social well-being if you don't make a change?

Advantages of change

- In an ideal world, how would you like to improve your thinking or actions towards the climate, natural environment and social well-being?
- What would be positive outcomes about reducing your greenhouse gas emissions?
- What form would you ideally like your ecological and social footprint to take in one or two years?
- If you could think and act from a climate-positive sustainable perspective right now, how might things improve for you?

Optimism for change

- What makes you to think you can make the change to sustainable thinking if you want to?
- How confident are you that you can make the shift to sustainable thinking?
- What personal strengths do you have that can help you to make the change to sustainable thinking?
- How is this change similar to other changes you have made in the past?

Intention to change

- What are your thoughts now about making a change in thinking about the climate, natural environment and social well-being?
- You seem to be stuck – what needs to change to allow you to move forward?
- How important is becoming a sustainable thinker to you?
- What are you willing to try?

Source: Adapted from Miller and Rollnick (2002).

questions to elicit change statements from an individual, the quicker the individual is likely to progress to the design stage of change.

Dealing with resistance

As previously mentioned, some people don't seem to be able to make a decision about whether or not to engage in sustainable thinking. They are chronic oscillators. Although oscillation indicates that an individual is considering a change, resistance to change can also remain high. The way in which a sustainable thinking change agent responds to resistance is likely to have a significant effect on the ability of the person to successfully work through oscillation and move to the next stage of change.

Recall that both ecological and social systems are structured to maintain the status quo. It seems paradoxical that systems are naturally resistant to change while also having the innate ability to adapt to change. When you think about it, however, the reasons for this irony become clear. The feedback, self-maintenance and repair mechanisms that help a system to maintain equilibrium also aid it in 'righting' the ship when the structure of the system is altered and change is required. Resistance, then, is not bad. It is a natural and healthy life-sustaining attribute of ecological and human social systems.

When resistance arises, rather than pushing harder, it's usually best for change agents to relax and work with it. Be empathetic and use your appreciative listening skills. One of the best ways of being empathetic is to agree with an individual when they voice resistance, but to do so by slightly reframing the issue. If someone says, for example: 'You're probably going to tell me I need to sell my SUV. I don't respond well to that type of pressure', you can respond by stating: 'I agree it would be very irritating if I were to give you a list of things you should do to reduce your greenhouse gasses. Rest assured I have no intention of doing that. It's ironic that just thinking about things you could be doing differently often overwhelms your ability to consider any of them.'

Many other approaches can be used to work with, rather than against, resistance. One method is to take sides and advocate for the position of the resistant individual. This type of paradoxical approach is reverse psychology at its best. The idea is to defuse resistance by agreeing with the resistant individual. For instance, someone might say: 'I'm not sure I want to reduce the energy use in my house. It sounds like it will take quite a lot of time and money to buy new appliances, replace old windows and take other steps.' You can respond by saying something like: 'It's definitely possible that after spending a little time and money on it you may decide reducing your home energy use is too much trouble. It doesn't make sense to pursue these activities until you are serious about wanting to help resolve global warming.'

The idea behind paradoxical approaches is to make statements that exacerbate the current views of others almost to the point of absurdity. Hearing their thinking pushed to the edge often causes people to disagree with your statements because they realize they are too extreme. As people find themselves taking a different viewpoint, they often become open to altering their views on other issues as well.

The bottom line is that resistance is natural in every change process. The way in which a change agent handles it is likely to have a significant influence on whether the individual makes a commitment to change or whether their mind frame stays frozen.

THE DESIGN STAGE OF CHANGE

CHANGE MECHANISMS FOR DESIGN

- Continued self-appraisal
- Continued helping relationships
- Commitment

At some point a sufficient amount of tension has accumulated and individuals feel confident enough in their abilities that they decide to resolve the discrepancy by saying to themselves: 'I will change.' The next step in the change process is therefore to design a plan to shift to sustainable thinking and behaviour in the near term.

Just because an individual has decided to design a plan, however, does not mean they are ready to become a sustainable thinker. In this stage, people are usually still oscillating back and forth over whether or not to make the shift. They may oscillate, for example, because they still lack sufficient confidence in their ability to make the change. In fact, people may exhibit their most extensive oscillation during this stage because as they design a change plan they are mentally imagining what the changes would look and feel like so their interest in going that route can move up and down. For this reason, the individual needs to design a sustainable thinking action plan that is within their capabilities.

'Slower is faster and faster is slower' at this stage. The more a sustainable thinking change agent pushes an individual towards quick action, the more likely they are to trigger that person's defence mechanisms and set the process back.

Role of the change agent

The first task of the change agent is to determine the level of the individual's commitment to making the shift to sustainable thinking. An individual will often voice readiness to engage in sustainable thinking and behaviours, but in reality has not yet solidified his or her commitment to do so. Their action plan may therefore include goals that they are not capable of meeting, which will lead to setbacks that erode their confidence in the ability to change. Continued self-appraisal can be helpful here. Change agents can continue to ask open-ended questions to help individuals decide whether the status quo will allow them to attain their most cherished goals and live up to the values they hold dear.

After an assessment is completed, the next task of the change agent is to help the individual design a realistic and effective change strategy. The plan should be constructed to take into account the individual's capacity, their past history with change and other similar factors. It should include clearly stated sustainability goals that the individual seeks to attain, the strategies to be used to achieve those ends, expected results, and a way of evaluating progress. The plan should also include projections of possible obstacles and pre-planned methods for responding to them. For example, mechanisms should be outlined that will prevent individuals from adopting sustainability thinking blunders or sustainably unethical behaviours. These tools help to build the individual's self-confidence in the ability to succeed.

Working with oscillation

The way in which a change agent responds to oscillation at this point is critical because it often determines whether an individual moves through it and firmly commits to sustainable thinking or retreats back to deliberation. The continual use of appreciative listening here can allow an individual to go further and deeper in their exploration of what becoming a sustainable thinker would mean for them. Empathy provides the supportive environment to continue the exploration. It is also possible to encourage more movement by commenting on statements about the intent to change in an affirmative way ('That's a great idea'), asking open-ended questions, delving into worst-case scenarios, and asking for more information. Advocacy in any form, however, can produce the opposite effect by triggering resistance.

Resolving oscillation requires taking responsibility and making a choice

Ultimately, an individual resolves oscillation by making a choice about what's most important to them. They must take responsibility and decide if continuing the status quo is more important than making the changes needed to allow them to attain their deeply felt aspirations and live up to their core values. In short, the individual must consciously choose the results they want to see come into being.

A change agent can assist an individual in clarifying their choices by encouraging them to verbalize what they want. When an individual actually states, in so many words, something like: 'I have decided to buy a hybrid vehicle' or 'I will walk to work once a week in good weather', a choice has been made and they are ready to move on to the doing stage of the process. Change agents can ask, for example: 'Have you made a decision about what you plan to do?'

Once a choice has been made, change agents should encourage the individual to let others know. As discussed in Chapter 7, making a commitment public energizes and helps the individual to stay focused on the future.

THE DOING STAGE OF CHANGE

CHANGE MECHANISMS FOR DOING

- Continued commitment
- Continued helping relationships
- Reinforcement
- Substitution
- Structural redesign

After a credible action plan has been developed and the individual has shored up their commitment, they enter the 'I am changing' stage of the shift to sustainable thinking. This involves translating the change plan into real world action. Although this stage can be an exciting period for people, it can also be difficult. We all know people who fail to actualize things they have worked on for a long time. In my job teaching college students, I know some who complete almost all of their coursework, then drop out just before graduation. In my work as a trainer and consultant, I see many projects grow and blossom only to fall by the wayside at the last moment. Some people just have a hard time 'closing the deal'.

Numerous mistakes and setbacks should also be expected at this stage. Less than 20 per cent of people successfully change longstanding problem behaviours on the first try. Multiple efforts are therefore usually needed to adopt the right path. Failures can be depressing and cause people to think about giving up.

The first two months of any change initiative are the most likely time for backsliding. The most common cause of setbacks is lack of effective planning for the resistance an individual gets from the people around them, or the obstacles thrown in their path by the unsustainable nature of the economic or social systems that they deal with. Effective reinforcement as well as behavioural and cognitive substitution strategies are therefore needed, along with a plan to redesign the structure of the systems within which they live and work as much as possible.

Role of the change agent

The change agent at this stage should make it a point to support the efforts of the individual to think and act in a climate-positive sustainable manner. A major focus should be on reaffirming the decision they made to engage in sustainable thinking, acknowledging accomplishments and providing rewards. Change agents should also continually look for opportunities to reinforce positive steps that the individual takes to substitute sustainable behaviours for unsustainable ones. Each of these steps should be aimed at building the individual's confidence in their ability to overcome obstacles, come closer to achieving their desired goals and values, and continue forward.

Offering advice

Sometimes an individual may seek the advice of a change agent when they begin to implement their sustainable thinking action plan. Until this point, I have suggested that you do not offer suggestions and instead draw out the individual's own thoughts and words about the situation. At this stage, however, if the individual gives you permission by asking for advice, you can offer suggestions as long as your real intent is to help expand the person's commitment to sustainable thinking, not to blow your own horn, pressure them or in other ways trigger their resistance mechanisms.

Change agents can guard against these risks by putting a caveat in front of each piece of advice you offer, such as: 'I'm not sure this will work for you, but I can provide my sense of ...' or 'I can only offer my own opinion. It may or may not be relevant to your situation ...'. The important point is to take great care to avoid putting an individual in a situation where they feel the need to defend themselves, which is likely to cause backsliding into oscillation.

Don't confuse action and change

It is also important at this stage not to confuse action with change (Prochaska et al, 1994). People can get busy doing things, but do so merely to appease others and not to actually make the fundamental shift in thinking needed to sustain a change. This is how 'greenwash' often occurs. No real change is made – just surface-level activity that gives the appearance of adopting environmentally and socially sound thinking and behaviours. All too frequently change agents make the mistake of thinking that people who are taking action have made the transition to sustainable thinking. They consequently fail to provide the ongoing support needed to help the changer maintain their new thinking and behaviour over time. Backsliding is a serious risk when people confuse action with change.

THE DEFENDING STAGE OF CHANGE

CHANGE MECHANISMS FOR DEFENDING

- Continued commitment
- Continued helping relationships
- Continued reinforcement
- Continued substitution
- Advanced structural redesign

After six months or so of active practice with climate-positive sustainable thinking and behaviour, the individual moves into the 'I have changed' stage of the transformation process. People must now defend their new approach to the climate, natural environment and social well-being against resistance from others and numerous obstacles long enough to allow them to become routine. Mistakes and setbacks are a certainty and people must work hard to keep their energy and commitment high, while preventing backsliding. If, however, an effective plan has been constructed and people have a sense of how to respond to resistance, setbacks will not be fatal. One step backwards can reveal important lessons that lead to two steps forward.

Role of the change agent

Sometimes people never look back once they start down the path of sustainable thinking and no longer need the help of a change agent. In this case, change agents should take credit for a job well done.

The most common cause of further involvement is often a setback that causes people to seek help in determining what to do. When a crisis occurs, the change agent should help the individual see that mistakes are natural, not a sign of failure, and that they provide an opportunity to learn and improve. Make the point that the knowledge and experience that the individual has gained through his or her efforts still exist. Encourage them to use double-loop learning methods, which will be discussed in the next chapter, to assess why the setback occurred and then to design a plan to resolve the issue and prevent it from being repeated.

As in the doing stage, the most common cause of setbacks here is the inability to plan effectively for resistance from others and for the obstacles produced by the unsustainable nature of the systems within which the individual lives or works. The change agent should therefore help the individual to continually assess those structures, and to make and continually update strategies for redesigning these new structures.

Through these steps, the change agent should help the individual renew his or her commitment to sustainable thinking and mobilize the energy to continue forward.

MAINTAINING MOMENTUM

The role that change agents play in motivating others to embrace sustainable thinking cannot be overstated. Often, the initial changes people make in their thinking and behaviour leads to deeper and deeper understanding of the causes, risks and solutions to global warming and other issues of sustainability and increased awareness of what they can do to help resolve the problems. Just as Rusty Rexius did, people often begin to continually think about how to reduce their environmental and social footprints. Time and again, sustainable thinking stimulates continual growth and change in people.

Change agents therefore play a very special role. By building motivation for change in others, you can help to launch a whole new movement towards climate protection and sustainability.

NOTE

1   Much of this chapter is based on the principles and concepts of *Motivational Interviewing* (Miller and Rollnick, 2002).

REFERENCES

Miller, W. and Rollnick, R. (2002) *Motivational Interviewing: Preparing People for Change*, Guilford Press, New York

Prochaska, J. O., Norcross, J. C. and Diclemente, C. C. (1994) *Changing for Good*, HarperCollins Publishers, New York

Reed, G. R., Velicer, W. F., Prochaska, J. O., Rossi, J. S. and Marcus, B. H. (1997) 'What makes a good staging algorithm: Examples from regular exercise', in *Methods, Issues, and Results in Evaluation and Research: American Journal of Health Promotion*, September/October, vol 12, no 1, pp57–66

Rodgers, C. (1961) *On Becoming a Person: A Therapist's View of Psychotherapy*, Houghton Mifflin, Boston

10

Motivating Teams and Organizations To Thinking Sustainably

The pessimist sees the difficulty in every opportunity; an optimist sees the opportunity in every difficulty.

Sir Winston Churchill

A few years back the mayor of my hometown, Eugene, Oregon, asked me to coordinate a project designed to engage local business and government leaders in sustainability. After years of warfare between environmental and business interests, the community had stagnated and Mayor Kitty Piercy was looking for a way to bring people together around a mutually positive agenda. After assessing the community's readiness to engage in sustainability, I concluded that we could not succeed just by motivating key individuals to engage in sustainable thinking. The Sustainable Business Initiative (SBI), as the venture came to be known, needed to foster change within the community's key business and government organizations.

Ray Anderson, Sue Klobertanz and Larry Chalfan came to similar conclusions. To successfully engage in climate protection and sustainability, they knew they needed to go beyond key individuals and alter the way in which their entire organization perceived the world and made decisions.

Organizations move through a similar series of stages as individuals do whenever they make a fundamental shift in thinking and behaviour. Catalysing change within groups, however, is a whole different kettle of fish than motivating individuals to think and behave in ways that protect the climate, natural environment and social well-being.

Because two or more people involved together constitute a social system, groups of people, whether they are a small group of friends, or a business, government or community organization, display properties that individuals on their own do not. For instance, social systems often display 'groupthink', which is the tendency to avoid honest analysis of issues in order to steer clear of conflict and maintain group cohesion (Janis, 1972). On the other hand, if groupthink can be avoided, the interaction that occurs between members of a social system can produce more imaginative ideas than any single individual can generate by him or herself. Group members can also serve as a check against the erroneous thinking of others. In this sense, teams and organizations have a mind of their own.

This chapter describes how an organizational mind frame comes about. It then examines how the 5-D staged approach to change can be used to mobilize individuals and teams to reorient the perspectives of their organizations towards sustainable thinking.

THE ORGANIZATIONAL MIND FRAME

Social systems are thinking organisms. Just as with individuals, organizations have mind frames that are composed of core beliefs, assumptions and automatic thoughts. A group's mind frame differs, however, from the cognitive views of any of its individual members. 'Culture' is a word often used to describe the mind frame of a team or organization.

An organization's mind frame, or culture, can be understood by its vision, values and norms. These shared perspectives synchronize thought patterns, perspectives and conduct across the group.

Vision denotes the sense of purpose and desired outcomes held by group members. It was during the Eugene SBI that I first met Rusty Rexius. It was during this process that I learned that prior to engaging in sustainability, a formal commitment to protecting the environment was not part of the vision of Rusty's company. After it made the transition, however, sustainability became an explicit organizational purpose and goal.

Values reflect beliefs about what is truly important. Some of the dominant values at Rexius Company are to ensure the continuation of the family business and to improve the community through its business practices and by giving back to those who support the company's existence.

Norms are the attitudes and behaviours required of participants. Group members are expected to conform to the organization's norms and failure to do so is usually a punishable offence. Honesty, commitment to the company, and excellent customer service are some of the core norms at Rexius Company.

Before reading further, take a moment to think about the mind frame – or culture – of your organization. First, list your sense of the group's vision, values and norms. Then, step back and speculate about how your colleagues are likely to see these issues. If a wide gap exists between your views and the way in which others are likely to see it, a discussion may be warranted among your group to clarify the differences. Box 10.1 can be used for this purpose.

HOW THE ORGANIZATIONAL MIND FRAME DEVELOPS

BOX 10.1 ORGANIZATIONAL CULTURE ASSESSMENT

- *Organizational vision.* What do you think is the overriding purpose and goal of your organization? _____
- *Organizational values.* What do you think the organization cares about most? _____

- *Organizational norms.* What attitudes and behaviours do you think your organization expects its members to demonstrate? _____

Just as ecological systems are shaped by the natural factors that surround them, an organization's mind frame is, in part, shaped by its external environment. Through the process of interacting with the exterior world and interpreting the feedback that it receives, groups begin to think and act in certain ways. At the same time, the way in which feedback is interpreted is influenced by the pre-existing beliefs, assumptions and automatic thoughts of its members, particularly those in positions of power. The thinking and behaviour of people involved in a group are also influenced by the information to which they have access, the power and authority they have to act, and the resources available to them to make things happen. These three factors constitute a group's governance system. Figure 10.1 describes a tripod of factors that form a governance system.

All too often, ineffective governance systems persist for a long time in organizations. Even though the conditions that the governance system was initially established to address have changed, the old system will persist for years. Inertia is part of the problem. However, the primary reason is usually that those who benefit from the existing governance system resist change because they do not want to relinquish those benefits, such as the power and authority that it provides.

Just as core beliefs and assumptions shape the way in which an individual sees the world, a team or organization's vision, values and norms constitute the lens through which group members interpret what they observe and experience. The world that an individual sees through the filters of their core beliefs and assumptions is, by definition, incomplete.

Similarly, unless they are extremely careful, the mind frame of an organization selectively screens incoming information, which means that it never obtains a true picture of reality. Instead, people must rely on second-hand information about the nature of the world around them, which often leads to erroneous assumptions and conclusions. Many organizations suffer from false feedback mechanisms.

During the Eugene SBI, I found that the city government had false feedback mechanisms related to their public involvement processes. City staff continually said

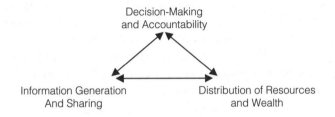

Figure 10.1 *Governance systems: A three-part interactive process*

Source: Doppelt (2003).

that 'we are very good with public involvement', while at the same time local citizens of all stripes would tell me that the city's processes were superficial and disingenuous. City staff was obviously listening only to who and what they wanted to hear.

GROUPTHINK

This is how groupthink materializes. Irvin Janis, one of the early researchers of the topic, described groupthink as a process that occurs when groups seek to maintain cohesion and avoid interpersonal tension by suppressing consideration of alternative views. Pressure is usually applied on anyone within the group who voices disagreement or fails to conform to the group views, seeing such behaviour as disloyal. Because of the fear of such social pressure, no one shares their true feelings if they conflict with group thinking. Because no one objects, an illusion of unanimity is maintained. Silence is viewed as agreement. And some group members usually make it their job to protect the group from information that might disrupt the group's cohesion (Janis, 1972).

Groupthink is a real risk in close-knit organizations, in groups that are isolated from outside influences, and in those who have homogeneous social backgrounds and ideology. Strong domineering leaders also tend to perpetuate groupthink because of their propensity to promote themselves and castigate those who may see things differently and threaten their authority (Janis, 1972).

Social systems caught in the grips of groupthink tend to exhibit certain types of behaviours. For example, they often believe they are invincible. As a result, they take extreme positions on issues and expose themselves to severe risks. Decisions that turn out badly are rationalized away or blamed on outsiders. Those in the grip of groupthink firmly believe they have moral authority (often issued directly by God), which leads them to ignore the environmental, social, ethical (and spiritual) consequences of their actions. Negative stereotypes are constructed about outsiders that serve to reinforce the group's belief in their superiority. In the most extreme cases, groupthink leads to the use of political or physical force or violence to persuade non-believers. The longer a social system is caught in the grips of groupthink, the harder it is to break free and the worse will be its decisions and outcomes.

Groupthink seems to be pervasive throughout the world today. Extremist groups such as al-Qaeda are clearly controlled by groupthink. However, so is the US auto industry (as demonstrated by their continued joint opposition to higher fuel-efficiency standards, using the same arguments the industry used during the 1970s, which proved to be dead wrong even then), the George W. Bush administration on climate policy (and, some would say, in almost every way it functions), and even many organizations taking steps to reduce their impacts on the climate, natural environment and social well-being.

Organizations controlled by groupthink are blind to the effects of their actions on the systems upon which they are ecologically, socially and economically dependent. Sustainable thinking blunders naturally result. It does not appear to me that the profound consequences of groupthink on the climate or other issues of sustainability are adequately understood. Unless sustainable thinking change agents assist the organizations with which they are involved to avoid groupthink, I fear this harmful pattern will block progress towards climate protection and sustainability, or produce even worse outcomes, such as wars.

Take a moment to ponder the extent to which your team or organization suffers from groupthink. Antidotes will be discusses at the close of this chapter.

CHANGING TEAM AND ORGANIZATIONAL MIND FRAME TO AVOID GROUPTHINK

In one of my previous books, *Leading Change Toward Sustainability: A Change Management Guide for Business, Government and Civil Society* (Doppelt, 2003), I identified seven key levers for altering the mind frame of an organization. These are described in Figure 10.2. The seven interventions correspond nicely with the stages of change discussed in this book. These leverage points constitute what I call the 'wheel of organizational change towards sustainability'. I will not repeat all of the details here that are described in *Leading Change*. Instead, I will provide a summary of the interventions and discuss how they can be used within the context of a staged approach to motivate organizations in adopting sustainable thinking and in protecting the climate, natural environment and social well-being.

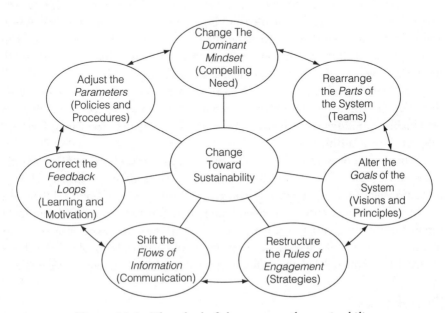

Figure 10.2 *The wheel of change towards sustainability*

Source: Doppelt (2003).

The disinterest stage of change

'Wheel of Change Towards Sustainability' intervention 1: Change the dominant mindset through the imperative of climate protection and sustainability

STAGE-BASED CHANGE MECHANISMS FOR DISINTEREST

- Disturbances
- Awareness-building
- Choice expansion
- Supportive relationships

Recall that in this stage of change people either deny that a problem exists, are unaware of the negative effects of their thinking and behaviour, believe the consequences are minimal, or have little confidence that they can successfully make a shift. In short, they are disinterested in becoming sustainable thinkers and business as usual remains the norm. No matter what new policies or programmes are established, if the mind frame of an organization is anchored in the myopic take–make–waste mental model, little progress will be made towards climate protection and sustainability.

Undermining an organization's controlling mental frame is therefore a vital step in moving towards sustainable thinking. Unless the dominant beliefs, values and norms of its members are challenged and people become aware of the team or organization's affects on the climate, natural environment and people, they will not move beyond disinterest to the next stage of change.

The change mechanisms that are most useful at this stage are similar to those that can be employed to motivate other people, and yourself, to shift to sustainable thinking: disturbances, awareness-building, choice expansion and supportive relationships.

Senior executives must eventually fully support the effort and be actively engaged. However, I find that lower and mid-level staff often initiate climate protection and sustainability change efforts and slowly expand them until they gain support from top executives. Top-level support is thus not essential to launch a sustainable thinking initiative. Change can start anywhere in the organization. Unit managers and specially assigned change agents often provide much of the direct service delivery once the change effort is formally endorsed by senior executives.

Disturbances

Just as with individual change, a disturbance of some type often serves as the genesis for re-examining the controlling organizational mind frame. In a private firm it could be threats to their market base posed by customers wanting to do business with a company that takes environmental and social welfare issues seriously. It could also be a chemical spill or other accident that causes a public outcry or leads to a fine from a government agency. In a public agency, the disturbance could be a natural disaster such as a major drought that makes the inadequacy of the team or organization's current mind frame obvious to all. Or it could be an egregious violation of human rights in the community that raises awareness of the need to address social equity issues.

Organizational leaders should continually be on the lookout for events that can serve as mind-frame altering disturbances. When they occur, rather than adopting a bunker mentality, leaders should seize the opportunity to help people see that the way in which the team or organization perceives and responds to the world has placed it at grave risk and that taking steps to alter the mind frame will benefit the organization as a whole and each of its members. Leaders should also make clear that protecting the climate and adopting a path towards sustainability is fully consistent with the team or organization's mission and values and that they are currently not meeting the standards they hold for themselves. These messages can be delivered through speeches by senior executives, discussions at staff meetings, internal memos, newsletters, intranet systems and other means.

Awareness-building

If team or organizational leaders use a major disturbance to open people to the possibility of change, group members will often become willing to consider new information about the causes, consequences and solutions to global warming, environmental degradation and social distress. They may also be willing to examine the role their organization plays in creating or exacerbating the problems through their use of sustainability thinking blunders, ethically unsustainable decisions, or other activities. Awareness-building is vital to move the members of an organization out of disinterest to the next stage of change. The goal is increased mindfulness. Talks by senior executives, guest speakers knowledgeable about the subjects, a constant stream of memos and bulletins, and other such actions can help build awareness of the risks and opportunities posed by global warming and other sustainability issues, as well as improve their connection to the organization's thinking and activities.

Employees can also be asked to complete change readiness assessments that measure people's knowledge of the issues, as well as their stage of change regarding them. By learning about climate change, environmental degradation and social distress and then answering questions describing their personal perspectives on these issues, people often become willing to consider a new approach. The information gathered through the assessments can then be used to design staged-based change programmes specifically tailored to where people are within specific units of the organization.

Choice expansion

Fear of failure often causes people to be back away from challenging the dominant beliefs, assumptions and norms of their team or organization. Helping line staff as well as decision-makers understand that they don't have to alter everything all at once, and providing them with a wide diversity of steps that they can take, often helps them to relax their defences and consider the possibility of new directions. Change agents should identify a menu of options that each unit within the organization can pursue in order to engage in sustainable thinking.

Supportive relationships

It is also important in this early stage of change to establish ways for people to share their angst about shifting their own and the organization's culture and activities. People can be encouraged to buddy up and talk with their supervisor or trusted co-workers. If one exists, the human resources department can also help. Special programmes can also be offered to help people cope with the stress of change.

Highlight the advantages of change

Remember that the ultimate goal of the mechanisms used in this stage of change is to build recognition of the need for the benefits of engaging in climate protection and sustainability. Change agents can make a list of the benefits of sustainable thinking for the team or organization with whom they are working. A sample list of benefits developed during the Eugene SBI for city government is provided in Box 10.2. Some of the benefits apply to the organization as a whole, while others apply just to specific units. For example, benefits for the facilities

---

BOX 10.2 SAMPLE BENEFITS FOR A LOCAL GOVERNMENT OF ENGAGING IN SUSTAINABILITY

- New strategies and techniques can be learned.
- Sustainable measures will help to reduce energy and water use and save money.
- The community will become more resilient to economic, social and environmental stresses.
- Public awareness will help to retain and attract leading-edge businesses.
- Creative young people who want to live in a progressive environment will be attracted by a sustainable community.
- Employees will become more excited about their work.
- Top-level employees will be drawn to local government.
- A sustainable community can become a leader in its field and share what it knows with other communities.

division emphasized new ways of reducing energy and water use and, thus, saving money, while the benefits for the community development department highlighted the new jobs that can be created in the community. Change agents should help people to identify unit-specific as well as organization-wide benefits.

Identify the team and organizational defences

Although it's important to identify the benefits of engaging in sustainable thinking, it is equally important to examine the defences that the team or organization uses to prevent people from becoming more knowledgeable about the issues. When a team or organization is disinterested in sustainable thinking, it often establishes explicit (but more often implicit) mechanisms that prevent its members from learning about the causes and consequences of, or solutions to, the issues. It is tough to make good decisions without good information. If the group screens out information that is inconsistent with their core beliefs and assumptions, they will only be fooling themselves.

Table 10.1 *Sample local government organizational defences*

Defence	Global warming	Environmental degradation	Social distress
Denying (Ignoring evidence)	It's not happening/ it's a natural phenomenon.	We don't have much impact upon the environment.	People are becoming wealthier, not poorer.
Reluctance (We don't know enough)	We need to know a lot more before we do anything.	We don't see how we can make a difference.	We tried to help in the past but failed.
Resignation (We are powerless)	We can't do anything to reduce our greenhouse gas emissions.	Our impacts are too small to make a difference.	Poverty will always be with us.
Rebelliousness (Don't tell us what to do)	We'll do something only when we decide it's worth it.	It's not our responsibility.	People need to take care of themselves.
Rationalization (I know doing)	Global warming will be good for the local area.	Our goods and services are not a problem.	These are problems in other regions of the world, not here.

Source: Adapted from Prochaska et al (1994).

Change agents can make a list of the defences that the group uses to block the inflow of credible information about global warming, environmental degradation or social distress, and the organization's possible role in exacerbating those problems. As with benefits, the defences may vary by unit and division, although the organization as a whole is likely to exhibit consistent patterns. Share the list with key individuals and ask them how they see the issues. The goal should be to elicit a discussion, not to create defensiveness. The more that people become aware of their team or organization's defences, the greater is the likelihood that they can be overcome. Table 10.1 offers an example of the defence mechanisms we identified within the City of Eugene during the SBI.

Decide if a change is warranted

By listing the benefits of change and acknowledging the defences that the organization uses to prevent people from becoming better informed, group members are likely to decide that sufficient risk or opportunity exists to consider the possibility of engaging in sustainable thinking and behaviours.

The deliberation stage of change

'Wheel of Change Towards Sustainability' intervention 2: Rearrange the parts of the system by organizing inclusive and powerful climate and sustainability transition teams

---

STAGE-BASED CHANGE MECHANISMS FOR DELIBERATION

- Awareness-building
- Choice expansion
- Supportive relationships
- Emotional inspiration
- Organizational appraisal

When group members begin to see the potential benefits of altering their team or organization's way of seeing and operating in the world, they will begin to deliberate over the benefits and drawbacks of a new direction. This does not mean that they are ready to engage in sustainable thinking – rather, that they are considering the possibility of making a change some time in the distant future. Recall that deliberation usually involves oscillating back and forth between whether or not to engage in sustainable thinking. Oscillation normally occurs because the downsides of a new direction are overemphasized and the benefits are underestimated (Prochaska et al, 1994).

One of the most effective interventions at this stage of the transition to sustainable thinking is to form teams that can examine the issues and develop climate and sustainability action plans. People from every section and level of the organization – and even key external stakeholders – can be brought together and asked to expand upon the change mechanisms begun in the initial stage, which include awareness-building, choice expansion and supportive relationships. In addition, the teams should be asked to place themselves in situations that allow them to become emotionally inspired by the harm caused by global warming, environmental degradation and related social distress or by the relief that comes from seeing ways of contributing to their resolutions. The team should also be tasked with completing an honest appraisal of the organization to determine if it is functioning in the way they desire. I call these groups 'transition teams' because they are often not permanent. Teams frequently disband when the climate protection or sustainability initiative is well under way or morph into new roles.

Team make-up should be broader than the usual planning groups. New people are important because they are unconstrained by the dominant mind frame of the customary decision-makers and thus can often see risks and opportunities that others can't. Active involvement in teams helps individuals to work through the upsides and downsides of change in partnership with others rather than on their own, and thus opens them to new ideas while also relieving some of the stress of change.

The most important step that each transition team must take early on is to get clear about their goals, roles and rules – what they are striving to achieve, the role each person will play, and the rules of decision-making that will be used to achieve those ends. Goals, roles and rules charting techniques can be used for these purposes.

Continued awareness-building

Team members should be encouraged to take a systems approach, meaning they should think about how their actions contribute to the success of the organization as a whole. A systems approach also means that people should be encouraged to think about how the actions of their team, and that of the organization as a whole, impact the ecological, social and economic systems of which they are part. Key questions must be asked about the affects the organization has and, just as importantly, why those impacts occur. The causes of the impacts, not just their symptoms, should be pursued. Full-cost life-cycle assessments can be used for these purposes. Stakeholders can also be asked to provide honest feedback to the organization about its activities and their effects.

Based on this information, the risks to the organization should be identified. Potential threats may include impacts on the supply chain, ability to obtain feedstock, revenues, future opportunities, public image, employee morale, retention and recruitment, the right to operate in a community and others. The direct and indirect impacts to the climate, natural environment and people now and in the future, locally and globally, should also be thoroughly analysed.

Take a few moments now and make a list of the risks that global warming, environmental degradation and related social and political distress pose for your team or organization.

Emotional inspiration

A powerful way of expanding the awareness of team members is to encourage them to place themselves in situations where they experience the negative emotions associated with the possibility of job losses or harm to their families or communities due to the effects of global warming and other sustainability crises, as well as the positive emotions stemming from envisioning what it feels like to successfully protect the climate and move towards sustainability. As long as the fear factor is not too great, people often become inspired to abandon business-as-usual thinking when their emotions are tapped.

As with individual change, site visits to communities that have experienced unusual wildfires, heat waves or drought allow people to personally observe the harmful effects of climate change. Movies such as *An Inconvenient Truth* and other means can also be used to help people become emotionally inspired to change. Eugene, Oregon, Mayor Kitty Piercy, for example, was emotionally inspired to engage her community in climate protection after visiting Alaskan villages and seeing first hand the negative impacts of melting tundra on native communities.

Organizational appraisal

After a good deal of awareness-building and emotional inspiration, team members should be ready to assess the degree to which they believe the organization is functioning in a way that they are proud of, or if changes are warranted. An honest organizational appraisal requires asking tough questions. For example, do team members want the organization to operate in a climate-positive and sustainable manner, or is it acceptable if it continues to have a large negative ecological and social footprint? How do people want the organization to be perceived by others – as harmful or environmentally and socially responsible? What do people want future generations of employees, customers or local citizens to say about the organization? What values do people want the organization to abide by? How would the organization look and function in an ideal state?

Once these important questions are answered, team members should compare the organization's current status with the desired ideals. If a big gap exists, change is warranted. This type of deep-seated assessment can be a powerful motivator of change.

Examine the downsides of change

Throughout these deliberations, transition team members are likely to start oscillating back and forth about whether or not to take steps to move towards sustainable thinking. People might be concerned about how the shift would affect their job, for example, as well as their current status and authority within the organization. They might also be concerned about what failure would mean, especially if, like many of the employees in Rusty Rexius's company, group members never thought of themselves as environmental or social activists before. Alternatively, they might be concerned that the needed changes will be overwhelming or that customers or constituents will resist.

To work through oscillation and move to the design stage of change, it often helps to involve team members in making a list of the downsides of adopting sustainable thinking. Box 10.3 includes a list heard during the Eugene SBI.

BOX 10.3 SAMPLE LOCAL GOVERNMENT DOWNSIDES OF SUSTAINABLE THINKING

- We will spend money on activities that do not pay off in the short term.
- It will take time away from other pressing issues.
- A bond measure will be required to raise money because we don't have extra funds.
- It will be difficult to become acknowledged for the positive things we have already done.
- We are likely to be blamed for problems that we cannot control.
- Time and energy will have to be invested in people who will not help themselves.
- Conservative members of the community will attack us.
- Cooperation from other local governments with whom we don't work well will be necessary.
- Sustainable thinking requires updating a strategic plan, which is an arduous process.
- Residents don't realize that there is not much we can do within the city limits.

Recast the downsides

After completing the list, the team should be encouraged to see the downsides in a different light. They can be asked, for example, to determine how many of the downsides are permanent. Just as with individual change, more often than not, the downsides of team and organizational change are temporary; yet people fail to realize this and consequently overestimate their importance. The stress and discomfort of engaging in climate protection and sustainability will fade the longer people are involved. Encourage team members to think of the downsides of the shift to sustainable thinking as temporary, rather than permanent, obstacles.

Table 10.2 *Example of local government reframing of downsides*

Loss	Reframed view
Money is spent on energy and water improvement that does not pay off in the short term.	We can increase energy and water efficiency and produce better long-term investment for taxpayers.
Time is taken away from other pressing issues.	Understanding of how issues are interconnected is improved.
It will be difficult to become acknowledged for our positive achievements.	We will be able to highlight our accomplishments because the community will be more focused on these issues.
We are likely to be blamed for problems outside of our control.	Engaging the community will help people to understand what city government can and cannot do.

Also look for the positive outcomes that the changes offer. Table 10.2 provides an example of how we recast the downsides of the transition to sustainability seen by staff from the city of Eugene during the SBI.

Build up the benefits of change

After reframing the downsides of a shift to sustainable thinking, ask team members to circle back and see if additional benefits are now apparent from altering the way in which the organization thinks and acts. New upsides may now be evident. Then, take the time to use the 'decision balance scale' described in Chapter 7 to compare the advantages of engaging in sustainable thinking to the disadvantages.

Continued choice expansion and supportive relationships

Throughout the entire process, the mechanisms established to provide a safe way for people to share their concerns about engaging in sustainable thinking should be evaluated, and new or expanded approaches established as needed. Continued effort will also be important to help people understand the range of choices available for engaging in the issues. Change agents should encourage people to surf the web, read books and talk with experts in order to identify a variety of ways in which the organization can begin to alter its approach towards the climate, natural environment and social well-being.

Moving to the design stage

Through these processes, team members may now see that the benefits of change are significantly greater than the downsides. When this occurs, the transition team is ready to move on to the design stage of change.

THE DESIGN STAGE OF CHANGE

STAGE-BASED CHANGE MECHANISMS FOR DESIGN

- Continued organizational appraisal
- Continued helping relationships
- Commitment

When the team has concluded that the pros of climate protection and sustainability greatly outweigh the cons, they should design an action plan for making the transition. As with individual change, at this point some people often want to immediately launch new projects. Mid-level executives frequently feel this way because they want to have something positive to show their bosses in quick order. Avoid this urge at all costs. Remember that action is not the same as change. In the design phase of the shift to sustainable thinking, transition team members and the senior executives who are monitoring their activities are likely to still be oscillating back and forth about whether or not they actually want to meaningfully engage in climate protection and sustainability.

Time invested in designing a thoughtful plan of attack is therefore time well spent because it affords people the chance to see what the changes would actually look and feel like. A more concrete commitment to sustainable thinking often results. The length of time invested in the design phase need not be long. The time period depends upon the level of change needed. The key point is to not to jump to action before people have thought through many of the key initial steps.

Two overall interventions are particularly pertinent at this stage: adopting a new vision and decision-making criteria for the organization (or unit if the team is focused on a subunit of the organization), and designing an action plan to achieve those new ends. Continued organizational appraisal, commitment and helping relationships support these interventions.

'Wheel of Change Towards Sustainability' intervention 3: Change the goals of the system by crafting a new vision and guiding principle of climate protection and sustainability

The first order of business is to develop a vision of how the organization would look and function when it thinks and operates in a totally environmentally and socially sustainable matter. A vision of a sustainable end state is essential for people to imagine what success would be like. A clear vision is also important for the development of an effective action plan.

Use backward thinking to develop visions

Developing an effective vision requires continued honest appraisal of how team members want their organization, and the goods and services that it provides, to look and function. It's often helpful when developing climate and sustainability visions to choose a time period in the future and to describe the ideal way, absent of constraints, in which people want the organization (or unit, product or service) to look and function if it were completely climate positive and sustainable. The ideal condition of sustainability is your vision. Once the ideal condition is described, look backwards and identify the closest approximation to the deal that can be achieved in relatively short order. The team must decide on what this means (e.g. six months, two years). The closest approximation to the ideal becomes the team's initial goal. After it has been described, work backwards again to your current condition to identify the most direct route towards the closest approximation to the ideal. This process is called 'ends-planning' (Ackoff, 1999).

Once the desired ideal future state is described, a vision can be articulated that depicts the intent of the organization to achieve this state. Visions usually begin with words such as 'We will be ...'; or 'Our goal is to ...'; or 'We commit to ...'.

Starting with the ideal and then moving backwards to the current state is counterintuitive to many people. Looking backwards from the closest approximation to the ideal, however, often points out obvious steps that can be taken to achieve this state. Ends-planning also helps to eliminate false paths. Dead ends that cannot get you to the ideal vision will become evident. Ends-planning also helps you to avoid getting trapped by decision-making tools that favour the status quo, such as standard cost-benefit analysis.

An effective vision is not just something written on paper. Success exists when people 'get it' in their gut. They intuitively know what they are striving to achieve.

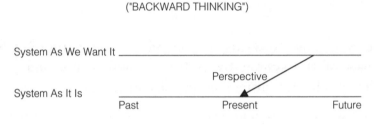

Figure 10.3 *Ends-planning ('backward thinking')*

Source: Ackoff (1999).

Develop a construct

After a vision has been established, develop a concept that captures the essence of the vision in simple terms. The 'construct' should provide the team with an organizing framework for the shift to sustainable thinking. A construct such as the Rexius Company's 'sustainable solutions' or others such as 'climate positive' or 'green living' can serve to define the purpose and goal of the change initiative, while also arranging a wide variety of actions under a central theme. A construct allows team members to continually ask themselves, for example: 'Is this action consistent with ... providing sustainable solutions ... or being climate positive ... or living green?'

Adopt decision-making guidelines

After a vision and construct have been developed, guidelines should be agreed upon for how decisions will be made to achieve these ends. The first decision-making screen should be the sustainability thinking blunders discussed in Chapter 4. Establish a mechanism for vetting decisions to ensure that they avoid 'linear', 'short-term, quick-fix', 'cheaper is cheaper' and the other forms of myopic climate-damaging thinking.

The second decision-making screen should be the use of the sustainable ethics guidelines discussed in Chapter 8. Use the process to ensure that decisions support ethically and morally sustainable outcomes.

Other decision-making guidelines can be used, as well, such as the four systems conditions of The Natural Step framework.[1] A new vision and decision-making guidelines can be powerful mechanisms for altering an organization's thinking and activities.

'Wheel of Change Towards Sustainability' intervention 4: Restructure the rules of engagement by adopting source-based strategies and action plans

Following the development of the new vision of sustainability and decision-making guidelines, action plans should be designed that provide a systematic approach for altering the way in which the team or organization thinks about, designs and delivers its goods and services. The right questions need to be asked when designing the action plans. Four core questions serve as a starting point:

1   How sustainable are we now?
2   How sustainable do we want to be in the future?
3   How do we get there?
4   How do we measure progress?

This is where an ecological and social footprint analysis becomes important. Measure the total amount of resources the organization consumes from initial resource extraction all the way through the manufacturing, product distribution, use and disposal stages. Assess the impacts of that consumption upon the environment, workers and communities. Quantify the organization's total greenhouse gas emissions, including those embedded in products used by the organizations that are manufactured elsewhere (such as in China), and the emissions produced at its facilities through its energy use, transportation, food, landscaping and waste management practices. If the organization wants to be totally honest about its emissions, it will also assess the energy demand and emissions generated from the use and disposal of its products by consumers or constituents. Although these types of analysis are complicated, they can be done.

After a baseline has been developed, the next step is to identify specific actions, including cognitive, behavioural, technical and operational changes that can point the organization in the direction of its ideal vision of sustainability. Assessments can then be completed to determine the stage of change of each group member or each unit regarding those actions and behaviours. The more precisely the desired changes are described, the greater the likelihood that the stages of change can be accurately assessed. Once the current position of group members is understood, 5-D stage-based mechanisms can be implemented to help people move systematically towards the doing and defending stages of change.

Remember that action plans should seek to establish truly sustainable processes, products and services, and not just 'minimize' those impacts or become a little 'less bad'. Measurement systems should be adopted to quantify progress towards the new ideal vision of sustainability and to enable continual learning and adaptive management.

Helping relationships

As with individual change efforts, some people are likely to struggle with the stress of the shift to sustainable thinking. Employees should be encouraged to talk with their fellow employees or supervisors about their concerns. Human resources professionals can also assist people in dealing with change-induced stress.

In this stage of change, however, a special emphasis should be placed on developing mentors. Learning how others have made the shift to sustainable thinking provides hope and energizes people. Encourage team members to participate in internal or external climate or sustainability networks of professionals working on similar issues. In addition, time-limited climate and sustainability trouble-shooting units can be established to help people work through problems. Through these activities, a safe and supportive environment should be established to assist team members in feeling comfortable in openly sharing their concerns and learning from others about how to make the transition to sustainable thinking.

'Wheel of Change Towards Sustainability' intervention 5: Shift information flows by committing to change and tirelessly communicating the vision and strategies

Through the processes of designing a clear vision of what it means to think and act sustainably, clarifying the criterion against which decisions will be vetted, and developing an action plan for pursuing these ends, team members are likely to have resolved their ambivalence about the shift to sustainable thinking. If the level of commitment is still unclear, a change readiness assessment can be used to measure the willingness of team members to meaningfully engage in the change effort.

Make a commitment

Once it becomes clear that a sufficient number of people are ready to make the shift to sustainable thinking, the team should make a clear commitment to do so. The commitment, along with the vision, decision-making criteria and action plan should then be announced to employees.

Senior executives must lead the way by publicly declaring their commitment to sustainable thinking. A relentless stream of interactive communication should then be initiated to inform people within the organization about the need, purpose, vision, strategies and benefits of the organization's new commitment. If people don't understand the reason for the new focus and its benefits, they will resist or feel resentful that a new direction is being imposed upon them. An unyielding flow of information is needed to build understanding and maintain commitment.

Make the commitment public

At the proper time, external stakeholders should be told about the new commitment. The organization may want to wait until the action plan has some traction. Remember, however, that the longer the organization takes to make its commitment public, the greater the chance that the initiative will flounder. Making the commitment public in short order will focus people on the new vision and energize employees.

A great example of the power of public commitments is the US Mayors Climate Protection Agreement that as of late 2007 had over 500 cities signed on. Signing the agreement commits a community to specific greenhouse gas reduction targets and to the development of an action plan to achieve those goals.

Few of the mayors who signed the commitment had developed an action plan prior to endorsing it. Instead, making a public commitment was the trigger that focused their community on climate protection.

THE DOING STAGE OF CHANGE

STAGE-BASED CHANGE MECHANISMS FOR DOING

- Continued commitment
- Continued helping relationships
- Reinforcement
- Substitution
- Structural redesign

Following a firm commitment, implementation of the action plan can begin. This is the most active stage of the change process. Lots of activity will normally ensue, and employees are likely to be excited. However, no plan unfolds perfectly. Numerous mistakes and setbacks are certain. People need help to overcome the barriers and constant encouragement to persevere. Advanced planning for these factors can help to smooth the way and avoid pitfalls that send team members and executives scurrying back into deliberation or disinterest.

'Wheel of Change Towards Sustainability' intervention 6: Correct the team and organization's feedback mechanisms by encouraging and rewarding learning and innovation

Numerous obstacles will emerge as the new strategies and action plan are put into place. Making the effort to think and behave differently will take a toll on many individuals. Some people or units will consequently be tempted to ignore the new direction and slide back into their old climate-damaging take–make–waste mental frame. For this reason, the use of continued commitment and helping relationships are important during the doing stage. In addition, reinforcement, substitution and structural change mechanisms become important.

Continued commitment

Senior executives and change agents should make it a priority to keep commitment high by continuing to talk about the importance of the climate and sustainability initiative. It should, for example, be one of the first issues discussed at every staff meeting. Memos and reports should repeatedly be circulated about the progress made, obstacles and learning processes. Noted climate and sustainability speakers and consultants can be brought in to share their ideas. Through these and other steps, team members must come to see that the climate and sustainability initiative is a top organizational priority.

Continued helping relationships

Because the doing stage of change is filled with new activity, it often helps to link together people who are engaged in similar climate or sustainability initiatives for support and learning purposes. Connecting with people who are engaged in similar activities offers the opportunity to compare notes, share solutions and discover new things. Individuals in the finance department of different organizational units, for example, can buddy up to talk about ways of calculating the full economic, social and environmental costs of the organization's processes, products and services.

Most importantly, an atmosphere of openness and acceptance must be established within the organization. People need to feel free to ask for help, make mistakes, get honest feedback without recrimination, and in other ways feel trusted and supported.

Reinforce positive thinking and activities

One of the most important ways to generate feelings of support is to acknowledge and reward people when they consciously avoid unsustainable actions and when they achieve successes. Praise and celebrations should become regular events within the team or organization.

In addition to recognition from others, people should be encouraged to become aware of the intrinsic rewards they get from their organization's new commitment to climate protection and sustainability. For example, urge people to think about their role in helping the organization to reduce its exposure to the risks of climate change and social instability, and thus protect everyone's jobs. Ask people to acknowledge the steps they are taking to protect the future of their children and the children of fellow workers.

Most importantly, create an atmosphere of *fun and excitement* within the organization! The organization is blazing a trail towards climate protection and sustainability. What an exciting activity to be involved in. Use humour, play, laughter and other ways to make the transition pleasurable. You have nothing to lose and everything to gain by turning the doing stage of change into a time when people can't wait to get to work because of the excitement and joy that permeates the organization.

Substitute sustainable for unsustainable habits

Behavioural substitutes

Eliminating factors within the organization that elicit myopic climate-damaging thinking and substituting sustainable factors in their place is one way to create an atmosphere of fun and excitement. Challenge employees to identify factors that make it hard to think and act sustainability and to offer alternatives that produce sustainable behaviours. Give awards to people when they identify successful alternatives.

For example, people may say that it's difficult to recycle paper without recycling bins close by. By placing bins near each desk throughout a building, recycling can eventually become as routine as the former practice once was of tossing used paper into the trash. If people must travel any distance to the facility, easy-to-use public transportation, vans, carpooling, bike or walking trails could be established to provide low-carbon alternatives for people who previously drove to work alone. People who come up with similar ideas should be acknowledged and rewarded in fun and meaningful ways.

Thinking substitutes

In order to alter the activities of a team or organization in any fundamental way, group members must realize what drives them. Ask people to examine when and why they ignore information about the organization's effects on the climate, natural environment or social well-being. Challenge them to think about how often and under what circumstances the organization reverts to take–make–waste thinking. Dare the group to identify the benefits that the organization gets from business as usual.

Transition team members should also make an explicit effort to become aware of situations and factors that trigger climate-damaging thinking and behaviour. Use the ABCD approach described in Chapter 7 for these purposes. Identify (A) *activating* events or situations that trigger (B) *behaviours* as well as their (C) *consequences*. Then identify ways of (D) *disrupting* those patterns.

Box 10.3 includes an example of an ABCD analysis we did for the city of Eugene during the SBI. We found, for example: (A) when a crisis of any significance occurred in the community, (B) city staff stopped working on the sustainability initiative, which led to (C) missed opportunities and less preparedness for the next crisis.

After team members become aware of their tendencies, steps can be taken to identify actions that can (D) disrupt their traditional patterns. In the example provided in Table 10.3, disruptions included making a conscious decision to continue the climate and sustainability initiative even when a crisis occurs, and for the organization to hire a sustainability coordinator who can help all departments continue forward even when budget cuts or other crises occur.

Table 10.3 *Sample ABCDs from a local government programme*

A: activating events	B: behaviours	C: consequences	D: disruptions
A significant crisis occurs in the community.	Work on the sustainability initiative ceases.	The result is missed opportunities and reduced preparedness for the next crisis.	Continue efforts even during a crisis.
Budget cuts are introduced within a city department.	There is reduced interest in collaboration between units.	One department goes further than another.	Hire a coordinator to help all departments.
		There is less cooperation and coordination.	

Seek stair-stepped successes and establish double-loop learning mechanisms

It's often best to start off by pursuing a series of step-wise successes. Taking on bite-size chunks allows the teams to test new thinking and approaches without major risk. Through these activities, the team and organization's feedback and learning mechanisms should be enhanced so that as obstacles surface, the skills, knowledge and understanding of employees and stakeholders continually expand.

In many organizations, learning is usually limited to 'single-loop' processes. A problem arises, individuals or small groups are assigned to deal with the issue, a fix is applied as quickly as possible, and then people move on to the next issue. Single-loop learning makes people dumb. They never examine why the problem occurred in the first place or what can be done to prevent those circumstances from occurring again in the future.

Double-loop learning, on the other hand, involves fixing the immediate problem and then spending concentrated time examining its root causes, including how the beliefs and assumptions of the people who are involved may have created the problem in the first place or exacerbated it. Conditions are then altered to ensure that similar problems don't occur in the future. Double-loop learning makes people smart. Explicit effort should be made to establish double-loop learning mechanisms throughout the organization.

Alter the structure

In addition to substituting climate-positive for unsustainable habits, pursuing star-stepped successes and forming helping relationships, team members should be encouraged to identify ways of altering the structure of the entire organization so that it naturally fosters sustainable thinking and acting. For example, examine ways of rearranging the physical setup of the office spaces to allow for more informal networking and face-to-face interaction. Look for ways of flattening the organization's hierarchy so that information and decision-making flows more quickly and easily between units. Identify suppliers who provide environmentally and socially sound products or work with your existing suppliers to make the shift to these goods. Develop more open and participative forms of governance so that employees feel fully engaged in the climate and sustainability initiative.

THE DEFENDING STAGE OF CHANGE

'Wheel of Change Towards Sustainability' intervention 7: Adjust the parameters of the system by aligning systems and structures with climate protection and sustainability

---

STAGE-BASED CHANGE MECHANISMS FOR DEFENDING

- Continued commitment
- Continued helping relationships
- Continued reinforcement
- Continued substitution
- Major structural redesign

After about six months to a year of active involvement in implementing the climate protection or sustainability action plan, effort should begin to embed sustainable thinking in the organization's systems and structures. The purpose is to align the signals that the organization sends to employees and stakeholders around a consistent and mutually reinforcing set of messages that makes it impossible to think or behave in climate-damaging unsustainable ways.

The change mechanisms employed in the doing stage of change should now be formalized, including the commitment to climate protection, helping relationships, reinforcement and substitution. These processes provide people with the tools needed to defend their new thinking and behaviours over time as they run into resistance from others and unforeseen obstacles. However, even more is now needed.

Major structural redesign

This is the time to institute new policies. For example, budgets should be prioritized to reflect long-term commitment to the new approach. Skilled staff, administrative support and office space should be assigned to the climate protection and sustainability effort. Job descriptions, hiring procedures, promotions, raises, bonuses and benefits should be redesigned to reward sustainable performance. Policies should be adopted requiring the design and production of zero-carbon and/or waste free products and services, the use of renewable energy and other actions. These and many similar types of policies serve to reinforce continued forward movement.

Major structural redesign is always hard work. Inertia as well as financial, technical and political obstacles must usually be overcome. One of the most important elements of any major redesign is to align the rewards and incentives of the organization. Frequently, organizations give mixed signals. They publicly acknowledge and reward people who succeed in finding innovative ways of reducing emissions, for example, but at the same time hire or promote individuals who do not have a commitment to sustainable thinking. Assessing and then aligning the messages that the organization sends about what is important is a vital step in any major redesign effort.

Leadership

Senior executives must demonstrate their support and personally lead many of these interventions. As long as executives make clear that climate protection and sustainability are top priorities, change agents within each unit can do much of the daily heavy lifting. Team efforts should remain a priority. Written materials and electronic training programmes can also be used. Although the involvement of senior executives is vital, ultimately the active engagement of employees throughout all levels of the organization will be the key to success. This is why it will be so important to continue to employ the 5-D staged approach to change. No matter where they are starting from, people should be helped to progress to the next stage of change until everyone within the organization is in the doing and defending stages. Similar efforts should be made to assist external stakeholders in making the transition to sustainable thinking.

Change can start anywhere

Your organization's climate protection and sustainability initiative can begin with any of the major interventions outlined in the 'wheel of change'. Remember that the shift to sustainable thinking will not be linear. It will be more like a corkscrew or rollercoaster ride from start to finish. Also remember that mistakes and backsliding will undoubtedly occur; but they do not signify failure. It normally takes multiple efforts for people to give up longstanding maladaptive habits. If effective learning mechanisms have been instituted, people can use a setback to expand their understanding and continue forward.

The city of Eugene example

The seven interventions of the wheel of organizational change towards sustainability formed the backbone of the strategy my students and I used when we coordinated the Eugene SBI. In this case, we used the framework to engage organizations throughout the community in sustainable thinking, not just a single group. The term sustainability was employed as the overarching construct to describe behaviours that would achieve the 'triple bottom line' of enhancing the environment, including the climate, as well as social and economic well-being.

For many years, the community had been polarized over environmental and economic development issues, so we decided that 'slower is faster and faster is slower'. We did not want to rush people into action because we feared pressure to engage in sustainable thinking would have the opposite effect of further entrenching people in their existing positions.

Although we did not explicitly label them this way, the mayor, members of the planning team, which included Rusty Rexius, a local businessman named David Funk, and my students and I decided to spend 12 months focused on the change mechanisms appropriate for the early stages of change, including building supportive relationships, expanding awareness and helping people and organizations to engage in self-appraisal. Our goal was to give people sufficient time to increase their understanding of the issues and to deliberate about the pros and cons of engaging in sustainability. We felt that once people moved to the design stage of change, they would be committed to developing an action plan for engaging in sustainable thinking. Fortunately, the strategy worked as planned.

To provide motivation and an initial vision for the SBI, the mayor kicked the process off by publicly stating her interest in having the community engage in and benefit from 'triple bottom line' sustainability practices that produce economic, social and environmental benefits. We used the mayor's vision as the reason to invite a group of 50 respected business, government and environmental leaders to spend a half-day discussing what sustainability could mean for the community. The group also discussed the pros and cons of growing businesses that use sustainable practices or produce sustainable products, and of expanding the use of sustainability practices within government.

We used a process called Appreciative Inquiry for these purposes, which focuses participants on the deeply felt ideal conditions they want to see in the community, rather than on how to resolve old problems.[2] This helped people to consider the benefits of sustainable thinking in a non-threatening way. Participants also had time to consider whether their current thinking and behaviour were consistent with the ideal vision and goals of sustainability that they and the group had identified.

My students and I then surveyed business, community and government leaders throughout the community to determine where they stood on sustainability issues. From the information we received, we were able to make a qualified assessment of the number of people and organizations who were in each of the stages of change regarding sustainability. We concluded that most business leaders were either disinterested or in the deliberation stage of change, although a small number of early adopters, primarily in the organic and natural food industry, were in the doing and defending stages. The majority of government employees were also in the early stages of change, with the exception of those involved with environmental programmes such as recycling, who were in the later stages.

The survey data was also used as the basis of a series of reports that were distributed throughout the community describing the vision people had of sustainability in key economic sectors, the benefits of moving in that direction, the obstacles and constraints they thought they would face, and what they needed from city government and others to make the transition.

Based on this information and the fact that the longstanding polarization had caused people on all sides to become very defensive, we decided that directly challenging the controlling mind frame of business and government leaders about issues of sustainability would not be fruitful. Instead, we felt the best place to start the SBI would be to form teams. We wanted to build supportive relationships, allow people to increase their awareness by hearing from others with different perspectives and provide a way for them to share their concerns about sustainability. Through this we wanted to provide a mechanism for everyone involved to consider the pros and cons of engaging in sustainable thinking.

The first team we formed was the SBI Task Force, which was composed of a diverse group of 15 respected business, government, education and non-profit leaders. Rusty Rexius and David Funk served as co-chairs. This group served as the steering committee for the overall project.

We then organized 15 'roundtables' where people from different business and government organizations discussed a variety of sustainability topics, such as renewable energy, green building, organic and natural foods, zero waste, sustainable healthcare and other issues. Each roundtable began with a summary of the survey findings as described in the reports. A special emphasis was placed on the ideal vision of sustainability that survey respondents wanted to achieve. A discussion then ensued on what the triple bottom line meant for participants in each sector, the benefits of achieving the vision, obstacles that were in the way, and what participants felt the city of Eugene could do to help them overcome the obstacles and achieve the vision.

More than identifying specific recommendations, the underlying purpose of the roundtables was to give people the opportunity to increase their awareness, become emotionally inspired, meet others involved with similar processes and decide if the benefits of engaging in sustainability outweighed the downsides.

At the close of each roundtable a report was produced and distributed to meeting participants with a request for feedback, which gave people yet another chance to think about the issues. A final report was then posted on the SBI website and widely distributed in the community.

Throughout the project a concerted effort was made on communicating the need, benefits and vision of sustainability that participants had developed to business and government leaders and the public at large. Opinion editorials were published in the local newspaper, presentations were made to numerous organizations, formal meetings were held with groups as diverse as the Chamber of Commerce, and local high school students, and public service announcements (PSAs) were run on radio stations over an 18-month period. A local Cumulus radio station became so excited about the SBI that it gave the project over US$250,000 worth of free air time that steered people towards the SBI website for information about what sustainability meant and how they could become involved.

After 12 months of intensive effort to help business and government leaders progress through disinterest and deliberation, we entered the design phase where the SBI Task Force drafted a plan for helping organizations throughout the community adopt a path towards sustainability. The SBI plan was entitled *Report and Recommendations to the Eugene City Council and Community of Eugene: From the Sustainable Business Initiative Task Force*.[3] With speed rarely seen on the city council, the first-tier recommendations of hiring a sustainability manager and establishing a formal city sustainability commission were unanimously approved. When these steps were completed, the city had formalized its commitment and entered the doing stage of the transition to sustainable thinking.

The SBI, however, had a much greater effect than merely gaining endorsement from the city council. Businesses, government agencies and private citizens throughout the community began to deliberate over, design plans for, and engage in sustainability and climate protection efforts. Businesses in the natural foods, green building and renewable energy fields formed ongoing professional networks that allowed them to learn from each other and to work together to overcome obstacles (in my work this is called cluster development).

Although the City of Eugene is just in the initial phase of the doing stage regarding global warming, and many organizations within the community are just now entering the deliberation and design stages, through all of this work the mind frame of many organizations shifted towards sustainable thinking. Continued effort will be needed, however, to keep momentum going and to help the organizations eventually enter and persevere through the defending stage of change.

The Rexius example concluded

Although it was not necessarily aware of it at the time, Rexius Company essentially followed the same framework when it made the transition to sustainability.

Increasing coverage in the media about climate change, peak oil and sustainability, combined with the challenge posed by a young employee who told Rusty Rexius that the sustainability field would inevitably grow and the company needed to get on the bandwagon or be left behind, served as the disturbance that dislodged business-as-usual thinking and moved Rusty Rexius and the other family owners beyond disinterest. These events led to a year and a half of sometimes-heated deliberations among the owners about whether or not to engage in sustainability.

A major part of the executive's deliberations revolved around the question of vision. The officers continually asked how the company would look and function if it fully embraced sustainability. They questioned tactical issues such as what it would be like to change their company colour from red to green in order to reflect their new commitment to the environment, including painting their trucks green. They also debated strategic issues, such as how the new focus would affect their customers, employees and suppliers, many of whom were in the timber industry and saw anything smacking of environmentalism as a threat.

The officers eventually came to three conclusions. First, the world is moving in the direction of sustainability and the company could either get out front on the issue or 'be squashed'. Second, their competitors were not doing anything in the field, which meant the company had a major opportunity to capture competitive advantage by embracing sustainability. Third, if they were going to embrace sustainability, they were not going to be tepid: they would make it public and go all out.[4] These deductions led to an extensive effort to help employees understand and apply sustainability in their units and jobs.

No specific actions were initially mandated. Instead, they started by creating a compelling case for change based on what Rusty called 'moral, financial and survival' imperatives. They also devised a new vision for the company.[5] At the core of this image was an honest appraisal of the way in which the company currently operated compared to how it wanted to do so in the future.

Rusty and his cousin and co-president, Arlen Rexius, relentlessly made the case for change by personally explaining the need for, and their vision of, sustainability to every single employee. They then asked their employees to work with the other members of their units to determine how to apply the principles and practices to their work. As a result, each of the company's units developed a vision of what sustainability meant in their own spheres of influence.

Over the next year or so Rusty repeatedly emphasized the new vision, strategies and benefits of the shift to sustainability. For example, Rusty shared the story of how their landscape construction manager nailed down a big job. As part of his commitment to the company's sustainability efforts, the manager had exchanged his fuel-hungry four-wheel-drive vehicle for a more efficient hybrid. One day he drove to eastern Oregon to bid on a job at a golf course. The hybrid immediately caught the eye of the prospective customer who asked the construction manager about it. They talked about the vehicle and what it meant about the company's business practices and commitment to sustainability. After two hours, with almost no discussion about the actual landscaping job, he got the contract.

This type of information, and the fact that 'my phone was ringing off the hook with new business' because of their new commitment to sustainability helped Rusty's employees see the benefits and eventually embrace the new approach.

Rusty also focused on continual learning. He told employees they should experiment and seek ways of creating solutions that were environmentally sustainable. The residential irrigation unit manager came to Rusty, for example, and said that he could not envision how sustainability applied to his work. He used polyvinylchloride (PVC) pipe, which is one of the worst forms of plastic from an environmental perspective and cannot be recycled, and the systems he installed were powered by electricity, which produced greenhouse gases.

In response, Rusty talked about the water conservation benefits of the manager's irrigation systems, which not only save water but reduce electrical use compared to regular lawn and garden watering techniques. Rusty also encouraged him to try other types of materials, such as high-density polyethylene (HDPE) pipe, which is non-chlorinated, requires fewer additives, has a much higher recycling rate and is considered a much more environmentally benign plastic than PVC. The irrigation manager used the new pipe in a green building project and found it harder to use but better over the long haul. In this way, Rusty helped his employees to overcome their resistance and learn how to think and act sustainably.

After a few years of engagement, the officers began to institutionalize the new vision, values and norms by formally embedding them in company systems and structures. The company's approach to cost-benefit analysis, for example, began to more explicitly include sustainability. 'I think at some level we have always done that', said Rexius: 'Early on, when biodiesel was substantially more money than low sulphur diesel, we went through quite a rigorous exercise in determining if it was 'worth it'. Obviously we determined it was; but it was not a simple 'which is less money' exercise. We had to weigh all sorts of factors: price, public perception and added business, mileage, maintenance, environmental costs, etc. We have gone through similar exercises with other things [since that time].'[6] In this way, sustainability has become firmly embedded in the culture as well as the policies and procedures of Rexius Company.[7]

It should be noted that the company's focus on sustainability has allowed it to attract high-quality talent. Rexius told me: 'The pool of prospective employees has grown since we went "public" with our commitment to sustainability. Folks have specifically sought us out because of our reputation in the field of sustainability.'[8] This underscores the benefits that accrue when an organization makes a firm commitment to sustainability and lets the world know about it.

The importance of a positive orientation

With this example as a backdrop, I want to say a little more about two issues: the importance of the orientation that an organization adopts during its shift to sustainable thinking and methods for avoiding groupthink.

I'll start with orientation. The Rexius example makes clear how important a positive point of reference is when seeking to change the way in which an organization thinks and acts regarding the climate, natural environment and social well-being. One aspect of a positive orientation is the creative versus problem-solving focus discussed throughout the book. The more people see climate protection and sustainability as an opportunity to create exciting new ways of meeting human needs, increasing prosperity and enhancing security, rather than as eliminating unpleasant evils such as greenhouse gas emissions, the more energized and committed people will be.

Another aspect of orientation has to do with purpose. I am not talking about mission or vision statements. I'm talking about the gut-level sense that group members have about what they are striving to achieve, why this goal is important and how these outcomes will be brought about.

Visions that, implicitly or otherwise, send the message that people are flawed and cannot be trusted to do the right thing, or that the real focus is business as usual even though the team or organization will do its best to 'minimize' its environmental and social impacts, are likely to produce mistrust, evasion and other dysfunctional qualities among employees and stakeholders that prevent them from moving beyond disinterest or deliberation.[9]

On the other hand, orientations that focus on expanding positive qualities and outcomes, such as creating and delivering truly sustainable products and services,[10] and empowering group members to use their innate skills and goodness to the fullest, bring out the best in people. Organizations that cultivate their members' best personal qualities perform at high levels.[11] They are also more likely to become leaders in the movement to develop the new circular borrow–use–return technologies and practices needed to establish a vibrant low-carbon global economy and to achieve sustainability.

Preventing and overcoming groupthink

This brings me back to the issue of groupthink. If a positive group orientation is important for protecting the climate and achieving sustainability, developing clarity over the goals, roles and rules required for open and participative governance is essential for overcoming groupthink.

For example, if people want to ensure that their organization avoids groupthink, they can start by engaging their group in an open dialogue about establishing an explicit commitment to making the most informed and effective decisions possible. If agreement can be reached on this point, a vision should be created of what an ideal decision-making process would look and function like. Talk about the type of information needed for good decisions, how it should be gathered, distributed and debated, and how decisions should be made.

You now know that if they have false feedback mechanisms, people often embrace the validity of feedback they receive only if it matches their existing views of themselves and the world (even when it's negative). In addition, people have greater confidence in feedback provided by someone who confirms their existing perceptions. The organization should become aware of these tendencies and devise a vision of effective decision-making that includes mechanisms to prevent self-selection from occurring.

With the new vision in place, an explicit discussion can occur about the potential causes, symptoms and consequences of groupthink. Group members can then be asked to compare their ideal vision to the group's historic and current decision-making patterns to determine the extent to which groupthink exists. Because the very nature of the dynamic makes people fearful of speaking up, surveys can be distributed that allow people to share their views anonymously. The views of external organizations and individuals that may have a good perspective of the group can be solicited.

Group members can also be asked to describe past situations when they openly challenged each other's ideas and in other ways followed the ideal vision of open and honest debate they created. The factors that led to and supported the successful approach should be identified. Then, a discussion can be held about how the group can enhance those positive cognitive and behavioural traits and avoid groupthink.

In order to avoid leader-induced groupthink, rules can be established that require organizational leaders to withhold their personal desires and expectations and remain impartial when the group first engages in important planning or decision-making discussions. The rule can also include the requirement that leaders give priority to contrasting views and criticism.

In addition, specific group members could be assigned the responsibility of openly questioning the perceptions, assumptions and decisions of the team or organization. This can be formalized by asking assertive group members to play the specific role of devil's advocate. Another way of ensuring that minority opinions are heard is to divide people into two or more groups and assign each the job of evaluating and promoting alternatives to the prevailing point of view.

Consistent with the goals, roles and rules of good feedback, outsider stakeholders and noted experts could be consulted on a regular basis and their perspectives openly discussed within the group. To overcome the tendency to seek feedback only from people who view the world the same way the group does, a rule can be established that requires the organization to explicitly request comments from those who are likely to be the strongest critics (Janis and Mann, 1977).

Lastly, a rule could be adopted that major decisions will always first be termed 'drafts', and that outside experts and stakeholders will be asked to comment on them, and their feedback meaningfully discussed, before a final decision is made. This allows the group to have one last go-around to consider alternative views before any type of formal commitment is made.

Throughout the entire process, the orientation should be positive. Just as sustainability cannot be achieved simply by eliminating unsustainable thinking and activities, groupthink cannot be overcome simply by removing its traits. Positive, honest, open and constructive ways of thinking and behaving must be adopted and continually cultivated.

Notes

1 In the US, information about The Natural Step can be found at www.ortns.org/. In Europe, information is available at www.forumforthefuture.org.uk/uk_homepage.htm.
2 For information on Appreciative Inquiry, see Whitney and Trosten-Bloom (2002).
3 The SBI report can be obtained at http://ri.uoregon.edu.
4 Rusty Rexius, pers comm, 26 June 2007.
5 Rusty Rexius, pers comm, 21 March 2007.
6 Rusty Rexius, pers comm, 29 June 2007.
7 Rusty Rexius, pers comm, 29 June 2007.
8 Rusty Rexius, pers comm, 29 June 2007.
9 One of the downsides of the four systems conditions of The Natural Step framework is that the focus is on 'systematically *reducing* societies' dependence on ...' (emphasis added) harmful resources and activities. This is a negative vision. Although The Natural Step framework has proven helpful to many organizations, especially in Northern Europe, it has failed to catch on to any great extent in the US. One possible reason is its negative focus, which fails to capture the imagination and entrepreneurial spirit of Americans.
10 See, for example, the Interface Corporation's sustainability vision at www.interfaceinc .com/.
11 This assertion is supported by the research of Collins and Porras (1997, 2001).

References

Ackoff, R. (1999) *Re-creating the Corporation: A Design For Organizations For the 21st Century*, Oxford University Press, Oxford

Beck, A. (1979) *Cognitive Therapy and the Emotional Disorders*, Meridian Books, New York, p240

Collins, J. and Porras, J. (1997) *Built to Last: Successful Habits of Visionary Companies*, HarperCollins Publishers, New York

Collins, J. and Porras, J. (2001) *Good to Great: Why Some Companies Make a Leap ... and Others Don't*, HarperCollins Publishers, New York

Doppelt, R. (2003) *Leading Change Toward Sustainability: A Change Management Guide for Business, Government and Civil Society*, Greenleaf Publishing, London

Janis, I. L. (1972) *Victims of Groupthink*, Houghton-Mifflin, Boston, MA

Janis, I. L. and Mann, L. (1977) *Decision Making: A Psychological Analysis of Conflict, Choice and Commitment*, Free Press, New York

Prochaska, J. O., Norcross, J. C. and Diclemente, C. C. (1994) *Changing for Good*, HarperCollins Publishers, New York

Whitney, D. and Trosten-Bloom, A. (2002) *The Power of Appreciative Inquiry*, Berrett-Koehler Publishing, San Francisco

11

The Power of Sustainable Thinking

The time for action is now. It's never too late.
Saint Exupery, The Little Prince, 1943

Global warming is the defining challenge of our time. The way in which this predicament is resolved will determine how all other environmental, social and economic challenges play out. Climate will decide the winners and losers of the future. It is the ultimate issue of sustainability.

Rarely has humanity faced a situation that called our deepest beliefs and assumptions so clearly into question. Global warming is not an energy, technological or policy problem. It is the result of the largest failure of perception and thought in human history. Global warming is also a moral dilemma related to the meaning we give to our lives, the lives of other people and organisms on the planet, and to those who follow.

We have assumed that the take–make–waste economic system naturally produces continued economic prosperity and that it can continue into perpetuity. But global warming makes clear how patently wrong this assumption has been. Humanity's lack of mindfulness about the harmful effects of the take–make–waste system on the Earth's sources, sinks and communities has brought the world to the edge of the abyss. If we are to avoid the ecological, economic and social calamities that uncontrolled climate change will bring, unconstrained freedom to do as we want without regard to the systems upon which we are all dependent for life is no longer an option.

One thing is certain. New perspectives and activities will not come about unless you believe it is possible. No matter whether we like it or not, global warming and today's other socio-economic dilemmas will foist major change on the world. If global warming is left uncontrolled, there will be no 'business as usual' in the future. We can allow our core beliefs, assumptions and thought patterns to remain the same and experience certain crisis, but this will precipitate a reactive form of change that will guarantee great harm and suffering. Alternatively, we can choose to alter our own thinking now because we understand the huge risks involved with our current mental frame and the positive benefits of planned change. If we choose the latter route, the transition costs will be manageable and all of humanity will eventually end up better off.

I know this from personal experience. Planned change is possible. I've pointed out how research has consistently shown that with effective change in thinking and behaviour strategies and persistence, even those most ardently disinterested individuals, such as drug addicts and alcoholics, successfully alter their thinking and behaviour. Most addicts break their habits with little to no formal treatment, meaning that change is self-induced. The vast majority of self-changers follow the 5-D stage of change approach described in this book.

You too can alter your mental frame and the rote behaviours that it produces and become a sustainable thinker. So can the people around you, and the groups and organizations with whom you are involved. The key is to accept responsibility for the consequences of your thinking and behaviour and make a conscious choice to adopt a more positive and effective approach.

History shows that rapid and large changes in economic and social conditions *are* possible. The transportation sector in the West was completely transformed during the first four decades of the 20th century, for example – from horses and coal-fired trains to electricity and gas-fuelled cars and tractors. Changes since that time have been related to growth, not structure. From this perspective, a 40-year time scale seems about right for a large-scale economic shift (Makhijani, 2007).

During 1985 to 1987, scientists, government regulators and corporations arrived at an agreement to protect the ozone layer that first required a 50 per cent reduction in emissions of chlorofluorocarbons (CFCs). The agreement quickly expanded, however, to the complete elimination of CFC emissions, which occurred ahead of schedule. Although the solution they chose at that time produced its own unintended consequences for the climate, the fact is that once the key industry and government players decided to make it happen, the changes were made rapidly and relatively painlessly.

The oil embargo in 1973 broke the longstanding lock-stepped relationship between economic growth and energy use in the US. For over a decade afterwards, economic and industrial growth increased without further upsurges in energy use. This demonstrates that it is possible to move the economy in the direction of greater energy efficiency without harming the economy in a very short time frame. Although the genesis of this change was a major disturbance, there is no reason why planned change aimed at resolving global warming and other sustainability dilemmas cannot produce similar results (Makhijani, 2007).

Recall that because humans live within a complex network of interlinked ecological and social systems, everything we do today has an effect. Continued use of the sustainable thinking blunders, and decision-making that violates the ethics of sustainability will aggravate global warming, ecological degradation and related social distress, and make planned change more difficult. Sustainable thinking, on the other hand, brought about with intention, will heal the climate and natural environment and reduce social distress.

Once you embark on the path towards sustainable thinking, experience shows there will come a time in the future when you realize everything is different. You will become much more mindful. As a result, you are likely to constantly think about your ecological and social footprints and no longer be capable of mindlessly contributing to the global climate crisis or other environmental or social ills. You are also likely to find that sustainable thinking makes you feel better about yourself and increases your personal health, effectiveness and well-being.

PERSONAL CHANGE LEADS TO SOCIAL AND POLITICAL CHANGE

Just as importantly, every change you make is likely to inspire others to examine and alter their thinking and behaviour. The best place to start when seeking to alter a system is where you sit. Not only will your new thinking trigger change in your personal circumstances, it is also likely to motivate others to change as well.

This type of synergistic 'systems effect' is vital because people and organizations steeped in an unsustainable mental frame today control most governments. Few public agencies are therefore capable of making the transformative changes needed to resolve today's challenges. Government will gain the capacity to protect the climate and advance sustainability only after a sufficient number of people, and the organizations with whom they are involved, alter their core beliefs, thinking and behaviours, and demand that government does the same.

This is why a planned 5-D stage-based approach to change is so important. Most political campaigns try to convince people who have not yet made up their mind on an issue or candidate to vote their way. The belief is that only a majority of voters are needed to shift the political scales.

This was clearly Cathy Zoi's frame of mind when I heard her presentation at a climate and behavioural change conference in late 2007. Zoi is the founding chief executive officer (CEO) of the Alliance for Climate Protection, a group organized by Al Gore to spearhead a campaign to persuade Americans of the importance and urgency of implementing comprehensive solutions to the climate crisis. Zoi shared recent polling data with conference participants that found that 18 per cent of Americans were in a state of 'ignorance and denial' on global warming; 38 per cent were in a state of 'fear and confusion'; 35 per cent were 'somewhat engaged' in climate solutions; and 9 per cent could be considered climate 'activists'. My interpretation of the data was that well over half the population (56 per cent) were either in the stage of disinterest of deliberation, with most being disinterested; a little over one third (35 per cent) were either in the design or early in the doing stage; and less than one tenth of the population (9 per cent) were solidly in the doing or defending stages of change.

Zoi said her organization's primary focus was to use polling, the media and other elements of a modern political campaign to move the 35 per cent of the population who were 'somewhat engaged' – those in the design or doing stages – towards action. When pressed by a question from an audience member, she said her group might focus some of their effort on the 38 per cent who were in a state of 'fear and confusion'; but they were not a priority because 'we can't get everyone and we only need a majority' to make the political gains she felt were necessary to resolve the climate crisis.[1]

Influencing those who are already supportive first is critical. However, was immediately struck by how much more powerful Zoi's approach could be if it focused on the whole population rather than just the early adopters. Generating the political majority needed to pass climate legislation is very important, and Zoi's organization is engaged in vital work. Al Gore and his team have done impressive work; his movie *An Inconvenient Truth* and relentless series of presentations are one of the primary reasons America began to take global warming more seriously in mid decade.

One has to wonder, however, what the downsides may be if 50 per cent of Americans are ignored through this approach. Disinterested and deliberating people can be powerful opponents. If global emissions must be reduced by 80 per cent or more in rapid order, everyone must become involved.

One approach Zoi's organization could take to address this need is a version of the 5-D staged approach to change described in this book. Rather than ignoring or waiting for people in the early stages of change to react, the Alliance could reach out proactively to the whole population, no matter what their current perspective may be on global warming. By engaging everyone in the process of learning about global warming, examining the pros and cons of climate protection, and building confidence that the problem can be resolved for the benefit of everyone, people can progress from whoever they are at to the next stage and eventually move towards doing and defending. This can stimulate widespread social change.

This is extremely important because research has shown that the more that people progress towards the doing stage of change, the more they support stronger policies. Research on smoking policy, for example, found that people in the disinterest and deliberation stages of change tend to oppose tough anti-smoking policies, while those in the later stages of doing and defending support them (Velicer et al, 1994, pp347–355; Prochaska and Velicer, 2004). The same dynamic is likely to hold true for climate and sustainability policies. This means that no matter where they are starting from, the more that communications and other instruments used by change agents help people to move to the next stage of change, even if it means just from disinterest to deliberation, the weaker their opposition will be and the more they will support strong climate and sustainability policies.

Said differently, if humanity is to resolve global warming and adopt a path towards sustainability, it is vital to reach out proactively to people who are disinterested or in deliberation, rather than hoping they will somehow jump on board on their own or at least not strongly oppose climate protection efforts. People in the early stages of change must become just as much of a focus as those who are in later stages of the shift to sustainable thinking.

The future will not look like the past

There is one thing you can count on: the past cannot guide the great work that lies before us. The policies and practices that proved so useful to us during the past century or so, and the mental frames that produced them, were designed for different times and circumstances. From decaying organic material that provides the nutrients for new plant growth to age-old fossil fuel deposits that today power our energy systems, the past has always influenced the present. For perhaps the first time in human history, however, the past cannot guide us in a future punctuated by the exhaustion of the Earth's sources and sinks, overpopulation, growing economic inequality and rapidly changing climate conditions.

We must remember and honour the traditions that came before us. The linear take–make–waste economic system raised millions out of poverty and produced tremendous wealth. The technologies that it produced provide a platform for the shift to circular borrow–use–return systems. But the linear economic model and the social systems that support it are devoid of wisdom of what is best over the long haul for humanity: wisdom of what should and must be if we are to thrive, rather than what is. We must understand that ours is a whole new time and a whole new set of circumstances that require very different ways of thinking and behaving.

Our great work, which we can start but which our successors must complete, is to take the next step in human evolution and adopt a sustainable mind frame that consistently accounts for the systems we are part of by protecting and restoring the Earth's sources, sinks and communities. We have been offered the gift of devising the new forms of cognition that shift the world from a climate-damaging linear take–make–waste economic model to a sustainable circular borrow–use–return system. Think of all the carbon-free goods and services just waiting to be invented. Imagine all of the quality employment opportunities that can sprout across the globe. Picture the tremendous personal and social well-being that will result from a stable climate and a sustainable path.

Only a few times in human history have a people been handed the opportunity to usher in a new era of global prosperity and security through new forms of energy, production, consumption and social organization. What a magnificent gift this is, if only we will take to heart the new thinking it demands and make the choice to change.

Sustainable thinking fundamentals

Before closing I want to summarize three points I made in this book.

First, all future thinking must be systems-based

The most important job before us is to account for, and live within, the systems we are part of. A systems approach forces us to remove the blinders that prevent us from seeing that humanity must live within the ecological constraints imposed by a finite planet. This starts with the realization that the path towards sustainability is not, at its roots, about new technologies or policies, or even actually about the natural environment. It's about new forms of human perception, thinking and behaviour. Only by developing better forms of human self-management can we protect and restore the Earth's sources and sinks. These actions must be explicitly coupled with efforts to increase prosperity and security for people around the world.

Most people today view the economy as well as local, national and international politics largely in terms of a variety of individuals and groups vying for their own self-interests. People have a difficult time seeing a common good that recognizes the interconnectedness of the economic, social and natural systems upon which we all depend for life. Systems thinking helps us to transcend this myopic view. Only by working for the common good of resolving global warming and increasing global prosperity and security will we all be able to meet our needs.

One imperative of systems thinking is that we must be constantly on guard against false feedback mechanisms and resistance to knowledge. Because of their defence mechanisms, people will go to great lengths to avoid acknowledging the unsustainable nature of their thinking and behaviours patterns. When you find yourself or others resisting, use the change mechanisms described in this book to examine your motivations. Is it resistance based on the reluctance to move beyond your comfort level, insufficient information, lack of self-confidence, rebelliousness, religious or political ideology, or just plain raw fear about what you may lose or what you will discover about yourself?

Remember that fear, projection, denial and other defence mechanisms are common reactions when our core beliefs, assumptions and automatic thoughts are challenged. Surfacing and replacing erroneous perceptions and thought patterns with accurate ones can overcome these personal fortifications. We need courage to face the great work that is before us.

Remaining blind to the ways in which our thinking and behaviours affect the systems we depend upon is a sure-fire way to disaster. A systems perspective will broaden our horizons, open doors to new ways of seeing and responding to the world, and unleash the creativity and innovation needed to resolve global warming and to adopt a path towards sustainability.

Second, a new ethics based on sustainable thinking is needed to resolve today's systems breakdowns

Ethics, which can be defined as self-imposed personal, organizational and political codes of behaviour, has taken a back seat in Western societies to the two polar opposites of governance: laws and unrestricted freedom to do as one wants. Although fair and firm laws are needed to protect the climate, natural environment and social welfare, it will also not be possible, or desirable, to regulate every activity that affects those issues. Yet, it is also no longer possible to allow people the freedom to do as they please if those actions degrade the systems upon which all life on Earth depends.

It is time that we all grow up and realize that uninhibited freedom to do what one wants, even if it negatively affects the climate, natural environment or other people now or in the future, is phoney freedom. It is driven by the control our internal impulses have over us. Humans are healthiest when they can restrain their inner urges and balance their need for autonomy with concern for the effects of that autonomy on the Earth's life support systems and other people. Something in the middle between total control and total freedom is urgently needed, which is sustainable ethics.

In today's overcrowded, overtaxed and interlinked world, sustainable ethics requires that we each put ourselves in the shoes of those whom our actions may affect today as well as in the future. The fundamental moral and ethical imperative of protection for the Earth's sources, sinks and communities must form the basis of all personal and organizational codes of conduct from this point forward. Sustainable ethics apply universally and must become a moral and political force.

Finally, success will depend upon our orientation

Things humans feel passionate about, they eagerly pursue and do well. Things people dislike, they avoid or do poorly. Just as the greatest motivation for personal change is the desire to resolve the tension between a current state and some unmet deeply held values and aspirations, the urgent need to close the gap between society's current thinking and practices and those needed to stabilize the climate offers society with the opportunity to transcend individual self-interest and rally around a higher calling.

The times ahead are certain to be marked by many new, never-before-seen types of disturbances. Although global warming and the disruptions that it will produce are certain to occasionally set us back, they paradoxically also open the door to new learning and growth if only we view them that way. Keep your eye on the ball. Remember that setbacks do not mean failure.

Put yourself in a position to excel, and do the same for other people whom you know and the organizations and teams with which you work. Understand the stages of change and utilize appropriate change mechanisms at the right time to help yourself and others move towards sustainable thinking. Power your journey with enthusiasm, grace and light-heartedness. Keep your sense of humour and catch yourself when you feel defeated or get uptight. Help others do the same.

At the same time, don't listen to the naysayers who, through sophisticated arguments of all types, will try to convince you that a change of course towards climate protection and sustainability is not possible. When this occurs, remember that resistance is natural, but that ecological and social systems also have an innate capacity to adapt and change. I'm completely convinced that humanity can – and will – make the shift in thinking and behaviour needed to resolve global warming and adopt a path towards sustainability. Societies have made big rapid changes in the past, and we can do it again now.

That being said, we have no time to lose. Today's challenges will not resolve themselves on their own. Humanity must rapidly alter its thinking and behaviours if we are to avoid the worst forms of climate change and the social and political distress that it will most certainly bring. Urgency, a positive orientation and light-heartedness are not contradictions. To the contrary, they offer a powerful combination for change.

So there it is. I've presented my case as well as I can. The rundown house my wife and I have been rebuilding is finally completed. And so is this book. You must now decide if you will choose your fate by becoming a sustainable thinker, or allow it to be chosen for you. I wish you all the best on your journey.

NOTE

1   Cathy Zoi's comments were made at the Behaviour, Energy and Climate Change Conference, Sacramento, California, 9 November 2007.

REFERENCES

Makhijani, A. (2007) *Carbon-Free and Nuclear-Free*, IEER Press, Takoma Park, MD, and RDR Books, Muskegon, MI

Prochaska, J. and Velicer, W. (2004) 'Integrating population smoking cessation policies and programs', in *Public Health Reports*, vol 119, May–June, pp244–252

Velicer, W., Laforge, R., Levesque, D. and Fava, J. (1994) 'The development and initial validation of the smoking policy inventory', *Tobacco Control*, vol 3, pp347–355

Index